PEDRO ALMODÓVAR
A Cinema of Desire,
Passion and Compulsion

PEDRO ALMODÓVAR

A Cinema of Desire, Passion and Compulsion

edited by
Arlene Kramer Richards
and Lucille Spira
with Merle Molofsky

IPBOOKS.net
International Psychoanalytic Books

International Psychoanalytic Books (IPBooks),
Queens, NY
Online at: www.IPBooks.net

Interior book design by Maureen Cutajar, gopublished.com

ISBN: 978-1-949093-10-0

One man scorned and covered with scars still strove with his last ounce of courage to reach the unreachable stars; and the world was better for this.

—*Don Quixote,* Miguel de Cervantes

Table of Contents

Listing of Pedro Almodóvar Films Discussed*

Labyrinth of Passion (1982)
Dark Habits (Entre Tinieblas)(1983)
What Have I Done to Deserve This? (1984)
Matador (1985/1986)
Law of Desire (1986/1987)
Women on the Verge of a Nervous Breakdown (1987)
Tie Me Up! Tie Me Down! (1989)
High Heels (1991)
The Flower of My Secret (1995)
Live Flesh (1997)
All About My Mother (1999)
Talk to Her (2002)
Bad Education (2004)
Volver (2006)
Broken Embraces (2009)
The Skin I Live In (2011)
Julieta (2016)

---

* Film dates from: *Almodóvar on Almodóvar (Revised Edition) 1996*: edited by Frederic Strauss. London: Faber & Faber and/or Pedro Almodóvar en.wikipedia.org.

Acknowledgments

There are many to thank for making it possible for us to bring this anthology, *Pedro Almodóvar: A Cinema of Desire, Passion and Compulsion* to fruition. First, we thank Pedro Almodóvar for creating films that are intellectually engaging and emotionally stirring. How readily our contributors signed on speaks to their generosity, and also to how well they regard Almodóvar's work. We are truly awed and grateful to each of them for enhancing the conversation not only about Almodóvar's films but about the human condition in all its breadth, depth, conflicts, and foibles that Almodóvar so beautifully captures.

We thank Arnold Richards from IPBooks and Tamar and Larry Schwartz for their support and help in executing this book. Bruce Sklarew, M.D. has our appreciation for allowing us to present and discuss a Pedro Almodóvar film at the American Psychoanalytic Association February, 2019 meeting in New York City. Most importantly, we thank Merle Molofsky for her overall support, delicate editing, and for coming on board.

We thank Marvin D'Lugo, Ph.D. for his support. It is our good fortune to have received pre-publication comments about this volume from Rosemary Balsam, M.D., Glen Gabbard, M.D., and Lois Oppenheim, Ph.D. (Please see the back cover.)

Arlene Kramer Richards

I thank Lucille Spira for her energy, patience and insistence on being a true scholar and doing the best possible scholarship. I also thank Arnold Richards for his unflagging support and kindness, my children Stephen Richards, Rebecca Richards and Tamar Schwartz for their willingness to put up with an often preoccupied mother. I especially thank Tamar Schwartz and Lawrence Schwartz for their generous help, support, back-up, research, and editorial work on this book. It could not have happened without them. I thank all of our contributors for their dedication and scholarship. And the readers for their attention.

Lucille Spira

My thanks to Arlene Kramer Richards for inviting me to co-edit and contribute to this book. Her enthusiasm for artistic works is contagious and made our project fun. Others deserve my thanks as well: Eve Golden for her eagle eye and much appreciated editorial commentary. To work with Merle Molofsky on this anthology was both a pleasure and learning experience.

I thank Miriam Pierce, Ed Fancher, Carol Thea, the NYSPP Board and membership for their years of support. The NYSPP Psychoanalytic Literary Group members—Roberta Espie, Ellen Henschel, Barbara Hertzberg, Barbara Lewis, Sandra Parness, and Maryam Razavi—thanks to all of you for helping me to appreciate and recognize the many dimensions of the wonderful stories that we read. I thank my patients for sharing about their life and teaching me more about the impact of history and memories on one's life.

On a personal note, I thank Bill Spira, with whom I have shared years of movie going and other adventures. Thanks also to Carol Munter, Lillian Berman, Lynne Herbst, Barbara Rauch, Patsy Turrini, Vicki Finkel, Paul Mulinski, Jeff Bird, Michael Sprung, Anan Ponnabalam, Laura Melano Flanagan, Carolyn Benbow Ross, Dotty Attie and other friends and colleagues for being there for me.

(With) Merle Molofsky

Thank you, Arlene Kramer Richards, and Lucille Spira, for inviting me to join in the realization of the project you created, this book dedicated to the cinematic creativity of Pedro Almodóvar. Your vision is inspiring. And thank you to all the contributing authors, whose chapters are so engaging to read, whose insights into the Almodóvar films they discussed are truly illuminating.

The editors would also like to acknowledge Kathy Kovacic of Blackthorn Studio for her front cover design and Lawrence L. Schwartz for his back cover design.

PERMISSIONS
We are grateful for permission to reprint the following material.

The Skin I Live In, by Arlene Kramer Richards, is published with permission from IPBooks.

Edinburgh University Press for allowing Julián Daniel Gutiérrez-Albilla to publish a revised selection of material from his book: *Aesthetics, Ethics and Trauma in the Cinema of Pedro Almodóvar*.

About the Editors and Contributors

Albert J. Brok, Ph.D., Board Div. 39, APA. Dir. Group and Couple Therapy, TIMH. Supervisor Derner Institute, Adelphi Univ. Guest Lecturer: Argentine Psychoanalytic Association. Past President, Section I, Division of Psychoanalysis, American Psychological Association. Guest lecturer, Asociación Psicoanalítica de Madrid. Author numerous books and articles. Most recent publication: Una travesía por la fabrica de sueños, intersección entre cine y psicoanálisis.

Sandra Cohen, Ph.D., Training and Supervising Analyst at the Psychoanalytic Center of California (PCC)in Los Angeles. Special interest in working with early trauma and complex clinical states. She recently discussed the films *Elle and Lady Bird at PCC's Saturday Cinema.* Dr. Cohen's blog, *Characters on the Couch,* offers her thoughts on the real human problems of characters in film.

Selma Duckler, Former actress. Artist-in-Residence Portland Public Schools. Advocate for the Arts; Member of the Portland Metropolitan Arts Council. Former President of APsaA Foundation and Former Committee Co-Chair of the Committee on Foundations; Awarded Distinguished Service Award, APsaA. Past President and Board Member Oregon Psychoanalytic Association. Contributing author: *100 Questions About Anxiety,* K. C. Attwell (Jones & Bartlett). Film and Book reviewer online: internationalpsychoanalysis.net

William Fried, Ph.D., FIPA, psychoanalyst and photographer. Member of the IPA and the Institute for Psychoanalytic Training and Research, past president and treasurer of Section 1 Division 39, and a former member of the Boards of Directors both of Section I and

Division 39. Published clinical studies, works on psycho-politics, group therapy, group dynamics, and analyses of films. Author of *Critical Flicker Fusion:Psychoanalysis at the Movies* (Karnac: Books 2017). He practices psychoanalysis and psychotherapy in Manhattan, NYC.

Nancy R. Goodman, Ph.D., Training and Supervising Analyst, Contemporary Freudian Society, Washington, D.C. and IPA. Faculty Wuhan, China Training Program. Authored publications on trauma, female development and enactments. Co-authored numerous volumes including: *The Power of Witnessing: Reflections, Reverberations, and Traces of the Holocaust* (2012)(with Marilyn Meyers); *Finding Unconscious Fantasy in Narrative, Trauma and Body Pain: A Clinical Guide (with Paula Ellman).* Founder and Director www.virtualpsychoanalyticmuseum.org with IPBooks.

Julián Daniel Gutiérrez-Albilla, Ph.D.,(Cambridge, UK). Professor of Spanish and Portuguese, Comparative Literature and Gender Studies USC; Author of numerous publications on Latin American and Spanish Cinema; Recent Publication: *Aesthetics, Ethics and Trauma in the Cinema of Pedro Almodóvar* (University of Edinburgh).

Danielle Knafo, Ph.D., Professor at Long Island University's Clinical Psychology Doctoral Program. She is also faculty and supervisor at NYU's Postdoctoral Program in Psychotherapy and Psychoanalysis. Dr. Knafo has written and lectured extensively on psychoanalysis, creativity, gender, perversion and technology. Corst Essay Prize (APsaA), 2014. Her most recent book is *The Age of Perversion: Desire and Technology in Psychoanalysis and Culture.*

Arthur A. Lynch, Ph.D., President and past president of the Board of Directors, Senior Faculty member, and Training and Supervising Analyst at the American Institute for Psychoanalysis. Member:

American Psychoanalytic Association; International Psychoanalytical Association. Adjunct Professor at Columbia University School of Social Work; Visiting Professor and Head of Training for the Chinese American Psychoanalytic continuous training program at the Wuhan Hospital for Psychotherapy, China from 2012 to 2017. Pioneered the Karen Horney – China Institute for Psychotherapy and Psychoanalysis in Guangzhou, China. Chair of the Psychoanalytic Symposium series from 2011–2017. Multiple publications. Recent Publications: *Selected Papers of Arnold Richards, Volumes 1 & 2*, Edited by Arthur A. Lynch (IPBooks).

Lourdes Rigual-Lynch, Ph.D., Retired as Director of Mental Health Services and Case Management for the Division of Community Pediatrics of Montefiore Medical Center (MMC). Assistant Professor of Pediatrics at the Albert Einstein College of Medicine affiliated with MMC (Ret.). Appointed by U.S. Attorney General Janet Reno (2000) to three-person mental health team to resolve Cuban refugee issue concerning Elián González. Published extensively on the health and mental health risk factors of homeless children and other underserved populations. Currently Accountability Review Panel – consultant for the New York City Administration for Children's Services.

Philip Matyszak, BA (Lon. Hons.), MA, D.Phil.(Oxon). Scholar of ancient history specializing in the classical world. He has a particular interest in ancient magic and mythology. Dr. Matyszak has written extensively on all aspects of the ancient world and the different shared perceptions of ancient and modern cultures. Teaches for the Institute of Continuing Education at Madingley Hall, University of Cambridge in the UK. Published a recent Chapter "Three Archetypes in Myth: The Goddess, The Witch and the Mortal" in *Myths of Mighty Women* (Karnac).

Merle Molofsky, MFA., Psychoanalyst, Private Practice, NYC. Faculty of the Training Institute of NPAP, and faculty and Advisory Board of Harlem Family Institute. Editorial Board of *The Psychoanalytic*

Review. Published numerous articles in books and psychoanalytic journals on film and other topics. A novel *Streets, 1970* (published by IPBooks, 2015); *Necessary Voices,* (IPBooks, in press). Chapters in: *Psychotherapy and Religion: Many Paths, One Journey* (Jason Aronson); *Myths of Mighty Women* (Karnac); *Living Moments: On the Work of Michael Eigen* (Karnac).

Adriana Prengler, LMHC, FIPA, Training and Supervising Analyst. Member of the Northwestern Psychoanalytic Society and Institute (Seattle). Sociedad Psicoanalítica de Caracas (Venezuela). International Psychoanalytical Association and Federación Psicoanalítica de América Latina. Faculty Wuhan, China Psychotherapy Training Program. Publications and interests in psychoanalysis and dictatorship, mourning and grief, immigration and loss.

Arlene Kramer Richards, Ed.D., Contemporary Freudian Society, Institute for Psychoanalytic Training and Research, American Institute for Psychoanalysis, Wuhan Psychotherapy Training Program, International Psychoanalytical Association. Numerous publications on gender, dreams, literature and film: Recent Books: *Listening to Understand* (IPBooks*);* Co-editor *Myths of Mighty Women* (Karnac)and *Encounters with Loneliness: Only the Lonely* [IPBooks(Gradiva Award, 2014)].

Arnold D. Richards, M.D., Member: New York Psychoanalytic Society and Institute; International Psychoanalytical Association; APA, Division 39, Section 10; New York Freudian Society. Editor: *Journal of The American Psychoanalytic Association* (JAPA, 1994 - 2003); Editor: *The American Psychoanalyst* (TAP, newsletter of APsaA). Faculty: MITPP (Adult Program). Training and Supervising Analyst: New York Psychoanalytic Institute. Recipient: Distinguished Contributor Award, American Psychoanalytic Association; Sigourney Award,(2000). Faculty, Tongji Medical College of Huazhong University of Science and Technology at Wuhan, China. Multiple publications. Recent Publications: *Selected Papers of Arnold Richards,* Edited by Arthur A. Lynch (IPBooks).

Bennett E. Roth, Ph.D., Graduate NYU Postdoctoral program in Psychoanalysis and The Postgraduate Center's program in Group Therapy. Member of the American Psychoanalytic Assoc., The International Psychoanalytical Association. Fellow of the American Group Psychotherapy Assoc., and the International Group Analytic Assoc. Published movie reviews and presented on Bion and Group analysis. Recent Publication: "Re-examining *Schreber* through the Lens of a present day case" *Psychoanalytic Quarterly.*

Lucille Spira, Ph.D., Member NYSPP. Presented on loneliness and literary works at APsaA, APA (Div. 39), and AAPCSW, etc. Co-Chair APsaA's Loneliness and Aloneness Discussion Group. Published in various psychoanalytic journals on loneliness and literary topics. Gradiva Award, 2014, with Arlene Kramer Richards and Arthur A. Lynch for co-editing: *Encounters with Loneliness: Only the Lonely* (IPBooks). Recent publication: Co-edited: *Myths of Mighty Women: Their Application in Psychoanalytic Psychotherapy* (Karnac).

Herbert H. Stein, M.D., Member APsaA, Faculty NYU School of Medicine. Former Director of the Institute for Psychoanalytic Education,(NYU). Editor *PANY Bulletin.* Published articles in the institute's society bulletin on Psychoanalysis and Film for many years. Published a compilation of film reviews: *Double Feature* and on Internationalpsychoanalysis.net. Recently, a compilation of some of these articles published as *Moving Pictures: Film Through a Psychoanalytic Lens.*

Jeffery Stern, Ph.D., English Literature, University of Chicago. Humanities Prize University of Chicago Doctoral thesis on Shakespeare's late romances. Supervising analyst at the Chicago Psychoanalytic Institute and Visiting Professor of Psychoanalysis at Wuhan University in Wuhan China. Associate editor of the *Annual of Psychoanalysis.* Numerous publications on self psychology, literature and film. A volume of his papers is planned for 2019.

FOREWORD

Marvin D'Lugo, Ph.D.

This is a unique compendium of intellectually stimulating and engaging commentary on major films by Almodóvar. The volume blends psychoanalytic, artistic, historical and social commentary into the intense exploration of the emotional core of Almodóvar's films.

What makes for the volume's distinctiveness is, as the editors argue, the extreme passions, even the compulsiveness of Almodóvar's characters. These emotions are, in turn, mirrored in the insightful readings of the various contributors who, shaped by their professional training as well as their cinephile fervor, engage in another kind of passion: the recovery of the cinematic object of desire. Beyond all the specifics of the analyses, this volume is a testament to the joy of cinema!

What unifies the seemingly diverse range of commentaries is the common task of each author to understand the relation of Almodóvar's films, and cinema in general, to the affective life of individuals. Ostensibly anchored in psychoanalytic readings, this volume goes beyond that framework to pose a range of questions of aesthetics and ethics, even identity politics.

Marvin D'Lugo, Ph.D. is a Professor Emeritus of Language, Literature and Culture and Research Professor of Spanish and Screen Studies at Clark University.

Selected Publications (2006). *Pedro Almodóvar*. Champaign: University of Illinois Press,

(2013). Co-editor: *A Companion to Pedro Almodóvar*. Hoboken: Wiley-Blackwell.

INTRODUCTION

Arlene Kramer Richards and Lucille Spira

Writing a book or movie script comes from a desire to communicate. The author wants someone to know about her feelings; even, perhaps, to feel the same feelings. Aristotle believed that tragedy was written to induce pity and fear in the audience. Comedy is written to produce feelings of surprise, joy, and satisfaction. The melodrama produces pity and fear until it reaches the happy ending which produces surprise, joy, and satisfaction. Comic elements in tragedy as in Shakespeare's tragedies allow the audience to bear what otherwise would be the unbearable. Surreal art and writing shocks as it reveals images like those in dreams, contradictions, weird juxtapositions, and the impossible. Pure or mixed, all of these forms are found in the work of Almodóvar.

The passion that drives the stories is the feeling that cannot be expressed in the experiential world of the artist. Rather, the work reflects the impact of the experiential world as filtered through and structured by the heart and mind of the artist. Trauma transformed by aesthetic structure becomes art. For Almodóvar, the passion is filtered through the Spanish artistic tradition of "duende". This is a capacity to move the audience to waves of emotion, even frenzy. Lorca discussed "duende" while in Argentina during the 1930s. He (1975) defined this as consisting of four parts:

1. irrationality;
2. a heightened awareness of death;
3. earthiness; and
4. the diabolical.

Death is universal; tragedy is universal; only the Spanish joy in death and dying is particular to the culture. In this way, Almodóvar is quintessentially Spanish. Bullfighting and Gypsy music use death as a celebration of pain.

The special "duende" form of art, epitomized by that Gypsy music Lorca calls "deep song" and by bull fighting defines what Almodóvar brings to movies that only the great Spanish director Buñuel had before him. The culture of the folkloric entailing a combination of passion and involvement with death that permeates Spanish art turns into a defense of camp and joy in the irrational in Almodóvar's work. In this way, he incorporates the past and the particular of Spanish history with a modern sensibility so that the shared past connects his work to South American and Mexican popular culture as well (D'Lugo M., 2006). At the same time he makes it universal as death and dying are universal. And he makes it contemporary by focusing on such phenomena as sex change surgery as an emblem of a non-binary view of the world.

We called the book *Pedro Almodóvar: A Cinema Of Desire, Passion and Compulsion* to explore these topics. Where does desire have the intensity of passion? Where does passion move over into the realm of compulsion? Are we all compulsive voyeurs when we watch movies? Is there a need for a sharp divide between them, or does one blend over into another? Is this a rainbow with varied colors, or a gradual blending so subtle that it is impossible to delineate where one turns into another? Almodóvar asks the question: What are we willing to sacrifice in order to gain the aim of our passion?

The contributors to this book were invited to choose a film from Almodóvar's work and discuss it from a perspective that had meaning to them. We include psychoanalysts, historians, and specialists in film theory and gender studies, and a former actress. Among the psychoanalysts are adherents of different theories: self psychology, psychoanalytic developmental theory, contemporary Freudian, Kleinian, and relational theories. Representatives of Spain, Canada, Argentina, Venezuela, Puerto Rico and the continental

United States are here. All come together in our love of movies, our passion for Almodóvar and our compulsion to write.

The book is organized sequentially so that Almodóvar's development is followed sequentially. The first chapter deals with the experience of film-going. We do not cover the earliest of Almodóvar's films shot in Super 8 format: *Fuck… Fuck… Fuck Me Tim* (1978). No one chose to write about *Pepi, Luci, Bom* (1980), *Kika* (1993) or *I'm So Excited* (2013). Two people selected *Talk To* Her (2002), and they write about it from very different perspectives. Two of the chapters find common themes in earlier and later films. Each of those two chapters is placed where the earlier film belongs.

All of the writers recognize the effect of trauma in the experiential world. Death in its various forms, the diabolical that wants only death, especially the death of the self, arises from the traumatic knowledge that for all life, death is the only ending. And in the art described and analyzed in our book, it is a joyful ending as the audience reflects upon the creativity of Almodóvar's films.

Watching Almodóvar's films, before reading the discussions here, we think, will better allow you to formulate your own views as you engage with the ideas presented by our authors. We invite you to join the conversation about the films and the contributions herein. To do so, you can email: psypsa@gmail.com and we will forward your comments and/or queries to our contributors.

References

D'Lugo, M. (2006). *Pedro Almodóvar*. Chicago & Urbana: Illinois University Press.

Lorca, F. G. (1975). *In Search of Duende,* C. Maurer (Editor and Trans). New York: New Directions.

CHAPTER 1

The Importance of Film for Psychoanalysis

Herbert H. Stein

"... say whatever goes through your mind. Act as though, for instance, you were a traveler sitting next to the window of a railway carriage and describing to someone inside the carriage the changing views which you see outside." (Freud, 1913, p. 135)

These are Freud's famous recommended instructions to his patient at the beginning of psychoanalysis. The patient is lying on a couch, reflecting inward and describing what passes before that inward gaze. The psychoanalyst attentively listens to the patient's words, forming her own thoughts, associations and images to what is being said. But what if the analyst could directly experience that inward gaze?

When we enter a movie theater, we sit down, lean back and try to relax. As the lights are dimmed, our focus is on the screen and we expect what we see and hear there to be the central focus of our minds. We don't completely shut out the rest of our world, but if the film is good, we hope to enter a different world, the world of the film.

If we are in the proper frame of mind to watch a film, we are prepared to allow our minds to enter into this manufactured world, hoping that it will engage us and knowing that at the end, we should be able to return to our daily lives, moved and perhaps enlightened.

In both settings, the movie theater and the analytic office, we are expected to experience the emotions and thoughts that come to us in a relatively free-floating way. If the film is effective, we will enter a somewhat altered state of mind. If it is particularly effective, we are absorbed by the lives of the people on the screen. We do not forget our own lives, of course, but in the moment, our lives recede into the background, except, of course, as aspects of them are mirrored or evoked on the screen.

Watching a film is like listening to someone on the couch, but with a direct view of that train window that Freud described, that inward gaze. It is as if we were seeing, hearing, and experiencing the world through someone else's mind.

For this to work, there must be a successful collaboration between the people who made the film and the people who watch the film. To accomplish that, the filmmakers must enlist our emotions. They must entice us to give up our own lives temporarily, and enter into the lives we see before us.

The psychoanalyst hopes to help patients transcend the superficial layers of personal experience in order to experience the inner workings of their minds. The filmmaker provides a template to help us enter into an alternate world, while the analyst attempts to help us find our own inner world. But the film, by creating the illusion of actual, immediate experience, also creates a free flow of internal reactions, emotions and thoughts that must move quickly to respond to the stimulating events set before us. In that respect, we might say that a good film is somewhat like a good psychoanalytic hour.

The Museum of Modern Art in New York City has a permanent film exhibit at which they regularly show old films in a small theater. Many years ago, my wife and I happened into that theater when they were showing the closing scenes of *The Blue Veil* (1951), about a nanny being reunited with her "children". We probably saw only about fifteen minutes of the film, but when it ended, we stood in puddles of our tears. The teenage girl who served as an usher looked at my wife's eyes as we were leaving and said, "Oh, you liked it!" (Stein, 2002) Similarly, in his classic book on psychoanalysis and film, Harvey Greenberg (1975), wrote about *Casablanca* (1941), "If I know it's schmaltzy then why am I crying?" Why indeed?

How do filmmakers like Pedro Almodóvar enlist our emotions and our attentions so that our minds are both drawn into another world and freed to come into contact with emotions, thoughts, images that are usually far from our awareness? Within the answer to that question lies the importance of film for psychoanalysis.

One answer to this question is that they touch upon unconscious fantasies that many of us share. We often don't understand why we react as we do, and we may even try to fight it, but we are responding to a hidden image evoked silently in ourselves that has deeper and more personal meaning than the image we see on the screen.

Fantasy holds a central role in psychoanalytic thinking. Our perception of the world and our reactions to it are continually influenced by personal fantasies that go back as far as early childhood. These fantasies are particularly evocative of emotions. At any given time, they may be more or less available to consciousness. Jacob Arlow, who wrote about the constant influence of fantasy on our perception, memory, and thinking (Arlow, 1969a, 1969b), used the 1966 film *Blowup* in a paper about primal scene fantasies, fantasies having to do with the child's experience of witnessing parental intercourse. (Arlow, 1980) It provides a striking example of how film can reinforce and bring to life expressions of fantasy. I became interested in film and psychoanalysis myself, after being impressed by a similar use of images suggestive of primal scene fantasies in Bernardo Bertolucci's *The Conformist* (1970), (Stein, 1997).

Films have tapped into commonly held fantasies from the beginning. In that, they are no different from other forms of literature and art. By connecting us with a basic fantasy, a film can capture our interest and link up with our most basic emotions. I would think that the most obvious of these are Oedipal fantasies that have to do with love and more pointedly rivalry between father and son, mother and daughter. Obviously, Freud took the name for the early father/son rivalry from Sophocles' play, which Freud clearly saw as a means to tapping the emotional life of most people. If you want a relatively early example in film, what better one exists than the classic *The Adventures of Robin Hood* (1938), with a young Errol Flynn fighting the authority of the evil Prince John and the Sheriff of Nottingham while idolizing the almost godlike King Richard, the loved and idealized father.

I'll cite another example from a classic film that most readers have probably seen, *High Noon* (1952). In that film, Gary Cooper's Marshal Will Kane faces the arrival on his wedding day of a gang of murderers to the town he protects. Throughout the film, we experience his struggle to be faithful to his bride and to the town. The film's theme song repeats over and over, reminding us of the central words, "Do not forsake me, oh, my darling, on this our wedding day."

Even a cursory glance opens up possibilities for complex fantasies around mostly Oedipal themes, but I want to make my point with one striking image. Throughout the film, we are reminded through glances at clocks, scenes at the train station and images of a moving train along with the dramatic music that accompanies all of this that the murderer Frank Miller is arriving on the noon train, hence the title. You don't have to be a psychoanalyst or a hyper-Freudian to connect the image of the train heading into the town to deposit Frank Miller with Will Kane contemplating his wedding night with his young, innocent bride.

Made and shown in the 1950's, *High Noon* makes no conscious reference to the anxieties this older toughened man (Gary Cooper) and his young innocent bride (Grace Kelly) face as they approach the coitus of their wedding night; but, the filmmakers give us an image that captures that anxiety in the "phallic" train plunging into the town to deposit the dangerous murderer. When we first see it, we don't make the conscious connection, but the image must work at some level. That is the power of film!

Recently, on hearing about someone who appears to lack empathy, with no real sense of what other people are thinking and feeling, I found myself wondering if she goes to the movies, where we are continually thrust into experiencing the world through others. Part of the success of many films comes from their ability to pull us into the perspective of the characters on the screen.

This form of empathic identification is not unique to film. We probably come closest to it when we read a good book. There, we are back to using words as an intermediary. Film is the best vehicle for it, especially when we see it on the "big screen." Unlike a stage play, film can put us directly into the perspective of the character. This is most easily seen in action sequences. In the film, *Gravity* (2013), we see the emptiness of space and almost have to experience the fright of being untethered and drifting in the vastness along with Sandra Bullock.

In fact, from early childhood we are trained to experience empathy through film. Filmmakers are adept at creating images that have universal appeal. Have you ever been in a theater watching the Disney cartoon, *Bambi* (1942)? There is a certain moment when it becomes apparent that Bambi's mother has died. First we hear one or two children crying, then it spreads as the young audience breaks out into a wave of distress. It is obvious that those small children identify with Bambi as she sees her mother shot to death, and in identifying with Bambi, they are experiencing empathy for another creature who is experiencing something that evokes fear and sadness.

I have chosen this simplest of examples, but we can move up to adult movies which pull us into a visceral experience. Horror movies provide a good example of this. Most people seeing the film *Psycho* (1960) for the first time will experience a fright when a knife-wielding figure suddenly appears accompanied by a high-pitched repetitive alarm sound. Here the sound is designed to reinforce the sense of shock along with the accompanying physiological reactions. If we don't have time to feel the heart pounding, we will nevertheless be certain that the pulse is rapid.

Almodóvar's films frequently bring us into the world of sudden and tragic loss and grief, much like *Bambi* does, but at an adult level. Through Almodóvar, we experience the world through a mother who has suddenly lost her teenage son, a doctor who has similarly lost the love of his life changing the nature of his work, a man blinded in an accident which also cost the life of the woman he loved, a nurse tending to a comatose patient. These films do not simply deal with normal grief. They take us to the limits of what people do to overcome tragic loss; and, in doing that, they bring to life fantasies and emotions of reparation and revenge that analysts hear as part of the inner working of their patients' minds.

As we examine films that evoke intense identification and empathy in many viewers, we can shine a light on the patterns of emotions and how they affect us. This allows us to both see and demonstrate these important motivational factors.

In an essay concerning Pedro Almodóvar's film, *Talk to Her* (2002), William Fried (2017) compares the four-year continual monologue of a male nurse directed at his seemingly comatose patient with an analytic patient on the couch free associating to his analyst:

"... the relative absence of cueing from the other makes it possible for the speaker to project aspects of her (his) inner world onto the other ..." (Fried, 2017, p. 81).

Fried's comatose "analyst" is an extreme representation of the so-called silent analyst who allows the patient to wander on his own, reaching out to an unknown listener. Watching films, we are not put off by such extremes. We expect, even delight, in the unusual. These curious looks at the patient/analyst relationship may reveal peculiar aspects of that dialogue.

I am thinking of such films as *The Silence of the Lambs* (1991) and *The Sixth Sense* (1999), each of which depicts an analyst at work under highly unusual conditions, and reveals something about the inevitable inter-connectedness of analyst and patient.

In *The Silence of the Lambs*, we see a psychopathic psychiatrist confined to a high security prison turning an interview by a young FBI agent into a therapy session. Hannibal Lector appears to be drawn by curiosity and a strange sense of therapeutic zeal into trying to help his interrogator, Starling, with her disturbing nightmares about the slaughter of sheep. But it goes awry at one point when his cannibalistic tendencies intervene, driving her away for the moment. What we learn if we look closely is that the film is shining a light on the link between this analyst's desire to understand, to take in as much as he can about his patients, and his more overt cannibalistic obsession, the desire to literally devour people. It is a reminder that the analyst has unconscious reasons for taking pleasure in understanding his/her patients (hopefully not so gruesome as Lector's).

Similarly, *The Sixth Sense* (1999), a film about a disturbed boy who can "see dead people," gives us a therapist who slowly discovers as he treats his child patient that he, himself, is dead, a ghost. The therapy gives insight to both patient and therapist, and can allow us to see that both of them must overcome resistances to learning the truth.

By drawing us into logically impossible situations, these films can provide us with insight and evidence concerning the more subtle realities of psychoanalytic therapy. We don't have to be cannibals to have unconscious motives for wanting to get into the minds of our patients and we don't have to be dead to have personal reasons for not wanting to see the truth. Films surprise us with insights into the workings of the mind and the therapeutic situation, but more importantly, they provide us with vivid demonstrations of these processes, ripe for the picking.

We see this ability of film to draw the audience into the give and take of psychoanalytically oriented therapy in more conventional depictions as well, such as *Good Will Hunting* (1998) or *The King's Speech* (2010).[1]

An old friend and colleague told me that in reading my essays on psychoanalysis and film he assumed that I had written them with the idea of using them for teaching about psychoanalysis. I can't say that

---

[1] *The King's Speech* is about a treatment by a speech therapist, but it has many qualities of an insight-oriented psychotherapy as depicted in the film.

I wrote them with that in mind, but I clearly understood what he was saying.

Films, I should emphasize "good films," offer us a unique opportunity to teach psychoanalytic concepts. The opportunity is unique in that the film can bring those ideas to life in a way that is rivaled only by going through detailed clinical reports of what patients say in analysis. With film, of course, we need not worry about confidentiality. With film, we can use material that has already been seen by a large audience and has already made an impact on them. We can show portions of the film as we use it to bring to life the particular psychoanalytic concepts.

With a well-crafted film, otherwise abstract sounding theoretical ideas feel immediate and meaningful. It is a central purpose of those making a film to evoke emotional responses and to do that they must at some point turn to the conflicts, fantasies, and identifications that we all share. As psychoanalysts and students of the mind, we may readily tap this goldmine of living theory to demonstrate it to others.

In doing so, we may also enrich our own appreciation of the complex, meaningful working of the human mind. Looking at a film through a psychoanalytic lens often opens up new insights and perspectives that come as a surprise to even the seasoned clinician.

What does that mean about the people who make the films? Does it mean that they know about unconscious fantasy, that they are experts in psychoanalytic theory?

I think not. And I also think yes. I suspect that although some directors have famously been in analysis and have an interest in psychoanalysis, that is not at all a pre-requisite. And yet, they give these wonderful demonstrations of what we work for years to understand.

Psychoanalysts and filmmakers[2] approach the problem from op-

---

[2] I am using the general term filmmakers because I am looking at the creation of the film as the work of many. Obviously, the director, like Almodóvar, is usually the subject of our scrutiny.

posite directions. The psychoanalyst is confronted with a patient who has problems. She listens to her patient and attempts to understand the internal workings of the patient's mind in order to discover what is contributing to those problems. The term "psychoanalysis" implies an analysis, a deconstruction, a search for complex patterns of mind that bring the patient to this point. The analyst takes a living, breathing human being and attempts to figure out the internal workings of the mind.

Filmmakers approach it from the opposite direction. It is their job to construct a whole person, a whole living situation, in some cases an entire world that is comprehensible, meaningful and evocative. To do that they must use those "parts" that the analyst tries to uncover. If the people they put on the screen are going to pass the test, they must exhibit those qualities that the analyst seeks. They must demonstrate the wishes, conflicts and fantasies that are the internal makeup of every one of us. And they must do it believably, so that we feel the emotions as we watch.

I used the ambiguous term, "pass the test". What does that mean? Passing the test doesn't necessarily mean passing the test of appearing real. For the film's characters, world, and plot to pass the test, it must do more than have them appear real. It must make us *want* them to be real. And to do that, the filmmakers must have an intuitive sense of what will engage us. They need not know the precise concepts they are invoking. They need not know the specific unconscious fantasies they evoke. They need only know that the audience will want to experience it as real, at least for that short space of time that we sit in the theater. Remember, the patient in the office doesn't understand all those concepts, but that doesn't stop the patient from embodying them.

So how is film important for psychoanalysis? We might say it brings the concepts that psychoanalysts use to understand people into living color. Film is useful in teaching, demonstrating, and even expanding our understanding. It does all of this jargon free and with immediacy.

To further understand it, I suggest you read this book. And then go to the movies.

References

Arlow, J.A. (1969a). Unconscious Fantasy and Disturbances of Conscious Experience. *Psychoanalytic Quarterly* 38:1–27.

———(1969b). Fantasy, Memory, and Reality Testing. *Psychoanalytic Quarterly*, 38:28–51.

———(1980). Revenge Motive in the Primal Scene. *Journal of the American Psychoanalytic Association*, 28: 519–541.

Fried, W. (2017). *Critical Flicker Fusion.* London, Karnac 160 pp.

Freud, S. (1913). On beginning the treatment (Further recommendations on the technique of psychoanalysis). *Standard Edition* 12:121–144.

Greenberg, H. (1975). *The Movies On Your Mind: Film Classics On the Couch From Fellini to Frankenstein.* New York: Saturday Review Press/E.P. Dutton 273 pp.

Stein, H.H. (1997). Hidden in the imagery: an unconscious scene in *The Conformist. International Journal of Psychoanalysis*: 78:1031–1033.

———(2002). *Double Feature: Finding Our Childhood Fantasies in Film.* New York: EReads, 264 pp.

Films

Bambi (1942) David D. Hand (Director) Walt Disney Studios.

Blowup (1966) Michelangelo Antonioni (Director) Bridge Films.

Casablanca (1942) Michael Curtiz (Director) Warner Bros.

Good Will Hunting (1998) Gus Van Sant (Director) Miramax Films.

Gravity (2013) Alfonso Cuarón (Director) Esperanto Film.

High Noon (1952) Fred Zinneman (Director) Paramount Pictures.

Psycho (1960) Alfred Hitchcock (Director) Paramount Pictures.

The Adventures of Robin Hood (1938) Michael Curtiz, William Keighley (Directors) Warner Bros.

The Blue Veil (1951) Curtis Bernhardt, Busby Berkeley (Directors).

The Conformist (1970) Bernardo Bertolucci (Director) Mars Film.

The Kings's Speech (2010) Tom Hooper (Director) See-Saw Films.
The Silence of the Lambs (1991) Jonathan Demme (Director)Orion Pictures.
The Sixth Sense (1999) M. Night Shyamalan (Director) Hollywood Pictures.

CHAPTER 2

Trauma and Memory in the Cinema of Pedro Almodóvar

Julián Daniel Gutiérrez-Albilla

How does a concern with trauma and memory offer a different and more profound way of engaging with the work of Pedro Almodóvar, one of the world's most critically acclaimed and commercially successful filmmakers? And what can Almodóvar's film practice offer ethically and politically to 'post-traumatic' cultures,[1] both nationally and globally – given that his work has been called 'apolitical' or 'ahistorical' (Smith 2014: 2)?[2] In this chapter, I want to provide a critical and theoretical reformulation of a neglected aspect of Almodóvar's cinema: its engagement with the traumatic past, subjective and collective memory, and the ethical and political meanings that result from this engagement. I explore how his cinema mourns and witnesses the traces of trauma and fragments of memory, paying attention to the toxic effects of these traces, as well as the transformative potential of encountering them in the present.

In 2007, the Spanish parliament approved the *Ley de memoria*

---

[1] The term 'post-traumatic' is used in Farrell (1998). 'Post-traumatic' implies a reconsideration of the prevailing effects of traumatic events on the present.

[2] Paul Julian Smith was one of the first Almodóvar scholars to contest this claim by foregrounding the significance of the Spanish sociocultural context in Almodóvar's cinema from the outset.

histórica (Law of Historical Memory) proposed by the former Social-
ist government of José Luis Rodríguez Zapatero. This legislation was
a response to what many historians and cultural critics have identified as the process of political, social and cultural mourning,
abreaction, and healing. This process was violently repressed under
Franco, consciously silenced during the political transition from
dictatorship to democracy, and historically negated by the political
Right. The new law afforded moral and symbolic recognition and
extended rights to those who suffered persecution and violence
during the Spanish Civil War and under Franco – but it did not take
legal action against the perpetrators. For some, the attempt to restore
legal rights to Franco's victims and to normalise historical inquiry
showed the health and strength of Spain's democracy. But, as Stephanie
Golob argues, the law also generated a range of controversial public
statements – by politicians, judges, and representatives of historical
memory associations – concerning the implications and efficacy of the
legislation, which was seen as anti-punitive (Golob 2008).

Many filmmakers and spectators in Spain are committed to using
film as a way to confront and work through the personal and collective memories of Spain's historical traumas: the silencing,
persecution, execution, exile, and exclusion of Franco's victims and
the victims of the Civil War. The memory debates have certainly
been ideologically instrumentalised and commodified by the Spanish cultural industry (Estrada 2013), but this has only given greater
significance to the commitment of filmmakers and spectators. In the
absence of institutionalised transitional justice, and the ambiguities
of the memory debates, filmmakers have become important political
and ethical figures.

The debates on historical memory were recently eclipsed, however, by the economic crisis, and they were completely excluded
from the political agenda of the conservative government since its
return to power in 2011 until the Spanish Parliament recently presented a vote of no confidence against the conservative Prime
Minister, Mariano Rajoy, in June 2018. The lack of interest in the
debates on historical memory on the part of the recent conservative

Spanish government does not mean, though, that the traces of the traumatic past have stopped affecting us, subjectively or collectively. Given these continued effects, we need to keep reflecting on how the terms of the debate can be defined, historically and theoretically, so we can see how the traces of trauma and fragments of memory function as an intervention in the neoliberal present. The current socio-economic conditions threaten the subject of neoliberal democracy (as Estrada contends in her study of Spanish documentary filmmaking); could that threat itself be a perpetuation of, or succumbing to, the dark shadows of the spectral past? Or could the fragments of memory, to the contrary, help us to a brighter future?

More specifically, can we focus on the aesthetic, ethical, and potential political implications of our affective and interpretive encounter with memory in Almodóvar's cinema, whether that memory be subjective, shared or both? To what extent in Almodóvar's work do we encounter or avoid subjective and shared traces of trauma and fragments of memory associated with, for example, state terror or patriarchal violence? Are these traces and fragments inscribed in his films, transmitted via the medium of film, and actualised in our body's memory? To what extent are we ethically and politically transformed by such encounters, or missed encounters, with the belated traces of trauma and fragments of memory? Do we remain afflicted by this experience of trauma? To what extent can we recuperate and re-inscribe in the present what was there before the trauma, to paraphrase Suely Rolnik (2008a), and so overcome the toxic effects inscribed in the body's memory, without submitting to a reductive teleology of resolution or cure?

Following these important questions, I need to point out that in both the Spanish and the Anglo-American academy, previous scholarship has considered Almodóvar to be the most modern (or (post)modern) of Spanish filmmakers. Cristina Moreiras proposes that his films – particularly those of the 1980s – have consistently contributed to the image of Madrid as a city of desire and tolerance. They present the city as one of Europe's most modern capitals, and Spain as a modern nation, throughout the post-Franco period. He is thus open to criticism for contributing to the culture of amnesia favoured by many Spanish institutions, because this culture itself was deemed necessary to create a modern, Europeanised phase in Spain's history (2002: 28). Accordingly, Moreiras notes that Almodóvar participated 'in an image of a democratic Spain that privileged subjects alienated by the spectacle of reality, oblivious to political processes, sceptical of any type of ideology (except that of the market), excluded from their own collective history, and exclusively immersed in an apparent superficiality and banality' (2002: 65, my translation).[3] Moreiras' rigorous attention to Spain's disavowal of the past, as made manifest in Almodóvar's 1980s cinema, raises very important questions. First, whether the celebratory embrace of (post)modernity on the part of Almodóvar (and of Spanish society as a whole) was a release from the psychic and social burdens of the recent past; and second, whether this embrace can be theorised in terms of trauma at the heart of everyday life in the (post)modern condition – which David Harvey, in a broader context, has associated with the advent of flexible capitalism and increasingly uneven economic development (1990).

Almodóvar's career (1980–present) began five years after the start of Spain's post-Franco, democratic period,[4] and scholars often argue that there is a clear distinction between Almodóvar's early films, which show a lack of political commitment, and his

---

[3] For a crucial critique of the Movida as an apolitical spectacle, see Subirats 2002. Subirats' critique of the Movida's apoliticism is due in part to an exclusive focus on the macro-political level. Txetxu Aguado identifies a transformative potentiality in the Movida in general and Almodóvar's cinema in particular by focusing on the micropolitical level, thereby foregrounding the production of new forms of subjectivity. See Aguado 2009.

[4] It is important to underscore the danger of reducing the democratic period in Spain to 'post-Francoism'. Cultural historians, for one thing, disagree on when the so-called post-Franco period ends. My intention here is not to define a clear-cut periodisation. Nor am I trying to associate the democratic period in which Almodóvar's films have been produced with post-Francoism. But there is a need to make sense of the traumas caused by war and totalitarianism. In this context, I underscore the belated effects of trauma and memory in the present.

latest films, which contain more explicit allusions to politics and to Spain's traumatic past.[5] According to Adrián Pérez Melgosa,

> the Civil War and Franco's dictatorship [are] two historical periods which Almodóvar had insistently declared to be located outside of his interests, but which have progressively gained a larger presence in his work, either tangentially through allusion, as part of the films' back-drops, or through direct political statements. (2013: 177)[6]

But, in line with Paul Julian Smith's argument (2014), Pérez Melgosa problematises the idea that Almodóvar's cinema was ever 'apolitical'. Rather, he argues, Almodóvar has been concerned with Spain's social, cultural, economic, and political transformations since he started making films. This requires a critical reappraisal of his oeuvre, which may 'register the presence of a quest that traverses all of his films, one that joins the personal and the political in the right embrace of the aftermath of a traumatic experience' (Pérez Melgosa 2013: 178). So the apparent distinction between an apolitical early period and an increasingly political later period overlooks the ways in which the past has irrupted, been evoked, or been registered, albeit obliquely, throughout Almodóvar's career.

For instance, Alejandro Varderi rightly suggests that Almodóvar successfully integrated the traditional *castizo* (authentic) culture into a (post)modern aesthetic through the use of camp and kitsch. Varderi calls Almodóvar's an 'estética heteróclita' (heteroclite aesthetics) (1996). It incorporates elements of popular Spanish culture, and reworks familiar styles and genres from Hollywood into a kind of

---

[5] Almodóvar has publicly supported demands from family members of the victims of the Civil War and the Franco regime. He has also explicitly supported Manuela Carmena, who represents a group of new left-wing political parties and social movements associated with Podemos, as a candidate in Madrid's municipal elections of May 2015.

[6] Pérez Melgosa rightly suggests that Almodóvar's critical engagement with the politics of memory in Spain was in part motivated by his concern with the memory of Latin American dictatorships, such as Chile and Argentina.

artistic pastiche. Almodóvar's characteristic collage appears as a clash of visual quotations, resulting in a cinema that cuts across genres and modes. Similarly, Alejandro Yarza focuses on Almodóvar's recycling of national stereotypes, such as bullfighting or flamenco, in order to rescue them from their reactionary Francoist connotations (1999). But Almodóvar's disavowal of the Francoist past could also be read symptomatically as the foreclosure of the symbolic order. Almodóvar's reinterpretation of reality, with a different kind of meaning outside the symbolic order, would then manifest that foreclosure. Could such a reinterpretation of reality palliate the disastrous effects of the foreclosure?

This is not to offer a psychological history of Almodóvar – one that re-discovers in the films the hidden truths of Almodóvar's unconscious. Nor should we approach the relationship between aesthetics, ethics, and trauma in Almodóvar's cinema by focusing on his conscious intention or ethical and political commitments; this chapter is not an auteurist argument. Despite the fact that Almodóvar's authorial signature is predicated on his appropriation and subversion of popular cinematic genres, auteurism remains the most common scholarly approach to Almodóvar's work. This can be explained by Almodóvar's 'determination from the very beginning to devote as much time to promotion as to production' (Smith 2014: 5). This chapter departs from a conventional auteurist approach; it thinks with, rather than about, Almodóvar.

But am I trying to perpetuate a psychoanalytically inflected understanding of contemporary Spanish society as haunted by the spectres of Francoism? My focus on trauma and memory might seem to be in line with the work of Hispanists whose sophisticated focus on hauntology has enabled them to engage productively with historical memory in Spain, by exploring how the spectres of Francoism belatedly return as residues of the collective amnesia, the erasure of subjective and collective traumatic memories, that characterised the Spanish transition from dictatorship to democracy.[7] In

---

[7] See Ibáñez 2013.

this case, my emphasis on the spectral past could limit my reading of Almodóvar's films to a continuous backward glance; back to mourning, to the traumas of the historical past, and the memory of the Franco dictatorship. My use of hauntology could seem to neglect the complex theoretical implications underpinning the concept of hauntology itself—spectrality as constitutive of the film medium, the vicissitudes of the present, or the promise of an incalculable future.[8]

I raise these points because, as a non-psychoanalyst contributor to this volume on Almodóvar's cinema, a psychoanalytically inflected approach to contemporary Spanish culture has already encountered some scepticism, if not outright hostility. In Jo Labanyi's seminal issue of the *Journal of Spanish Cultural Studies* dedicated to the politics of memory, Ángel Loureiro questions the value of trauma theory and psychoanalysis in work on the historical specificity of the Spanish context, hence establishing a division between the psychic and the political, or between subjective and shared experiences. The distinction between structural trauma, which is caused by psychic events, and historical trauma, which is caused by external events, is attributed to psychoanalysis itself. The latter is understood as a science or epistemology that focuses on individual subjectivity at the cost of collective history. Loureiro argues that cultural critics who use psychoanalysis run the risk of resorting to simplistic metaphors of physical and psychical pathologies which, he claims, fail to take into consideration the complexity of social, political, cultural, or historical processes (2008: 225).

However, Mignon Nixon reminds us that psychoanalysis cannot be dissociated from traumatic historical events. The theory itself is inextricably linked to historical trauma and to the exploration of the impact of traumatic events upon the self (2007). For instance, Freud's 1920 'Beyond the Pleasure Principle', which is a crucial source for trauma studies, was stimulated by the destruction that Europe suffered during the First World War. Freud's work continued to

---

[8] See the fascinating issue of the Journal of Spanish Cultural Studies dedicated to Spanish film and spectrality edited by Steven Marsh (2014).

consider questions of collective, historical trauma, as in his 1933 correspondence with Albert Einstein, published as *Why War?* (Nixon 2007). *Moses and Monotheism* (1964 [1937–9]) is another critical reference for the study of trauma. Freud established an analogy between the effects of trauma on the individual and the collective guilt at the core of Jewish culture due to the event of the murder of Moses, the founder and giver of Jewish culture and laws (Luckhurst 2008; Gutiérrez-Albilla 2011).

More specifically, *Moses and Monotheism* is a source for Derrida's conceptualisation of the archive, which Griselda Pollock calls 'the textualisation of cultural memory populated by our own ghostly projections and phantasies, the encryption of both a conscious record and an unconscious impression' (2013b: 12). Derrida questions the historian of psychoanalysis Josef Hayim Yerushalmi's lack of engagement with psychoanalysis in a study devoted, paradoxically, to the founder of psychoanalysis. In this argument, the archive both perpetuates authority and questions it. For Derrida, Freud's theory that compulsive repetitions are caused by the death drive is the condition for the possibility of the creation of the archive; the archive either records and preserves information, or erases it. Derrida situates the archive at a tensional point between monumentalising and documenting the past, and revealing the haunting traces of the past. Even though they may be effaced from the archive, these traces carry the promise of a hidden secret in an unpredictable *futurity* (1995).

Given this, and following Jeffrey Skoller, I ask: does not psychoanalysis enable us to think about how our underlying unconscious structures impact the present at both a subjective and collective level, thereby becoming an important element in the production of the social field (2005: xviii)? From this perspective, as Joshua Hirsch has put it, psychoanalysis can mediate 'between individual and collective experiences of history' (2001: 9). Pollock reminds us that, for Derrida, culture, history, and tradition always already depend on the way spectres inhabit the archive. Psychoanalysis, as both a clinical and an epistemological practice, conceives the psyche as a kind of archive of the archaic (past) desires and fears that, as inaccessible spectres encrypted or carved in our psyche, unconsciously determine our present and future (Pollock 2013b: 11). Such underlying, unconscious mechanisms are extracted through repetition in the psychoanalytic encounter.

But our emphasis should not be on a detached scientific method that attempts to find the historical truth from an outside position. We should pay attention to the traces, the affects or, to use Derrida's term, the impression of history and memory inscribed precariously in subjectivity and leaving its (invisible) mark on the body. Traces of historical trauma are, I argue, extracted through our encounter with Almodóvar's cinema in an already 'out-of-joint' present, and brought into a presence that cannot be reified beyond signification. So psychoanalysis remains a promising epistemological framework and critical resource for thinking about traumas, both subjective and shared, in relation to the film medium.

At the same time, it is important to underscore Almodóvar's own ambivalent position vis-à-vis psychoanalysis. This is manifest, for instance, in the way his films depict psychoanalysts, psychologists, or psychiatrists. *Laberinto de pasiones* (*Labyrinth of Passions*, 1982) parodies Lacanian psychoanalysis in the figure of an Argentinian analyst who can only offer a facile explanation of the main female character's obsessive sexual addiction.[9] In *¿Qué he hecho yo para merecer esto?* (*What Have I Done to Deserve This?*, 1984), the psychoanalyst, whose house is cleaned by the main female protagonist (Carmen Maura), is portrayed as unprofessional, dysfunctional, and apathetic, while in *Hable con ella* (*Talk to Her*, 2002), Alicia's psychiatrist father reduces the main character's emotional, social, and

---

[9] Moreiras emphasises Almodóvar's critique of psychoanalysis as an epistemological discourse. She argues: 'submitting both psychoanalysis (as a discourse about the formation of subjectivity and identity) and trauma theory to parody through the character of the psychoanalyst and the primal scene of Sexi and Riza (cause of their current sexual positions – nymphomania and homosexuality), deeply questions the dominant discourses and ideologies through which the constitution of the subject is produced, as well as psychoanalysis' value as an epistemological discourse' (2014: 150, my translation).

affective problems to a symptom of his closeted homosexuality. Yet, in *Matador* (1986), the female psychologist (Carmen Maura) *responds* to the main character's traumatic experiences in an intimate, compassionate manner; she is an effective witness to the unknown other's painful experiences.

Of course, Almodóvar's engagement with psychoanalysis cannot be reduced to a simple discussion of how characters associated with this profession are positively or negatively represented in his films. Psychoanalysis is part of the dramatic, or anti-dramatic, construction of his films, and a theoretical resource for thinking about his films, even when those films problematise psychoanalysis as an effective epistemological discourse. I contend, rather, that my use of trauma theory and psychoanalysis embraces and replicates Almodóvar's own ambivalent attitude towards psychoanalysis, as well as the (unfulfilled) promises of psychoanalytic study for an incalculable and unpredictable *futurity*.

But, any reading of Almodóvar's cinema must pay attention to the idea that some of the formal and thematic concerns and *leitmotifs* in his latest films may have originated in and developed from those of his early films – without thereby implying a straightforward, linear approach. Marsha Kinder has described this organic, creative arc in Almodóvar's cinema and the practice of reading his films with the term 'retroseriality'. Kinder explains: 'I am arguing that his films increasingly perform an evocation of earlier works (both his own intertexts and intertexts of others) that leads us to read them as an ongoing saga. And to regroups them into networked clusters' (2009:269). The films, hence, help us to think about the relationship between repetition and difference beyond a framework or logic associated with the thought of the Same. Particularly in his later films, such as *La mala educación* (*Bad Education*, 2004) or *La piel que habito* (*The Skin I Live In*, 2011), our encounter with Almodóvar leads us to reflect more explicitly on the way the cinematic image witnesses and re-experiences the traces of the traumatic past, and mediates between or encounters individual and shared experiences in the complex relationship between aesthetics, ethics, and trauma.

This relationship between aesthetics, ethics, and trauma raises the question of how Almodóvar's cinema negotiates cinema's mimetic properties and its affective properties, thus problematising the division between what can be represented and non-represented, or the relationship between representational mediation and ethical immediacy. Interestingly, Rancière criticises Jean-François Lyotard's emphasis on the inability of art to capture the (traumatic) event through his concept of the 'différend'. Rancière argues that Lyotard's concept of the 'différend' subjugates the aesthetic regime to the ethical dimension. Since Rancière is interested in the affirmation of new forms of political subjectivities, he objects to what he considers Lyotard's (and, more broadly, (post)modernism's) ethical turn. He sees this as disallowing the possibility of thinking aesthetics in relation to unpredictable, emancipating political actions in the future (Rancière, 2007). But, like Pollock, I identify the 'aesthetic' as a process of knowing beyond cognition and as a sensorial process beyond perception (2013b: 12). So, by focusing on perceptible and imperceptible traces, we can associate Almodóvar's cinema with a cinematic/aesthetic practice that encounters 'some affective elements capable of shifting us both subjectively and collectively that do not arrive at containing the event in finite forms' (Pollock 2013a: 26–7).

I am inspired by Bracha Ettinger's emphasis on a 'matrixial' psychic resource which may or may not be used to think about *response-ability*: our ability to respond to the suffering of the other. In other words, the trans-subjective preconditions of our subjectivation, which in Ettinger are associated with our 'intimated co-human-subjectivity' (cited in Pollock 2013b: 16), may potentially lead to our ethical way of being in a tangible world inhabited by a plurality of beings. Instead of overlooking the political, whether the macro- or micro-political levels, we should emphasise the transformations of our perceptions through the aesthetic experience, and of our ethical way of relating to irreducible others. Such transformations at the unconscious, micro-political level may potentially lead to macro-political, conscious, yet incalculable political decisions and actions in an unpredictable future. Our engagement with Almodóvar's films evokes the traces of trauma and fragments of memory by provoking a reverberation in our subjectivities and bodies, without making us succumb to an over-identification with others' suffering.

But to return to the supposed distinction between an early, 'apolitical' period and a later, more 'political' period in Almodóvar's work, some critics have associated Almodóvar's early period with eccentric and spontaneous filmmaking, explicit gay thematics, and a hedonistic vision of Madrid as the city of desire (Smith 2003: 150). By contrast, Smith informs us, Almodóvar's recent cinema has been associated with austere and experienced filmmaking, a mastery of narrative and cinematic form, heterosexual thematics, and a more sombre vision of the city as marked by social alienation and violence, disease, and death (2003: 150). Drawing on Pierre Bourdieu's work on distinction, Smith suggests that Almodóvar's cinema has moved into a higher cultural register by displaying increasing formal perfection, thematic seriousness, and social prestige (2003: 153).

Almodóvar's integration of literary or performance pieces, such as, for instance, Pina Bausch's dance pieces in *Hable con ella*, can be associated with what Saša Markuš has defined as Almodóvar's 'etapa de sublimación' (period of sublimation). This period is characterised by the integration of various poetic experiences that are less clashing than in his earlier work (2001). Although Almodóvar does not dismiss popular autochthonous cultural expressions, this integration of literary and performance pieces could reveal a desire to embrace modernity and high – in other words, European – culture. Although, as I have said above, my approach is not auteurist, it is important to underscore that Almodóvar's embrace of European culture both reflects and contributes to his international status as one of the last European 'grands auteurs'. As is well known, Almodóvar was denied the status of an artist in Spain until his cinema had become commercially successful and critically acclaimed on a global level.

Smith accordingly identifies Almodóvar as the only remaining European auteur who balances critical and commercial success (2003: 153). However, he notes, there is a continuity in Almodóvar's cinema. Almodóvar's early cinema focused on the impossibility of love, the irrevocable nature of loss, and the persistence of traumatic experiences that resulted in the death and/or loss for his characters (2003: 150). By contrast, Smith rightly suggests that some of his latest films, such as *Todo sobre mi madre* (*All About My Mother*, 1999) and *Hable con ella*, focus optimistically on the possibility of redemption (2003: 150–1). Smith also suggests that *Hable con ella*, 'apparently so straight in its premise of twin heterosexual couples, does continue Almodóvar's oblique investigation of queer sexualities' (2014: 175). By contrast, some critics have seen the recent *La piel que habito* as evidence for a distinct break. They read it as symptomatic of Almodóvar's increasing alienation from social reality, and an increasing obsession with his own cinematic oeuvre and formalist concerns. I propose, to the contrary, that Almodóvar's increasing self-reflexivity (and thus apparent withdrawal from social concerns) actually encourages the spectator to ponder how the fragments and traces of memory and history endure in the present. Almodóvar's cinema thus embraces a modernist conception of autonomous art *as well as* a heteronomous conception of art. In other words, his art intervenes in life while maintaining its distinctiveness as art.

Almodóvar's cinema sits between mainstream and art cinema, between genre cinema and auteur cinema. Instead of perpetuating a conservative nostalgia for utopian modernism, his work underscores the ethical and potential political implications of aesthetic practices and experiences. Nelly Richard argues that the aesthetic valorises a 'distinction between the respective *motivations* and *accomplishments* of meaning, between different reading *experiences* that mark each practice' (2013: 140, emphasis in original, my translation). Almodóvar's cinema is an aesthetic practice in which the traumatic event may or may not reverberate in our subjectivity and body, by means of our affective and interpretive encounter with the traces of the irreducible other (see Ettinger 2000). It shows how traces of trauma and fragments of memory 'impinge upon concrete reality, but also upon [...] intangible reality' (Rolnik 2008b: 155), and affect us on a spectral and material level.

So we enrich our reading of Almodóvar's films by paying attention to recent arguments about 'the recuperation of historical memory', thus reconceptualising some of the debates on trauma and memory. For instance, the Franco regime changed dramatically over its life. Yet, using Rolnik's theory, we can still insist that there is almost no space, physical, or symbolic, that can escape the omnipresence of a military dictatorship. Such a regime restrains almost any 'vital movement [...]', creates 'a state of permanent alert [...]' and an almost 'total impossibility of rest [...]' (Rolnik 2008a: 134). The state terror that characterised the Franco regime for much of its existence imposed itself onto almost every space and the subjectivity of almost every agent. Given this, trauma can be a useful concept for thinking about how the sensory mark or effects of trauma – as well as its traces and fragments of its memory – can be actualised in our bodies and psyches, without necessarily perpetuating a melancholic repetition of traumatic symptoms or leading to a closure of the past after the process of working through.

Freud distinguished between mourning, in which the subject gradually accepts the loss of the object, and the more pathological state of melancholia in which the hated-loved object is seen in the self. Although Freud's distinction between mourning and melancholia seems to imply a teleological 'cure', Tammy Clewell argues that the loss of the loved object and the traumatic impact of the event leaves a residue in the subject. The residue, the alterity, makes it impossible to completely work through a trauma.[10] And the presence of alterity is often argued to be the precondition of subjectivation. Darian Leader, for instance, argues that 'the very process by which Freud characterized melancholic identification was later used to describe the actual constitution of the human self. Our egos, he wrote, are made up of all the leftover traces of our abandoned relationships'

---

[10] I am indebted to Tammy Clewell's discussion of Freud's 'Mourning and Melancholia' (1917 and 'The Ego and the Id' (1923). See Clewell 2004. Clewell argues that Freud proposes a theory of endless mourning beyond melancholia in 'The Ego and the Id'. Joseba Gabilondo also refers to Freud's own revision of his early distinction between mourning and melancholia to explore the way Almodóvar mourns the loss of the Movida and the Spanish Transition (2005).

(2008: 55). Leader enables us to think of the constitution of subjectivity through our experience and registering of loss.

Idelber Avelar applies the distinction between melancholy and mourning, and the problematic presence of a residue, to the context of post-dictatorship Latin America. He argues that mourning implies an active forgetting, as the subject carries out a 'metaphorical operation whereby the lost object is subsumed under a newly found object of affection' (1999: 4). Avelar is highly critical of this process. He sees this subsumption as a pathological symptom of the post-dictatorial society's passive forgetting. The current neoliberal order, implemented by the dictatorships themselves, is predicated on forgetting the past, and life in a perpetual present. But successful and complete mourning is (or should be) an impossible task. For Avelar, literature reveals the residue or trace left behind in the substitution of new for absent objects, and in doing so reveals the ethical and political potentialities of mourning.

This is not to say that we should instrumentalise traumatic events or advocate a depressive, melancholic position – one that would imply remaining immobilised by the impact of traumatic events, whose untransformed effects are buried or encrypted in the psyche or the body (Abraham and Torok 1994). In their study of 'encrypted identification', Abraham and Torok use the concept of the 'phantom' to explore how traumatic events remain buried (encrypted) in the psyche without the subject being able to process them cognitively, thus producing painful, untransformed, affective and sensorial effects in the damaged ego (1994). The concept of 'encrypted trauma' does not relegate trauma to oblivion, however. Instead, traumatic encryption implies that the traumatic experience remains entombed, frozen, untransformed in our psyche. When the crypt collapses, the affective intensity of trauma disintegrates the structure in which we had tried to contain the traumatic experience. Instead, we should foreground the impossibility of complete working through in order to articulate an affirmation of the ethical and political potential of mourning, both subjectively and socially. The traumatic event can be transformed aesthetically in and through Almodóvar's cinema without forming a fiction of redemption. Rather, in his work the perceptible and imperceptible affects and effects of the traumatic event become an inassimilable, radical alterity. This alterity resists the commodification of memory, as, for instance, in commemoration, to which Estrada (2013) refers; it also threatens the obfuscation of the past. And such an obfuscation is what our current neoliberal order, and the political agenda of Spain's conservative government, in particular, is predicated on. The neoliberal order in Spain can be seen as one of the consequences of the Franco dictatorship's 'stabilisation plan' of 1959, a series of economic policies that paved the way for the political transition to democracy in the 1970s.[11] The transition is often understood as a grand success in economic, cultural, and political terms; the state moved from an economically backward, politically authoritarian and isolated country to a democratic nation fully integrated into the European Union and global capitalism. But, as Txetxu Aguado notes, 'the past did not exist, it should not have existed, because all it could do was intrude with its demands for reparation, the paying-off of debts and the undertaking of justice' (2009: 27, my translation). In this context, memories that cannot be commodified are simply ignored.

My emphasis on psychoanalytic time – what Freud called *Nachträglichkeit* (Laplanche 1999) – may appear to overlook more historically focused accounts of power. Instead of emphasising historical time–a linear conception of homogeneous time that implies unidirectional historical development – can we focus on how some of the horrors of the past inform and are translated into forms of violence inherent to modern sovereign power? But does this approach reduce complex, multi-layered and contentious historical, social, and cultural

---

[11] I am applying this term retrospectively. Although the term often refers to the economic policies implemented from the 1970s and 1980s, and traced back to the 1930s, I suggest that the late Franco government implemented a free market economic system that paved the way for the hegemony of consumerist capitalism in the post-Franco period. Instead of thinking of a transition from a 'pre-modern' Francoist period to a '(post)modern' democratic period, I suggest that the post-Franco period is the logical *consequence* of the economic transformations that took place in the late Franco period.

processes to a single category of trauma? Does such a reduction pre-clude the critical recognition and understanding of the historical past and run the risk of translating individual into collective trauma?

Thinking of the imbrication of the individual with the collective, Pollock and Silverman argue that 'the magnification of individually experienced trauma [...] can lead to collectively shared experience' (2011: 30). Pollock notes that a focus on trauma allows us to under-stand how traumatic events take place without us fully registering or processing them, due to a lack of representational and cognitive resources. Yet, whether we have participated or suffered from those traumatic events or not, we may collectively and belatedly re-engage with the residues of such painful experiences. Here, the distinction between individual and collective experiences is undercut. After all, individual traumas are transmitted by collective culture, while, on the other hand, the collective legacy of traumatic events impinges on individual subjects.

Trauma's belated nature can be inscribed in the film or transmit-ted in the encounter with the cinematic/aesthetic practice. Trauma also implies a non-lineal conception of time. Anti-teleological tem-porality can be understood as a kind of 'palimpsest'. Silverman claims that, in the non-lineal temporality of trauma, traces of indi-vidual or shared experiences may be confused with latent traces of another, earlier or later event. In this way, 'the whole becomes a superimposition of interconnected traces', of individual and shared experiences of different yet similar events (2011: 206). Hence, ap-proaching the complexity of individual and shared traumatic experiences in and through the cinema of Almodóvar requires that we move beyond a linear narrative of historical progress and a teleo-logical conception of history.

But I am aware of the danger of reducing the richness of Almodóvar's cinema to a critical or theoretical framework that may exclude other perspectives. Seguin rightly argues that Almodóvar's films cannot be conceived as structures pointing to a single, founda-tional centre. Instead, his cinema undercuts any possible homogenisation; it is constantly and endlessly formed and de-formed of heterogeneous fragments in a state of suspension and becoming (2009: 9). Seguin suggests that Almodóvar 'rejects in some ways any structuring proposition – any structure contains in its genesis its fascisms and dictatorships [...] [Almodóvar] escapes from certitudes to open up a space for fluidity, margins, borders, fringes or frontiers' (2009: 10, my translation). Pérez Melgosa insists that we should not let memory and trauma 'become the master signifiers through which Almodóvar's work must be interpreted', but rather 'add these concepts to the multiple layers of interpretation that his films instigate' (2013: 181). In line with Melgosa, we should establish productive connections and tensions between our methodologies and Almodóvar's cinematic practice in order to show how Almodóvar's cinema offers a reflection on, pushes back against or moves beyond the theoretical debates on the relationship between ethics, aesthetics, and trauma.

For instance, connecting theories of trauma and Almodóvar's cinema foregrounds the impossible process of working through traumatic events, and an awareness of this impossibility paradoxically becomes the condition of possibility for thinking about the ethical and political transformations in an incalculable future yet to come. Our encounter with the traumatic event through Almodóvar's cinema does not just lead to a calculable, responsible commitment to the past. The relationship between aesthetic practice and aesthetic experience may create the conditions of possibility for *wit(h)nessing* (that is, to witness to and with the other the traces of trauma and fragments of memory) and sharing the suffering of an irreducible other. This bears comparison to Lévinas's and Derrida's concept of hospitality and Ettinger's concept of 'compassionate hospitality'. In hospitality, the autonomous subjects do not make a calculable decision on the conditions for receiving the other. Instead, hospitality implies an unconditional openness to the irreducible other. It acknowledges a heterogeneity that cannot be captured within knowledge, and foregrounds the vulnerability of the subject. The irreducible traumatic event vibrates in our bodies and psyche as an index of an 'im-possible' (that is both possible and impossible), unconditional hospitality, which is predicated on respect for the uniqueness and singularity of an incalculable and undetermined event's rupture (Fernández Agis 2009; Raffoul 2007). In the case of Almodóvar's cinema, this openness and hospitality derives from perception and cognition as well as affect and sensation.

If the cinematic medium participates in the transformation of our consciousness of reality, an 'ethics of listening and seeing' may help us sustain a variety of human life, a kind of otherness, and encourage us to work towards a national and global culture that pays much deeper attention to caring and com-passion. Only such a culture can sustain the safety and dignity of all others and their different ways of 'being-in-the-world' (Pollock 2008).[12]

References

Abraham, N. & Torok, M. (1994). *The Shell and the Kernel*, Chicago: University of Chicago Press.

Fernández Agis, D. (2009). Tiempo, política y hospitalidad. Una reflexión desde Derrida y Lévinas. *ISEGORÍA Revista de Filosofía Moral y Política* 40:191–202.

Aguado, T. (2009). Pedro Almodóvar, La Movida y La Transición: Memoria, Espectáculo y Anti-Franquismo. *Letras Peninsulares* 22(1):23–44.

Avelar, I. (1999). *The Untimely Present: Postdictatorial Latin American Fiction and the Task of Mourning*. Durham: Duke University Press.

Clewell, T. (2004). Mourning Beyond Melancholia: Freud's Psychoanalysis of Loss. *Journal of the American Psychoanalytical Association* 52(1):43–67.

Derrida, J. (1995). Archive Fever: A Freudian Impression. *Diacritics* 25(2):9–63.

Estrada, I.M. (2013). *El documental cinematográfico y televisivo contemporáneo. Memoria, Sujeto y Formación de la Identidad Democrática Española.* Woodbridge: Tamesis Books.

---

[12] This chapter is based on the introduction of my book: 'Encountering the Trace', in *Aesthetics, Ethics and Trauma in the Cinema of Pedro Almodóvar* (Edinburgh: Edinburgh University Press, 2017). I would like to thank Edinburgh University Press for giving me permission to publish a modified version of my introduction.

Ettinger, B. (2000). Art as the Transport-Station of Trauma, in *Bracha Lichtenberg Ettinger: Artworking 1985–1999,* Ghent: Ludion, pp. 91–115.

Farrell, K. (1998). *Post-Traumatic Cultures: Injury and Interpretation in the Nineties.* Baltimore: Johns Hopkins University Press.

Freud, S. (1962 [1923]). *The Ego and the Id,* trans. James Strachey. New York: Norton.

——(1964 [1937–9]). *Moses and Monotheism, An Outline of Psycho-Analysis and Other Works (1937–1939).* London: The Hogarth Press.

——(2003 [1920]). Beyond the Pleasure Principle, in *Beyond the Pleasure Principle and Other Writing.,* London: Penguin Books, pp. 45–102.

——(2009 [1917]). Mourning and Melancholia in Leticia Glocer Fiorini, Sergio Lewkowicz and Thierry Bokanowski (eds), *On Freud's 'Mourning and Melancholia'.* London: Karnac Books, pp. 44–59.

Gabilondo, J. (2005). Melodrama atlántico y migrancia maternal. Apuntes sobre *Todo sobre mi madre* in Zurian, Fran and Vázquez Varela, Carmen (eds), *Almodóvar: El Cine Como Pasión.* Cuenca: Ediciones de la Universidad de Castilla-La Mancha, pp. 287–306.

Golob, S. (2008). Volver: The Return of/to Transitional Justice Politics in Spain. *Journal of Spanish Cultural Studies* 9(2):127–41.

Gutiérrez-Albilla, J.D. (2011). Children of Exile: Trauma, Memory, and Testimony in Jaime Camino's Documentary *Los niños de Rusia* (2001), in Davies, Ann (ed.), *Spain on Screen: Developments in Contemporary Spanish Cinema.* Hampshire: Palgrave Macmillan, pp. 129–50.

——(2017). *Aesthetics, Ethics and Trauma in the Cinema of Pedro Almodóvar,* Edinburgh: Edinburgh University Press.

Harvey, D. (1990). *The Condition of Postmodernity: An Enquiry into the Origins of Cultural Change.* Malden, MA: Wiley-Blackwell.

Hirsch, J. (2001). *Afterimage: Film, Trauma, and the Holocaust.* Philadelphia: Temple University Press.

Ibáñez, J.C. (2013). Memory, Politics, and the Post-Transition in Almodóvar's Cinema, in D'Lugo, Marvin and Kathleen Vernon (eds), *A Companion to Pedro Almodóvar.* Malden, MA: Wiley-Blackwell, pp. 153–75.

Kinder, M. (2009). All about the Brothers: Retroseriality in Almodóvar's Cinema in Epps, Brad and Despina Kakoudaki (eds), *All About*

Almodóvar: A Passion for Cinema. Minneapolis: University of Minnesota Press, pp. 267–94.

Laplanche, J.(1999). Notes on Afterwardness' in John Fletcher (ed.), *Essays on Otherness*. London: Routledge, pp. 260–65.

Leader, D.2008). *The New Black: Mourning, Melancholia and Depression*, Minneapolis, Minnesota: Graywolf Press.

Loureiro, Á.(2008). Pathetic Arguments. *Journal of Spanish Cultural Studies* 9(2):225–37.

Luckhurst, R. (2008). *The Trauma Question*. London: Routledge.

Markuš, S.(2001. *La poética de Pedro Almodóvar*. Barcelona: Littera.

Marsh, S. (2014). Untimely Materialities: Spanish Film and Spectrality. *Journal of Spanish Cultural Studies* 15(3):293–98.

Moreiras, C. (2002). *Cultura herida. Literatura y cine en la España democrática*. Madrid: Libertarias.

Moreiras, C. (2014). *Laberinto de pasiones:* lógicas de mercado global y simulacro identitario. *Miríada Hispánica* 5:135–52.

Nixon, M. (2007). Wars I Have Seen: Louise Bourgeois and Gertrude Stein, unpublished paper given at the Louise Bourgeois Conference, Tate Modern, London (October).

Pérez Melgosa, A. (2013). The Ethics of Oblivion: Personal, National, and Cultural Memories in the Films of Pedro Almodóvar, in D'Lugo, Marvin and Kathleen Vernon (eds), *A Companion to Pedro Almodóvar*. Malden, MA: Wiley-Blackwell, pp. 176–99.

Pollock, G. (2008). Feminist Shamelessness, unpublished paper given at 'Sex and Shame in the Visual Arts', Tate Modern: London (December).

——(2013a). *After-affects/After-images: Trauma and aesthetic transformation in the virtual feminist museum*. Manchester: Manchester University Press.

——(2013b). Editor's Introduction, in Griselda Pollock (ed.), *Visual Politics of Psychoanalysis: art and the image in post-traumatic cultures*. London: IB Tauris, pp. 1–22.

——& Max Silverman (2011). Concentrationary Cinema, in Pollock, Griselda and Max Silverman (eds), *Concentrationary Cinema: Aesthetics as Political Resistance in Alain Resnais's Night and Fog (1955)*. New York: Berghahn Books, pp. 1–54

Raffoul, F. (2007). Derrida et L'éthique de l'im-possible. *Revue de métaphysique et de morale* 53(1):73–88.

Rancière, J. (2007). *The Future of the Image*, London: Verso.

Richard, N. (2013), *Crítica y política.* Santiago: Palinodia.

Rolnik, S.(2008a). 'A Shift Towards the Unnamable', in Guy Brett (ed.), *Cildo Meireles.* London: Tate Publishing, pp. 132–37.

Seguin, J.-C. (2009). *Pedro Almodóvar o la deriva de los cuerpos.* Murcia: Tres Fronteras Ediciones.

Skoller, J. (2005). *Shadows, Specters, Shards: Making History in Avant-garde Film.* Minneapolis: Minnesota University Press.

Silverman, M. (2011). Fearful imagination: *Night and Fog* and concentrationary memory, in Pollock, Griselda and Max Silverman (eds), *Concentrationary Cinema: Aesthetics as Political Resistance in Alain Resnais's Night and Fog (1955).* New York: Berghahn Books, pp. 199–213.

Smith, P.J.(2003). *Contemporary Spanish Culture: TV, Fashion, Art & Film,* Cambridge: Polity.

——(2014). *Desire Unlimited: The Cinema of Pedro Almodóvar,* London: Verso.

Subirats, E. (2002). Transición y espectáculo, in Eduardo Subirats (ed.), *Intransiciones. Crítica de la cultura española.* Madrid: Biblioteca Nueva, pp. 71–85.

Varderi, A. (1996). *Severo Sarduy y Pedro Almodóvar: Del barroco al kitsch en la narrative y el cine postmodernos.* Madrid: Pliegos.

Yarza, A. (1999). *Un cannibal en Madrid. La sensibilidad 'camp' y el reciclaje de la historia en el cine de Pedro Almodóvar.* Madrid: Ediciones Libertarias.

CHAPTER 3

Navigating Almodóvar's *Labyrinth of Passion*

Bennett E. Roth

Discussing Almodóvar's *Labyrinth of Passion (1982)* involves entering the labyrinth of a movie, a particular movie, and thus, encountering the labyrinth of Almodóvar' cinematic imagination. We must share in his journey, marveling at where we are being led. Will we be lost in the labyrinth?

For many of us, you can't simply psychoanalyze a movie; you must first pass through its sensuous barrage, trying to make sense of the visual and aural stimulation. As sophisticated audience members we have learned cognitive methods of making sense of the fragmented stimulation: suspending disbelief and using our cognitive and intuitive skills to comprehend the story, action, plot or narrative trajectory through the separate and disjointed visual scenes. The movie screen stimulates the audience in multiple ways through a complex orchestration of group cinematic techniques transforming a series of acted scenes into a visual story that is held in an envelope of sound and moving images.

A moviemaker may best be viewed as someone who fantasizes while wide awake, creating a fictive realm, and then transfers that realm onto film, allowing other people to fantasize and (day) dream along with him (Freud, 1908). Movies work best when they reveal a part of the human condition while satisfying deeply felt regressive needs for stimulation of the mind, the emotions and imagination through evocative images, action and sound. Analyzing a movie need not destroy its vicarious pleasures. I analyze a movie only to increase my pleasure and appreciation of it, to enhance my understanding of its artistry of the movie, and to understand my premeditated judgments of plot and image. When seeing a stimulating movie more than once my emotions rule over my intellect, yet I believe insight into a movie can only happen when accompanied by my senses and emotions, for they inform and contribute to my judgments (Langer, 1988).

It is important to note that a film cannot be treated analytically as if it is a dream, as the conventions of narrative predominate and it is a collective project with many tasks not in evidence on the screen. Importantly, a movie is only manifest content and its depth is created in the minds and memories of the audience. To overcome this limitation, I use Bion's concept of selected fact (1970), an interpretation that explains some of the sensuous data in the film.

Selected Fact: The plot and narrative structure in movie tales are usually created and experienced as a journey or a passage through time and geography. A narrative film has an introduction or exposition, a middle and an end or a solution to the narrative.

The Almodóvar film *Labyrinth of Passion* takes the audience on a tour of the sexually ambiguous world of Madrid immediately after the demise of Franco and his repressive regime. We have two guides, one female and the other male and the film's "climax" is a bawdy sexual joke about sex on an airplane. The female is Sexilia, a pop star and a nymphomaniac; and the other is Riza, the gay son of the imaginary Ex-Emperor of the imaginary country of Tiran. From this start we are in a Spanish carnival of gender confusion that contains a mockery of conventional Spanish sexual mores, hidden jokes and a visual parody of transgender comedy. All this set in a milieu of drug dealers, scientists, psychoanalysts and high-class queens and transvestites.

Selected fact: the film is a Spanish language film. *Labyrinth* is not only set in Spain, it is in Spanish, establishing the movie's frame as

Spanish gendered culture. In this context there are four elements that are significant in the Spanish culture: the Civil War in Spain, Francisco Franco and his regime, the representations of the labyrinth, and the geography of gender relationships in Spain. In pre-Christian religions the symbolism of a bull in the labyrinth had special significance. The Minoan representation of the bullfight, the symbolic use of the bull and the labyrinth are mythic elements suggested by the title of the Almodóvar film (Grotjahn, 1959). These elements form part of the cultural underpinnings of the Spanish masculine culture. For the Spanish, Theseus and Christ are joined in the imagery of the bullfight. Throughout the Mediterranean cultures, sacrificing bulls is a practice dating back to pre-historic times. In Greece, for example, killing the Minotaur is a symbolic reference to a bullfight and also suggests the labyrinth built by Daedalus. Given these references, sacrifice can be considered a theme (Grotjahn, 1959) in this movie, and the act of escape from Spain can be compared to a pilgrimage.

Selected fact: There are secondary meanings of Almodóvar's term "Labyrinth". In prehistory the labyrinth was a place where evil spirits were believed to be trapped; in later years it has come to symbolize a difficult path to God or cosmic order with a clearly defined center (God) and one entrance (birth). Labyrinths can also be thought of as symbolic forms of earthly pilgrimage; people can walk the path, ascending towards salvation, enlightenment or death and on the path out one is born anew. As many people lacked the means to travel to holy sites and lands, the use of labyrinths and prayer fulfilled that need. Later, the religious significance of labyrinths faded and they were used primarily for entertainment and meditation.

It is also possible in this film that Almodóvar assumed a connection between Madrid and a symbolic labyrinth as a pathway from the rural areas of Spain to the freedom of sexual choice and masquerade in Madrid. In Almodóvar's cinematic world all sexual boundaries are violated but seemingly without any visual transgressive pleasure or the experience of pain. The wayward paths of the characters suggest a pop-style cult film embedded with a fascination for sexual ambiguity merged with sexual license: but oddly without either real pleasure or guilt. The film has a self-conscious gossipy amorality that contributes to an exhibitionistic impostoring without revealing sympathy for its characters. Is sexuality without emotion the demon bringing people to Madrid and then releasing them to escape on the path out of Spain?

The Plot

The narrative structure of this film is a series of micro-plots. Central is the great Argentinean actress Cecilia Roth, who plays Sexilia (Sexi for short), a carefree nymphomaniac whose father (Luis Ciges) is a world-renowned fertility specialist. Hoping to exorcise her fear of sunlight (which she associates with her father), Sexi consults a therapist who determines that her chief problem is an incestuous attraction to her father. Then another patient confesses her attraction to her father. She also desires her stepson Riza and is in Madrid looking for him.

Riza just wants to cruise the gay bars and straight discos incognito, but he has difficulty maintaining a low profile, let alone anonymity. Reading the newspaper *El Pais*, Riza focuses on four stories, shown by Almodóvar as inserts à la Hitchcock. The first depicts the flight of Tiran's Emperor to Paraguay; the second concerns Sexi's father, a Spanish bio-gynecologist who has experimented with cloned canaries that cannot sing, and the third is an advertisement for porn star Patty Diphusa, (which is also the name of Almodóvar's literary alter ego, whose adventures he wrote about in a column for the Spanish magazine *La Luna*). The fourth is the wimpish and seemingly defenseless daughter of Sexi's dry cleaner. Abandoned by his wife, the somewhat peculiar man rapes this daughter every other day with the aid of an aphrodisiac. She protests that she is his daughter, not his wife, and he counters that even if she has four personalities he loves them all. The theme of splitting of identity as a primitive psychoanalytic defense will reappear throughout the movie. Riza's activities create scandals, especially after he goes to bed with Sadec (the young Antonio Banderas) and soon, revolutionary student-terrorists plan to kidnap him for ransom.

Riza finally meets Sexi in person in the nightclub Carolina, in which both Fabio de Miguel (Fanny McNamara) and Almodóvar himself perform a song titled "Suck it to Me," with the camera revealing Almodóvar in fishnet stockings and Fabio in drag. The name of the second song, which is lip-synched by Riza, is also suggestive, "Gran Ganga" ("Big Bargain"). Another song heard during this episode includes the lyric: "Looking for your warmth I went down to the sewers, and the rats gave me their love." Following the tradition of Carnival, the ribald or openly suggestive lyrics in the songs are accompanied by bumps and grinds. The lyrics provide an open pleasure in avoiding censure while alternately arousing and condemning the behavior they describe imitating the songs of the Carnival.

Predictably, the duo Riza and Sexi immediately fall madly in love in a broad imitation of American cinematic romance stories à la Rock Hudson and Doris Day. Also predictably, the course of their love is not smooth. The satirical movie targets also include test tube babies, Islamist influences in Spain, and tyranny, virility cures, medicalization in general, incest, psychoanalysis and plastic surgery.

The opening montage sets the tone of the film focusing on Riza and Sexi cruising in the Madrid flea market by showing that their perverse desire characterizes homosexuality just as much as heterosexuality. This is accomplished by the camera's obvious focus on men's crotches rather than the female body, in an obvious parody of the male gaze at the female body

Film Theory

For more than 50 years, no other area of academic and cultural theory has been so dependent on its concrete utilization of psychoanalytic theory as Film Studies. Classical psychoanalysis has provided a set of core intellectual concepts or models that have been used to frame film theory while the study of cinema has become established as an academic discipline. However, in this academic domain film was not considered to exist in the same domain as an individual or social dream and not subject to the same rules or processes of interpretation. The 1970s and 1980s witnessed the emergence of a feminist challenge to the image of women on the screen. The film theorist Mary Ann Doane (1991), among others, noted that the significant emergence of a psychoanalytic feminist film theory spear-headed by Laura Mulvey (2009), Juliet Mitchell (Mitchell and Mishra, 2000), and others, was constructed on the assumptions of a "perfect fit" between a feminist revision of Freudian theory and cinematic narrative. Because of the perception of the clear narrative divergence between films geared toward male and feminine audiences it was necessary to revise film theory and criticism that relied heavily on the somewhat more gender neutral dynamics of gaze, voyeurism, fetishism of the woman's body, and audiences' identification. It was recognized by these critics that the hero or heroine as ego ideal in film was conceived exclusively for the audience in the culturally dominant masculine terms (Doane, 1991); likewise the male gaze dominated the female gaze (Mulvey, 2009) and went unchallenged in most films. While psychoanalysis evolved in response to some essential questions regarding gender, it is not yet true for the film industry until recently. The American studio system has remained mostly driven by money profit/male interests with some inroads by the "Maternal," or female heroines.

Classical Freudian theory is central to the application of this psychoanalytic model that has been appropriated by film studies, heavily influenced by Lacan's particular view of subjectivity embedded in French philosophy and film theory. The representation of and attention to sexual difference in the cinema has drawn on what is seen as Lacan's deterministic account of the triangular Oedipal construction as the child's entry into the symbolic system — language, law of the father, and culture. This is presented as coterminous with the construction of the achievement of sexual difference between the sexes, the representation of the body and the cinematic dramatic conclusion. This in turn rested upon the historic pattern of film censorship that was likely influenced by the theoretical dynamics of castration anxiety in men and women with the possession or not of the phallus representing presence and authority or loss ('lack') (Mulvey, 1989). To allay the threat of male castration or loss of status within a cinematic narrative and its dramatic closure, the woman must be found either morally damaged or 'guilty'. Patriarchal Hollywood cinema and melodrama with its required resolution seemed perfectly made for this purpose, cinematic narratives were organized by means of a male-based language, separation from the female as maternal followed by conquest and heterosexual desire. Movie thematic narrative trajectory could be divided into four acts: set-up: complication, development and climax, following the structure of dramatic narratives in many other genres. In cognitive and dramatic terms, the problem established at the opening has to be solved by the end of the film as in the realistic novel. Classical editing, deriving from D. W. Griffith, separated reality and time into succession of shots or scenes that were organized as a series of either logical or subjective points of viewpoints of a narrative. The perception of time as a constant baseline in reality was mysteriously and magically transformed by film techniques that signaled shifts in time among present, past and future.

This conventional dramatic structure was often not followed by innovative European filmmakers. Metz (1975) focused on narrative structure and confounded the problem by reminding the theorists that the events on the screen were fictive although the act of watching was real. What is perceived in a film is not really the object; rather, it is a replica in a new kind of technical mirror (pp 443–445) that works by reproducing and enunciating the dominant ideology, thus stimulating by a chain of memory traces from which the audience makes meaning. Importantly Metz tied meaning and memory together in a rapid loop. This moving mirror was constructed to arouse emotion within our own subjectivity. Metz (1974) went on by quoting Ingmar Bergmann, who wrote: 'I … use … an apparatus with which I can sway my audience in a highly emotional manner—make them laugh, scream with fright, smile, believe in fairy stories, become indignant, feel shocked, charmed, deeply moved or perhaps yawn with boredom." When we set out to experience a film, we consciously prime ourselves for illusion" (P. 387). Cinema requires participation in the imaginative possibility, given by the mechanical-passive and unchanging camera, to extend vision beyond the boundaries of individual subjectivity to intimacy, voyeurism or another domain. When a film is viewed for the second time the film does not change but its perception is altered and the audience more aware that they are watching a cinematic construction.

One example of the problems of male and female genre from this earlier perspective is that Western films were viewed as a celebration of overt American masculinity and benign homosexuality; however the form of male loving male is hidden behind cultural ideas of hyper-masculine individualism which is also present in the patriotic war film with the brotherhood-of-men motifs. From this perspective, war films present both a homoerotic bonding and violent killing of men. The classic male image in both film genres is also stoic, Midwestern and charismatic, violent when provoked, and at the same time chivalrous: in a word, an American emblem of secure manhood facing a crisis in a narrative without women. Not so in films by Almodóvar, who claimed in an interview, "Men are boring", and "Madrid is the center of the World". In *Labyrinth*, men are reduced to nearly absurd icons as is the incestuous cleaner repeatedly at the steam presser.

Two important concepts in film theory are the concept of the scoptophilic drive and the codification of objects of fascination within the cinematic text. In psychoanalytic theory the nature of the gaze, or the audience's pleasure in looking (Mulvey, 1989) was reductively seen as male, with the images on the screen symbolizing a replication of the parts of the female body or the primal scene. That pleasure in spectatorship informed directorial strategies of camera movement and editing which were "knowingly" intended to place the spectator in a particular position, thus stimulating or intensifying the desire to look at the staged visual representation. In summary, psychoanalytic discussions of symbolic meaning within conventional film were severely limited by a set of restrictive psycho-analytic notions such as the master plot of male desire, the surrender of the female or the return of the primal scene (Roth, 2007). Additionally, in prior theorizing, the spectator was assumed to be heterosexual. Almodóvar's *Labyrinth* moved that assumption in a new direction by presenting homosexual masquerade and the vibrantly colorful sexual carnival to be gazed at. *Labyrinth*, while acknowledging the existence of the patriarchal order or status through parody and rule breaking, still contains the seeds of its criticism and transgressions in which perverse ruptures are the essential rule rather than the exception. This results in an opposition between patriarchy (oedipal), a variety of females' problems and homosexuality, with the unfolding struggle among the three positions in the film. Since, I assume, homosexual men are socialized differently from both heterosexual men and women, the homosexual men are situated in a different and perhaps fractured position in both patriarchy and matriarchy. This unique position calls into question the usual gendered spectator's capacity for empathic gaze and identification with Almodóvar's characterizations. Who desires whom in the film?

Humphrey (1975) in his classic study of impersonal gay public sex in the United States offers something significant here. He describes his adoption of the position of "watch queen," a homosexual who watches gay sex acts but does not participate, in his sociological study. This complex gaze position enjoys the primary position of looking without participation and enhances the pleasure of those looked at. The secondary simultaneous position is directed at the heterosexual world outside the public toilet; here he was a lookout. The duality of this role, as noted by Smith (1994), suggests a model for understanding Almodóvar as director: voyeur and lookout. In addition, Almodóvar suggests, through characters and camera movements in his film, that hetero- and homosexuality are identical in their aim. Madrid becomes his cinematic labyrinth inhabited by sexual eccentrics preoccupied with incest, reproduction, and exhibitionistic performance. Sexi as an actor blurs the lines between perverse and the normal with her theatricality and audacity that will somehow magically cure Riza of his love of men. All this is happening on the screen while the emotion that is revealed on screen is nullified, and doesn't fit into the actors' bodies or dialogue, but overflows into the mise-en-scene: the exaggerated colorful costumes, and the score, creating cinematic conflict regarding modes of performance, comedy and acting styles. The audience as well as this reviewer is forced to consider a clash of modes of representation of identity within each character leading to a basic confusion about Almodóvar's intent. Almodóvar does not tolerate grasping either political or psychoanalytic ideas concerning gay life in this film, preferring to confuse and over-stimulate the audience and play against cinematic expectancy.

Masquerade

Masquerade has a long tradition in Spain and theater. It is defined as "an action or appearance that is mere disguise or show." It is to pretend to be someone you are not, or to knowingly put on a deceptive appearance. The psychological latent key is that masquerade simultaneously creates anonymity as well liberation from restrictive social norms, thereby facilitating expressions that are otherwise suppressed (Gargano, 2007). Masquerade is an essential element of Carnival in which men masquerade as women, witches, and devils. In *Labyrinth*'s masquerade the characters' masculinity and femininity becomes arbitrary and fluidly interchangeable—often dependent on a matter of style, performance, or the people of the moment. I believe that the use of masquerade in this film is intended to raise the question of whether masculinity and femininity are defined by biology or if they can be contrived in a laboratory or worn as a costume. This confusion and ambiguity echoes the gender interchangeability of the characters in the Spanish Carnival. This destroys the public objectivity of the event, making it meaningful only as a lived moment in time and aiming to eliminate the political and the psychological aspects of gender (Gilmore, 1998) by showing people as either maternal clowns or loathsome. This double image degrades people, but may also free them.

One result in this film is that sex; gender and social status are ambiguous and at the same time are fought over. The film becomes a series of seeming moral dialogues between Almodóvar's characters, between people of different social status and ambiguous gender identification that define them to themselves. It serves as an assault, as all comedy does, against the ruling orders and normative structures of reality and in particular the role of the father. In Spain, Carnival is revolutionary and reactionary at the same time, subversive and conservative at the same time. It reveals an impulse to degrade and ridicule those with status while also acknowledging their status. The ingredient of "spice" or exaggeration in dialogue and costume is necessary, and the movie is as scandalous and provocative as a gossip magazine, meant to arouse the audience, yet delivered in a flat dead-pan style in *Labyrinth*. This style exhibits a dis-inhibition and promiscuity as well as a casual indifference to any social transgressions in reality. In another polarity, tragedy and comedy intertwine into melodrama that causes emotional confusion in the audience. Through this merging Almodóvar added another salient feature with sexual inversion presented in a parade of rapid scenes depicting people changing gender without interludes for the audience to digest what just happened. Which gender is real? Or, what is the acceptable reality?

This constant ambiguity may be explained by Doane's (1991) concept of female masquerade, which helps to explain the importance of masquerade for the woman on the screen. Doane relied on Riviere's idea that woman who found themselves in the role of "male authority" put on a mask of femininity that compensated for their masculinization and that mask creates interpersonal distance. Clover (2015) also offers a foundation for understanding Almodóvar in her analysis of horror films,. These films attempt to "feminize" the audience. Not only is all the audience feminized, but Almodóvar engages in a celebration of exaggeration and sexual excess: the good mother and the whore. Feminization may also carry with it the wish to create a homoerotic appeal to the woman spectator to initially identify with the victim and the victim turned savior of the gay man. This is accomplished by what Saddik (2015) called the freedom of (cinematic) exaggeration and excess often expressed in cross dressing and a celebration of what she called 'the strange, the crazed, the queer' as celebrity or hero. Daniel Harris (2005) in his book, *Diary of a Drag Queen*, suggests that people are generally more tolerant of drag queens (who may or may not be homosexual) than they are of homosexuals per se, because drag queens have become staples of Hollywood films and are "therefore an endearing object of amused pity."

From another perspective there is an unquestionably strong emphasis on mocking hyper-femininity and ridiculing female gender stereotypes that occurs in a Mediterranean culture that celebrates legitimate biological motherhood. The Virgin, as a moral model of the good Spanish mother among the pantheon of male saints, puts macho men at some disadvantage while sanctifying the mother-son connection and their inherent femininity. In Carnival the men "steal" a piece of their mother's clothing to flaunt. Almodóvar, who was by all accounts more deeply attached to his mother, displays a range of erotic cinematic inventiveness and the grotesque acceptance of the breakdown in sexual prohibitions by producing discordant images with muted emotional reactions regarding the suggestion of sexual acts.

European film, when compared to the dominant American cinema, was more invested in European philosophy and in the possibilities opened up by a new artistic medium, its impact on perception, and the strong power it can have on audiences. The impact of different national traditions and traditions in theater and philosophy influenced the approaches to film theory and what films were made. The central importance of the director as auteur had roots in Europe, while in America this was modified by the studio's power, then reestablished by the director-as-celebrity.

As one of his earliest films, *Labyrinth* established Almodóvar in the genre of the carnivalesque, the grotesque, and the psychoanalytic.

As such, he is a ripe subject for feminist and queer theory. On the surface Almodóvar pokes fun at conventional sexual mores and celebrates the freedom of Spanish Carnival, with its glorification of "the strange, the crazed, the queer." He also emulates the spirit of Carnival as social resistance by ignoring the limits of gender, utilizing comic violence and bawdy, exaggerated language, and presenting (even celebrating) acts that are deemed to be morally repugnant and outrageously perverse according to traditional mores, in order to mock what is held to be sacrosanct and normal. This style tends to deride the entire culture, and the society that produced it, as a perverse game.

This attack reveals an assault on the narrative formulaic structure on which dramatic realism is based. Caricature and parody are related creative forms of the attack on conventions. In aesthetics they are generally viewed as inferior to serious artistic efforts, and the elite and critics of the artistic community give their creators grudging condescension as second-class citizens. Caricature refers almost exclusively to distortions of the image of personal physiognomy, while the terms parody and travesty are applied to similar treatment of literary or dramatic productions.

Macdonald (1965), a literary critic, points out that the dictionaries cannot be relied upon to concur in the subtle distinctions of meaning in the various terms. All three forms as well as burlesque have certain critical features in common but vary in different cultures and languages. In this film they exaggerate or minimize certain aspects of the object for the purpose of mockery while leaving the illusion of recognizability of the original object intact. Travesty usually refers to a caricature of dramatic or literary form, while parody satirizes the content of the literary production. Burlesque is considered by some to be an even more "degraded" relative of travesty. Cult films may rely on a Guignol device of comic caricature, which when successful allows the aggressor(s) to insult his victim without malice and the victim to feel some pride in being insulted; why is this important? These forms of dramatic technique raise questions about Almodóvar's targets.

As American filmmakers were struggling to include overt sexual material in the movies and to make homosexual material acceptable to the Hays Office and the Legion of Decency, "sissy" characters were suggestive of homosexuality, In *Pillow Talk* (1959), very much admired by Almodóvar and perhaps serving as a template for this screen play, Rock Hudson played a character who posed as gay in order to seduce a woman. It was highly ironic, to depict a gay man impersonating a straight man impersonating a gay man to seduce a woman. I believe that these plot devices in the hands of Almodóvar are meant to deepen the audience's emotional and gender insecurities and emotional needs or to cultivate again both an exhibition of and rejection of the eccentric world revealed. At the same time Almodóvar offers his imaginative queer theory. Sexi and Riza met as preteens, each felt betrayed by the other and she becomes promiscuous and he turns to boys. When they meet again they do not recognize each other (amnesia), memory returns and they fall in love.

The critics' initial reaction to this film was one of confusion. I believe they expected a more traditional comedy in that pre-AIDS culture. Almodóvar's eccentricities were larger than his screenplay could contain, and spilled out in the film's dialogue. In later films he began to master his cinematic technique and his wish to shock the audience. It is tempting to offer pathological explanations from his childhood (Greenacre, 1957) for all the symbolic interactions; unfortunately they would be my reverie….

References

Bion, W.R. (1970). *Attention and Interpretation.* London: Tavistock Publications.

Clover, C. (2015). *Men, Women, and Chain Saws: Gender in the Modern Horror Film,* Updated Edition. Princeton: Princeton: University Press.

Doane, M. A. (1991). *Femme Fatales: Feminism, Film Theory and Psychoanalysis.* London: Routledge.

Freud, S. (1908). Creative Writers and Day-dreaming. *Standard Edition* 5:142–153.

Gargano, E. (2007). The masquerader in the garden: Gender and the body. In: Angela Carter's The Magic Toyshop. *Women's Studies* 36:57–78.

Gilmore, D. (1998). *Carnival and Culture: Sex Symbol and Status in Spain.* Yale University Press: New Haven.

Greenacre P. (1957). The childhood of the artist: Libidinal phase development and giftedness. *Psychoanalytic Study Child* 12:47–72.

Grotjahn M. (1959). On bullfighting and the future of tragedy. *International Journal of Psycho-Analysis* 40:238–239.

Humphreys, L. (1975). *Tearoom Trade: A Study of Homosexual Encounters in Public Places.* New York: Aldine Publishing.

Langer. S. K. (1988). *Mind: An Essay on Human Feeling.* Baltimore: The Johns Hopkins Press.

Macdonald, D. (1960). *Parodies: An anthology from Chaucer to Beerbohm.* New York: Random House.

Metz, C. (1990). *Film Language: A Semiotic of the Cinema.* Chicago: University of Chicago Press.

———(1986). *The Imaginary Signifier.* Bloomington: Indiana University Press.

Mitchell, J. & Mishra, K.M. (2000). *Psychoanalysis and Feminism: A radical reassessment of Freudian Psychoanalysis.* New York: Basic Books.

Mulvey, L. (1999). *Visual and Other Pleasures.* New York: Palgrave Macmillan.

Riviere, J. (1929). Womanliness as Masquerade. *Iinternational Journal of Psychoanalysis* 9:303–13.

Saddik, A.J. (2015). *Tennessee Williams and the Theater of Excess: The Strange, The Crazed, The Queer.* New York: Cambridge University Press.

Smith, P.J. (1994) *Desire Unlimited: The Cinema of Pedro Almodóvar* (2 ed.). London: Verso.

Film

Almodóvar, P. (Director). (1982). *Labyrinth of Passion.* [Motion Picture]. Spain: Alphaville.

Gordon, M. (Director). (1959). *Pillow Talk.* USA: Arwin.

CHAPTER 4

Dark Habits and Lost Souls:
The Struggle within the Struggle

Arthur A. Lynch, Lourdes Rigual-Lynch, and Arnold D. Richards

Introduction

Entre Tinieblas (1983), loosely translated as *Dark Habits*, is Pedro Almodóvar's third feature. In this film he continues to experiment with content and form, while deeply exploring the time period he has lived through–"La Movida Madrileña". This is the counter-culture backlash (a reactionary response) that was centralized in Madrid and later moved throughout Spain in the late 1970s. It emerged at the end of the "Spanish State"(*Estado Español*),(a.k.a. the Francoist era) (1939–1975), and the return of democracy with a titular monarchy. As with every period of transition, the people of Madrid[1] and Spain[2] had to divest the traumatic remnants of living under an oppressive government and invest in solutions that addressed the question: What's next for us? The answer depends on a preceding question: "How have I lived through this era?" In the interim, the inhabitants of this transition had to wait and embrace the uncertainty of a future not yet determined.

---

[1] 1980 Madrid Population: 4.25 million inhabitants. worldpopulationreview.com/world-cities/madrid-population

[2] 1980 Spain Population 1980 – 37.7 million inhabitants. www.populationpyramid.net/spain/1980

Story Narrative

The scene opens with a view of Madrid's congested traffic at the end of the day. It is about 6:00 p.m. when darkness falls and we meet Yolanda, a struggling cabaret singer walking home. She brings her boyfriend some heroin, which he injects and dies from. Without too much thought or emotion Yolanda picks up a few things and quickly leaves for the cabaret. After a brief encounter with the police, who are at the cabaret looking to question her, she takes flight. She finds shelter at the "Convent of the Humiliated Redeemers" after finding a card that the Mother Superior, a fan of hers, had given her earlier. Yolanda becomes part of the convent's community and finds safety with five unconventional nuns, an off-beat priest, and a pet tiger. The previously busy convent that used to welcome, protect and redeem prostitutes, drug addicts and murderers, has fallen into disrepair. They are facing serious financial problems, and their main source of protection, a greedy Marquesa who studies cosmetology, is discontinuing her deceased husband's endowment to the convent. She tells Mother Superior that she would rather use the funds to live in luxury. In the past the convent had sheltered their troubled daughter, "Virginia", who became a nun to escape her father's tyranny. Virginia later went to Africa, where she was eaten by cannibals.

Mother Superior tells Yolanda that the business of the convent is "Self Mortification and Humiliation". She explains this is the reason why the nuns have bizarre names: Sisters Manure, Damned, Snake, and Rat of the Sewers. Yolanda befriends the nuns. The Mother Superior instantly falls lustfully in love with her. They form an attachment through their shared use of heroin and cocaine until Yolanda declares that they both should quit. For Yolanda, withdrawal provides painful but important insights. For Mother Superior, withdrawal only confirms her sinful life and she is unable to quit. Yolanda then distances herself from Mother Superior and becomes friendly with Sister Rat.

As the threat of Yolanda's rejection and the closing of the convent looms, Mother Superior devises a plan to blackmail the Marquesa with a compromising letter she has recently received from Africa about her daughter Virginia. When this attempt fails, she turns to drug trafficking in order to keep the convent open.

In the midst of this turmoil, the sisters continue to plan a party for Mother Superior's birthday. The Marquesa, the Mother General of the Order, and nuns from other convents, are invited. During the party Yolanda and some of the sisters sings a foreboding salsa, "Sali porque sali" ("I left because I left") for Mother Superior. Yolanda's warning is crystal clear. She does not make strong or reliable attachments.

The Marquesa manipulates Yolanda and Sister Rat into getting the letter about Virginia, which Mother Superior has hidden in her chambers. The letter reveals that the Marquesa has a long-lost grandson who was raised by apes. In gratitude, at the end of the party the Marquesa invites Yolanda and Sister Rat to live with her. Also at the end of the party, the newly appointed Mother General of the Order declares the convent closed. Mother Superior has now lost both Yolanda and the convent. Sister Dammed makes plans to return to her native town and leaves her boy/tiger to Sister Snake and the priest. They are in love and adopt the tiger as their son. Mother Superior collapses under the terrible heartbreak of losing Yolanda and the convent and only Sister Manure remains to provide solace.

Conflicts In Culture

From the very beginning of the film, with the introduction of the title, we are given hints of the deeper allegorical nature of this tale. *Entre Tinieblas*, translated as *Dark Habits* (Habitos Oscuro is a wonderful pun). Almodóvar's choice of *Dark Habits* is more fitting for the film's use of dark comedy. The habitualized patterns of living in the darkness during the fascist era leave most uncertain about their future. With the dawn of a new era, hidden desires begin to burst through. *Dark Habits* could be interpreted as the illegal, sinful, hurtful behaviors flaunted by all the characters in the film. All these behaviors are barely hiding under their "habits" as if literally trying to contain the individuals' flagrant impulses. For example, the headdress of the nuns could be seen as appearing to keep all their fears contained in "darkness" (i.e., the illusion of the Church's protection). Likewise, we see how the abuse of drugs, pervasive at the time, contains the distress and miseries in the characters' lives. Almodóvar juxtaposes the incongruities of life to make his point. The story takes place in a "Humiliated Community of Redeemers". Each character comes with a story and a personal "negative habit".

Another possible translation of the title that could carry Almodóvar's broader message would be "In Between the Shadows" (Entre las Sombras). His choice of *Dark Habits* introduces the pulls between the gentle, playful, comedic nature of the story and its darker dimensions. "In Between (the) Shadows" far better suits the painful and brutal realities of the story, leaving us at times with only a brief respite when we are entertained by its comedic soap-operish form. This title brings us closer to the heart of the film's message (i.e. *oppression and/or any rigid ideology is a grotesquely malignant force on personal development*). These two perspectives, in the suggested titles, capture the essence of the challenge for those caught up in "La Movida Madrileña" and are central to Almodóvar's story. Each aspect of the transition reveals the potential for conflict and a need to dismantle the old life and rebuild a new one. This rebuilding can only be as good as the resources/resolve available.[3]

Almodóvar enhances this conflict, not only by his use of satirical form in the film, but also by delivering the content through the mixture of intense genres of music (e.g., salsa, boleros, merengues, tangos, rancheras). He strategically uses music to express intense emotional moments between the film's main characters, Mother Superior and Yolanda. This is best seen in the music/song choices at three key points in the movie: in Mother Superior's office ("Encadenados"), at her birthday party ("Sali Porque Sali") and at the end of the film ("Encadenados").[4] These enhancements exaggerate the confrontation

---

[3] Some see this as the unfolding of a "divestment/investment" process (Medalie, 1981).
[4] Lucho Gatica's "Encadenados" - English translation "Chained together." Cheo Feliciano's "Sali Porque Sali" - English translation "I left because I left").

that occurs between the old and new, the right wing Nationalists and the new Republic, and Mother Superior and Yolanda's responses to conflicts about cultural mores and moralities. This was a time of experimentation when heroin consumption, and other drugs, became common, and liberal sexual exploration fuelled the AIDS pandemic worldwide. Almodóvar leans heavily on a genre of dark comedy to convey and manage the film's difficult and unpleasant content, which consists of the raw, bleak and harsh choices that emerged in the disillusionment process: Spain is no longer the country it once was and all its adaptive solutions and promises offered during the Francoist era are now gone.

The film uses a subculture (e.g., nuns in a convent) within a national culture to emphasize the fact that the effects of rigid oppression flows from many sources and affects everyone. Of course, this is all reflected in the background of the story—unseen but felt by the viewer.

The characters we meet are visibly struggling with their newfound freedom internally and externally, psychologically and culturally, as they try to adapt to the new reality of the post-Franco era. They seem stuck in their attempts to attain different solutions. Some remain stuck (e.g. Mother Superior and Sister Manure), and others die (e.g. Jorge [Yolanda's boyfriend] and Virginia). Some try to return to the mores of the past (e.g. Sister Damned), and still some try to find new more constructive solutions (Yolanda and Sister Rat, Sister Snake and the priest). However, none get to avoid the painful underlying realities (e.g. both near past and far past) that have brought them to this moment.

The Characters

There are seven major characters in the story, Yolanda and six religious members of the convent: four nuns, the Mother Superior and the priest. Spiritless and lacking in people to redeem, the sisters are forced to delve into their peculiar interests and have difficulty controlling their individual "negative habits".

Almodóvar sets the stage for *Dark Habits* through a series of paradoxes or juxtapositions that are played out among and within the six main characters. Broadly defined the paradoxes include: life/death, love/hate, sadism/masochism, good/evil, feminine/masculine, unknown desires/socio-cultural pressures, activity/passivity, integrity/deception, serving oneself/serving others. These come into play throughout the film.

To say something meaningful about these fictitious characters is challenging. All we know about them is what they say and do. There is no supportive historical information about their lives. Where did they come from? What was life like growing up? What contributed to making them the women and man we meet? Nor is there any information about what it was like for each of them to go through the Francoist era. All we know is that they are a representation of something Almodóvar wants to tell us, about living through this period. Almodóvar, however, provides two possible ways to understand his characters. The first is to view their unusual behaviors as a statement of how badly people needed to behave in this era. Another is to wonder what did go wrong for them that they developed some very skewed characteristics and odd or strange behaviors. At the end of the day, these behaviors served them as a useful means of getting what they needed or wanted. We will use both lenses (the psychological and the cultural) to discuss the characters.

Sister Damned has a compulsive need to clean and nurture animals, including a tiger. Do these devotions carry more than hygienic and loving needs?

On some level one must ask: What drives her to nurture and be nurtured by a ferocious male animal that continually hurts her? She cares for a pet tiger and calls him her "boy". As we look at this behavior, we are trying to sort out what these feelings are about. What does she hope to get from or give to the carnivore? What does she expect in return from the animal and from herself? What allows her to remain so insistent that this is an innocent and caring child/cat? Is this a need to be a mother or something more sinister, like keeping a check on her own cruelty toward men by guarding it in the tiger?

Certainly, as she confesses to the Marquesa, she is in a constant struggle with her "boy", who is always after the "little ones" (i.e., the other small animals she cares for – chickens and rabbits). This is a losing battle, which she persistently returns to and seems repeatedly defeated by. In this sadomasochistic relationship the elements of masochism appear to dominate. Even her name gives us a signification of her accursed and loathsome fate. She has a need to be seen as good, caring and holy but desires punishment from the beast. The pull to satisfy her own deep sense of destructive aggression, one can conjecture, is being both contained and satisfied as she repeatedly makes herself the target for it. Where this is suggested as one possibility for Sister Damned, on an individual level, it can also be explained as a cultural mandate in a time of war. Here she sides with the Nationalists and the Church against the "cruelty" of the Republicans. She is a victim of her religious devotion. Yet she allows herself to have great sympathy for the aggressors. She wants everyone to live in a harmony that is unattainable, even during the counter-culture explosion.

Next we meet the rigid and self-punitive **Sister Manure.** She takes acid to calm her guilt about murdering a man. We have no evidence as to the reasons or circumstances for this murder. She also punishes herself for this sin by walking on broken glass and sleeping in a bed of thorns. Nevertheless, she devotedly cooks and bakes for the community. At times while baking, she hallucinates a vision of the face of Jesus in the dough. She considers these drug-induced hallucinations "religious visions" that allow her to feel closer to her adoring Father (Jesus). These visions bring her some mild sense of redemption. She is also deeply devoted to Mother Superior because the latter saved her from prison by lying for her in court.

We need to begin the discussion of this character with the obvious, her taken name. Manure, as a substance, notifies us of a potential threat. The smell of manure stimulates a sense of disgust and repulsion that may be hardwired into our biology to protect us from the risk of disease and should therefore be avoided (Curtis, et al., 2004). Its bad odour may also signify a deeper repulsion about her sense of self. One can easily conjecture that she is living not only with guilt but also with a deeper sense of shame about the murder. We are compelled to ask: What does this mean to her about herself, as a person, a murderer? How does this inner self-sense lend to her experience around others?

We also need to attend to her needs regarding the self-injurious symptoms. What needs are satisfied by walking on broken glass and sleeping in a bed of thorns? These appear tied to her "Father." Do these behaviors serve as a form of penitence? After all Jesus's golden rule was "love your neighbour as yourself" (Luke 10:27) and "do unto others as you would have them do to you" (Matthew 7:12). Murder does not quite fit into this proposition.[5] Also are these actions tied to her devotion to Mother Superior, or simply a devotion to a "Mother?" One way to understand this special form of self-punishment is to divide it into two phases. The first phase consists of a wish for something (e.g., the wish to murder, for someone to be dead, or the wish to possess another for their own desires) and the second phase brings a need for punishment for having had the wish (Loewenstein, 1945). For Sister Manure, this punishment can be protective of the greater personality, especially as it preserves moral guidance and allows for some hope or relief from the guilt or shame of the sin. In this case, the pain of stepping on broken glass or sleeping on a bed of thorns may mitigate the guilt and shame of having taken a life.

At this point, we can see Sister Manure's character representation as symbolic of a cultural dilemma. How did those young warriors of Spain's Civil War react as grown adults to Movida Madrileña? How did they live with their war crimes? As early as World War I we have repeatedly witnessed the mental trauma and its debilitating effects of combat in posttraumatic stress reactions and syndromes. We see ethnic purges as the basis for most violent forms of war (H. Graham, 2012). Fighting an enemy, as debilitating as it can be, is one thing. Fighting, killing and torturing countryman, neighbours, family

---

[5] An exception might be made for the person that feels the death of one's soul at the hands of another.

members is entirely something else and weighs far heavier, as we have seen in the aftermath of so much ethnic violence. Sister Manure kept her habit on to manage this anguish. What did others with no habit do?

Sister Sewer Rat works in the garden and writes "dirty novels" under a pseudonym. These are stories about the "redeemed" girls who came through the convent. She sneaks the new novels out when her sister comes to visit her. She doesn't realize that her sister, who uses the profits from the books to live in luxury and fame, is exploiting her. One can understand Sister Rat as in search of a way to view herself in the world. She is a nun with her religious vows of humiliation and mortification, but she is also the ghost-writer of sensational novels. Here she struggles to answer the question: Who am I? Am I Sister Sewer Rat (with all the disease and contagion one brings)[6] or am I the writer Concha Torres? This conflict of identity is mainly at rest when she is living in self-mortification and humiliation, but as she dwells in her writing the struggle intensifies.

Yolanda, Almodóvar's central character, is given sanctuary in the convent and she remains conflicted, confused and frightened as she tries to kick her "habits". Yolanda shares the same conflict as Sister Rat and has been searching for something more meaningful in life since the beginning of the story. She has been an academician, horticulturalist, bolero singer, and drug dealer. She has dabbled with the nuns' struggle and in the end leaves the convent to continue her personal search.

What is interesting in the cultural interpretation of these characters is the similarity between the two (Sister Rat and Yolanda). At first they seem very different. Even the path that led them to be invited to live with the Marquesa seemed very different. Sister Rat is

---

[6] A recent study (Firth, et al.,2014) from Columbia University found that the average New York City subway rat carries 18 viruses previously unknown to science, along with dozens of familiar, dangerous pathogens, such as C difficile, hepatitis C and the bubonic plague (in India). This is the plague that killed 25 million people in five years during the 14th Century. Collectively, rats are responsible for more human death than any other mammal on earth.

able to hold onto her identities for long periods; whereas Yolanda leaves them in search of more, without much attachment. However, both characters came through a period of personal struggle defined by the search for a self, which had not reached full realization. Both, also, find a deeper insight. Sister Rat goes through long periods of self-mortification and perhaps self-loathing. This is reinforced by the wretchedness of her sister's deception. Clarity emerges as she discovers that her readers love her writing and that she has become acclaimed. Affirmation has a strong effect in supporting her decisions to leave.

Yolanda too gains a deeper insight into herself from the detoxification she was able to achieve. She no longer believes that she has to rely on others, or even substances, to attain what she needs. This frees her to leave the convent with assurance. In short, both Sister Rat and Yolanda seem to have a greater sense of resilience than the other characters through these difficult times.

On a cultural level we can see these two characters, Yolanda and Sister Sewer Rat, as representing "La Movida Madrileña". They are both going through a "moratorium" state often necessary for people to begin the struggle with the questions raised by Spain's civil war and its dictatorship. "What do we as a nation do now?" "How do we go forward?" "Who as Spaniards are we?" and "Who qualifies as a Spaniard and who does not?" These conflicts of inclusion and exclusion based on ethnicity continue to gnaw at their identity. It is easy to see how this period a time of uncertain norms and expectations was complicated by the exploration and experimentation with what was once taboo (i.e. sex and drugs). This could provide a spectrum of responses from: a sense of direction and certainty through a sense of insecurity, diffusion and havoc. Now that it is over what is next? How do we understand ourselves as individuals and as a people? Can we achieve some semblance of our worth and value in a world of others? Or will we be left to the crisis of only those old solutions that leave little room for non-Spaniards and do not work well as a reflection of our better self?

Sister Snake and **the priest** also share a similar dynamic with one another. They sew garments for the Virgins to cover their bodies. They use their piety as a way to distract themselves from their intense erotic love for one another. This is not just compulsive sewing. It goes into broader knowledge of fashion design, trending, conceiving and creating designs of the near future. In developing their relationship within these parameters they form an adaptive prohibition and a nobler form of love. She gets to fuss over the chainsmoking priest's dark habit and he confesses that he took up sewing to be near the woman he loves. Sister Snake and the priest both represent the older, pre-war, adaptive familial path of the culture, which remains available even during Movida Madrileña. Sometimes the old patterns suit us best.

Mother Superior – She uses the convent and pseudo charity as a way of bringing in frightened and desperate young women. She uses heroin and cocaine to help modulate her overwhelming lesbian erotic desires and, as we have seen, shares these with the residents. She states: "From admiring them so much I have become one of them". In the end, in fact, she has become one of them, deteriorating to the point of blackmail, extortion and drug trafficking.

Mother Superior is a cultural icon for most power-centered organizations. She is the symbol of opportunistic greed and perhaps a destructive envy that drives it. Driven by her intense desire she will use any ploy to attain what she wants. Her moral compass, like the Franco regime and the Church, is broken. Even the Church's multitude of possible adaptive strategies is only used in the service of her desires. So we can see how she could go unnoticed by the government or its partner – the Church, because, in effect, she is one of them. By being unable to directly confront or challenge them in any way she has conformed to their cause. How many citizens lived in this shallow conformity; or worse, complied with Franco's rigid ideology which threatened imprisonment or death to anyone found supporting the Republic's values[7] during the dictatorship?

---

[7] These included: regional autonomy, social democracy, free elections and women's rights, including the vote.

Conclusion

The majority of films are a product of their time. The ones that endure are those that continue to inform or stimulate questions about life and living. Even though it was not as well received as other Almodóvar films on initial release, *Dark Habits* does continue to caution us about those who would repress us or use us solely for their own purposes.[8]

By opening the film in the heart and heat of "La Movida Madrileña" at 6:00pm when darkness falls, Almodóvar is calling out to the people of Madrid to "Move" (to act or engage) faster then the crawling traffic. It was in this counter-culture movement that people composed the wake-up calls to Madrid: "Madrid nunca duerme" ("Madrid never sleeps"), "Esta noche todo el mundo a la calle" ("To-night everybody to the street") or "Madrid me mata" ("Madrid kills me").

Through this cinematic expression he forces us to summon up its catalyst. It is through this very vague remembrance of the impact of the Spanish civil war and the 36 years of military dictatorship that follows, that we can appreciate Yolanda's terror of being blamed for her boyfriend's death. This was only four years into post-Francoist Spain[9] and its new counter-culture movement with a new freedom of expression and transgression of the Franco taboos. The participants of Movida Madrileña were attempting to construct a new Spanish identity, albeit a very vulnerable one. Assault, imprisonment and death lingered in aggressive readiness around each corner. This was best demonstrated by the ex-enjeu (love interest) of the Mother

---

[8] Even today as the ink dries on the page 300 Roman Catholic priests are accused of sexually abusing male children in Pittsburgh. The Pope is moved to not abandon the "little ones". Sister Elizabeth (Liz) Murphy of Ireland is calling for a greater role of women in the Church's authority. She might be asking the question: How can we expect a male dominated institution to find success with male members' sexual abuse of boys? Is it not mostly women worldwide who protect the "little ones"?

[9] The "Concierto homenaje a Canito" ("Canito Memorial Concert"), which occurred on February 9th, 1980, is considered the traditional start date of *La Movida Madrileña*.

Superior, who was arrested and dragged from the convent shoeless, with Mother Superior carrying the shoes and pleading with the police to let her put them on. A more subliminal example of this fragile transition can be gleaned in the Marquesa's character. She perhaps illustrates the small community of the remaining repressed wealthy class in Franco's era. She was doubly repressed; first internally by the brutality of her husband ("he is a monster", she is thrilled he is dead) and secondly, by the cultural regime's severe restrictions. After her husband's death, which coincides with the end of the Franco regime, she bursts into an unrepressed world of freedom by living in "luxury" and doing whatever pleases her, even becoming a cosmetologist. In her conversation about the endowment to the convent Mother Superior reminds the Marquesa that she is a millionaire. The Marquesa responds: "You have to be one to survive, and I don't want just to survive. I want to live life, now!"

With this newly attained freedom, she also becomes an advocate for Yolanda and Sister Rat by enabling them to further search for their personal identity and freedom.

Almodóvar goes beyond the issues of universal pleasures (e.g. sex, love, and happiness) by elevating another universal state – unpleasure or pain. He does this by rendering sadomasochistic dynamics into his characters' desirous pursuits, attempts at moral vindication, and relationship to the broader culture. However, he softens their impact through the use of dark comedy, which somewhat prepares his audience to these painful moments. Even slightly blunted, the audience is left with how to manage the reality passed on by Franco's restrictive government while confronting yet another dark period of the Church's failings. La Movida Madrileña provides answers from one perspective while Almodóvar provides suggestions from yet another. He searches out the restricting consequences on human growth by institutionalized aggression that lingers in our personality and interferes with our appreciation of others and ourselves. Hence, those who are the victims often become the perpetrators and the vicious cycle continues.

References

Almodóvar, Pedro (1983). *Entre tinieblas.* Release date: Spain - March 10, 1983. USA February 4, 1984 under the title of Dark Habits.

Curtis V., Anger R., Rabie, T. (May 2004). "Evidence that disgust evolved to protect from risk of disease". *Procedures of Biological Sciences* 271(4 Suppl): S131–133.

Firth C, Bhat M, Firth MA, Williams SH, Frye MJ, Simmonds P, Conte JM, Ng J, Garcia J, Bhuva NP, Lee B, Che X, Quan P-L, Lipkin WI. (2014). Detection of zoonotic pathogens and characterization of novel viruses carried by commensal Rattus norvegicus in New York City. *mBio* 5(5):e01933–14. i:10.1128/mBio.01933–14

Graham, H. 2012). "The memory of murder: mass killing, incarceration and the making of Francoism." *In War Memories, Memory Wars. Political Violence in Twentieth-Century Spain.* Eastbourne: U.K. Sussex Academic Press.

Loewenstein, R.M. (1945). A Special Form of Self-Punishment. *Psychoanalytic Quarterly* 14:46–61.

CHAPTER 5

Pedro Almodóvar: Women Searching For a Man Searching For What Women Want, in *What Have I Done to Deserve This?* and *Julieta*

Merle Molofsky

Freud famously asked, "What do women want?", and, perhaps, Pedro Almodóvar offers the answer, since his films seem to be the work of a man who obsessively focuses on just that question, therefore offering an answer, "that man", the man who focuses on discovering what women want.

Almodóvar apparently knew early what he wanted: to be a filmmaker. Before he was 20 years old, he sought what he yearned for at the National School of Cinema in Madrid, but that opportunity for formal education ended abruptly when Franco closed the school. Yet his passion was fulfilled, since he was able to immerse himself in the cultural milieu to be found in Madrid. Throughout the 1970's, he became part of the intense Madrid cultural world, "la Movida Madrileña", and made short films with a hand-held camera.

Almodóvar made his first feature-length film, *Pepi, Luci, Bom*, in 1980, starring his beautiful and brilliant friend Carmen Maura, who had befriended him when he first sought to become a filmmaker. That film emblemized the ethos of la Movida Madrileña, defiantly, brazenly sexual, and sympathetic to the plight of women, who could be free, but whose freedom included the freedom to be abused. He was on his way to carving a natural niche for himself in the world of "art film", as a man who indeed seems to understand "what women want".

He quickly followed up with three more films, *Labyrinth of Passion* (1982), *Dark Habits* (1983), and *What Have I Done to Deserve This?* (1984). Somehow, with all the emphasis on the brave new world of sexual freedom (although that brave new world had many antecedents!), with *What Have I Done to Deserve This?*, Almodóvar was moving toward a deeper understanding of what women want, with an intensifying focus on socioeconomic circumstances that limit what a woman who wants could get. The sexual quirkiness persists, but the title alone evokes a smoldering sociocultural morass – what have women done to deserve misogyny and abuse?

What Have I Done to Deserve This? (*¿Qué he hecho yo para merecer esto?*) once again stars the beautiful and brilliant Carmen Maura. She not only is a brilliantly talented actor, she was a philosophy and literature student at the École des Beaux-Arts. In her depiction of Gloria, a young, amphetamine-dependent mother who works as a cleaning woman, she captures a "desire for more", the aspirations of a woman who has to invent her "more", because her choices are so limited.

Gloria. The name choice is so evocative. It means the same in Spanish as it does in English – glory. Where is the glory of youth, of young womanhood, of motherhood? If it is embodied in this young, impoverished, abused mother, it is embodied in her sense of her bodily boundaries, despite the conditions of her life. Her body more and more belongs to her, even as it/she becomes more and more compromised. Almodóvar provides the story line, the possibilities, and Maura embodies the embodiment of Gloria. The results are painfully glorious.

The film's opening shot, and immediate events following, define limits, and how to defy limits. The first shot is a panoramic sweep of a plaza. What is a plaza? An open space set among buildings and streets. It is open, yet boundaried, limited. The title appears against a red background. What is red? Oh, so many things... red is open to hours of free association. Blood? Passion? Violence? Love? A torero's taunting cape? War? Mars, named for the Roman god of war, is the red planet.

Bernardo Bonezzi's music throughout the film was composed specifically to intensify the meaning of the themes of the plot, of specific scenes, essentially a musical twinship with what the visuals convey. *What Have I Done to Deserve This?* is the first mutual venture with Bonezzi and Almodóvar, and was so successful that Almodóvar continued to work with Bonezzi throughout the 1980's (p. 196).

The plot unfolds. We first see a kendo class in a dojo. The red background showcasing the title of the film is a foreshadowing of what seems to be the formal discipline and control of kendo, a civilized war game. Swords kill. Do we, the viewer, know that? Does Almodóvar want us to know remember that the practice of martial arts is training for the art of war – for murder?

A cleaning woman – whom we will get to know as Gloria, a passionate, angry, sexual woman – is watching, as she cleans, the kendo class. We see colorful credits against the austere black uniforms of the martial arts practitioners. As I watched, without knowing how the story was going to unfold, something came to mind – the famous song that Pirate Jenny sings in Berthold Brecht and Kurt Weill's *The Threepenny Opera,* with the lyric, "You gentlemen can watch while I'm scrubbing the floors, and I'm scrubbing the floors while you're gawking...."

This indeed is an Almodóvar film. Soon enough, there is a sex scene, with the cleaning woman and the kendo sensei. He reaches a climax, she doesn't, he's done, she isn't, he gets dressed and leaves, she picks up a kendo sword and practices what she has learned, watching. We don't yet know what she has learned about war, about death, while watching kendo as she cleans, day by day, we don't yet know that practice makes perfect.

But Almodóvar knows. He knows what women want, before we

know what we need to find out about what Gloria wants. Of course Almodóvar made a film with the title, *Talk to Her*. Whenever I've heard that famous quote attributed to Sigmund Freud, "What do women want?", I've always thought, well, duh, ask women! Talk to her. Listen to her.

Gloria's husband Antonio wants glory. Once a chauffeur for a wealthy German woman, he now is a cab driver. He remembers a fragment of a German song he heard, "and women, when they want something...."

The film wanders into many situations confronting what ordinary women and ordinary men want. All too often, it seems that ordinary men want to be dominant, and ordinary women want something else. We meet Gloria's family, Gloria's neighbors. Gloria has two teenaged sons. Toni is a heroin dealer. Miguel is homosexual, and, since Gloria and her family need money, in essence she sells her son to the family dentist. Her son becomes the dentist's sex toy, and the braces the boy needs are now free. Almodóvar is openly gay, and is sympathetic to the many varieties of sexual desire, to LGBTQ people. The sense of this event in the film is of empathy for the boy – but not for the dentist. The boy is a child, albeit a sexual child. Freud indeed let the world know that children are sexual creatures – but that does not mean that they are sex toys for pedophiles.

One of her neighbors, Juani, mistreats her own little daughter, in essence to accustomize the child to what her role as a woman will demand of her. The little girl has an uncanny, unrecognized talent, telekinesis. She is a human poltergeist, moving objects with her mind. Poltergeists are considered to be malevolent, tormenting spirits. What does Almodóvar offer us with this odd child? Does she represent the repressed malevolence of tormented women, an eruption of strength that defies what we believe is reason, the vengeance of the seemingly helpless? Are the seemingly helpless not as helpless as they seem?

Another neighbor is a prostitute, Cristal, a good friend of Gloria's. The name choice seems meaningful. What is a crystal? The atomic structure of crystal extends in all directions. Crystals are ubiquitous.

Salt, diamonds, and ice, are crystalline. Once upon a time, salt was hard to obtain. Roman soldiers were paid in salt, hence the English word "salary", derived from the Latin word "sal". "Ordinary" people, Jesus said, are the "salt of the earth" (Matthew 5:13), giving the life of humanity its flavor. Diamonds are expensive. Ice preserves, and ice can kill. Crystals can be transparent. Crystals are used as transmitters, in electronics, in radio.

What is Cristal's function as a prostitute? Like salt, she gives lonely, desperate men a flavor they seek, but cannot find elsewhere. She serves as a transmitter, fulfilling men's sexual fantasies.

Cristal enlists Gloria's help in her work. When a man wants a third person present, a witness, Cristal asks Gloria to watch. When a man wants to be whipped, she asks Gloria if she has a whip she can borrow. No, Gloria doesn't have a whip. What else can a woman use to beat a man? A stick. There's always a stick.

Is Cristal herself a representation of telekinesis, manipulating men's minds and bodies, changing the physical universe, uncovering her own malevolence, the malevolence of women abused by men, by catering to the sexual fantasies of men in a way that allows her to reverse the social order, and punish men? The man who wants to be beaten, a not unusual masochistic fantasy famously named for the author of *Venus in Furs*, Leopold Von Sacher-Masoch, foreshadows the fate of Gloria's husband Antonio.

Gloria and Antonio get into a bloody fight. She is defiant, he is punitive, he strikes her and draws blood. This is what the opening scenes foreshadowed. The plaza is not as open as space as it seems, the blood-red background to the title, *What Have I Done to Deserve This?*, is the color of Gloria's blood. Gloria's kendo practice has prepared her to defend herself. She grabs a ham, bone in, she has prepared for dinner, and smashes Antonio in the head. He stumbles, crashes into the window, and his neck breaks. He is dead.

Gloria visits her neighbor Juani, creating an alibi. When she returns, asking her neighbor Cristal to come home with her, oh heavens, alas, she finds her husband dead, and calls the police. She feeds them the dinner she had been preparing for her husband, for her family, and the police eat the evidence.

What do women want? One thing they want is that they don't want to believe that they have done anything to deserve violent, scornful, misogynistic treatment.

More than 30 years after making *What Have I Done to Deserve This?*, Almodóvar made a very different sort of film, *Julieta*, 2016, his 20th feature film, based on short stories from *Runaway*, by the Canadian writer Alice Munro. According to the *Los Angeles Times* (2017), in a previous film, *The Skin I Live In* (2011), the book itself can be seen on a bookshelf, prefiguring this film. One important difference in the two films separated by 30 years, of course, is that he drew the plot of the film from a woman writer. Apparently, he was listening, and reading! He tried to discover more about women by paying attention to what women were saying about being a woman.

Different? Yes. But, plus ça change, plus c'est la même chose, the film begins with red. Red fabric. Perhaps the fabric of our lives is the fabric of the passions, of the extreme emotions, of love and hate, sex and death, Eros and Thanatos.

The red fabric of our lives is a dress the main character, Julieta, is wearing, as she is undertaking the next phase of her life, beginning with her wrapping up a small statuette of a seated figure. The statuette will take on a particular significance, but we don't know that yet. Perhaps we should. If Almodóvar opens a film with a particular image, we should know it is going to be truly meaningful. Julieta is going to abandon Lorenzo, her lover, for the sake of something that resonates with what women want – for the sake of reuniting with her daughter Antia, who is estranged from her. If we weren't familiar with all of Almodóvar's work, would we recognize a mini-theme suggested in *What Have I Done to Deserve This?*, the theme of a mother and daughter dissonance, embodied by Juani and her telekinetically-gifted little daughter, who rebelled against being told what to do, if being told what to do was training for what it meant to be a girl who would grow up to be a woman? A mini-theme, yes. But this story is different. "Almost 30 years" makes a difference. Although, about that statuette... it is a phallic figure. But, never mind. We'll get to that eventually.

As so much time has passed for Almodóvar himself, in the 36 years between making his first feature film and *Julieta*, it is fitting that so much time passes in the film that Julieta is portrayed by two actors, Adriana Ugarte as the young Julieta, and Emma Suárez as an older Julieta. The older Julieta is discovering, meeting an old friend of her daughter's in the street, who has seen her daughter on vacation at Lake Como that she is a grandmother, that Antia, her long-estranged daughter, has three children.

Julieta is going to give up going on a long-planned, long-desired vacation with Lorenzo, in essence abandoning him, in order to track down her daughter, and grandchildren.

The story of estrangement is the dominant theme. What happened? It's complicated. The theme is the eternal triadic conflict, what Freud called the Oedipal conflict, which is an appropriate term for a little boy's development, but not for a little girl. What do women want? One thing might be resonant language.

When Antia was 18, she went on a three-month religious retreat in a remote mountain area, before she was about to begin university. She experienced a shock to her very core, and never went home again. She abandoned her mother. She and her mother seem to have been very close, very loving. Yet something disrupted this closeness, leading Antia to end the relationship, without any explanation. Julieta goes to the mountain retreat to pick up Antia, but Antia is gone.

Once they were a happy family. But not really. Julieta's "happy family" originates in Julieta's unhappy family. She is estranged from her father. Generational estrangement is perpetuated. Young Julieta, who teaches classical Greek literature, meets a handsome stranger, Xoan, on a train ride, and they have sex/make love. Woman, man, sex, love, ergo Antia. Xoan is a fisherman, living in a fishing village, and Julieta lives with him.

The train ride is of utmost importance to Almodóvar. The sexual intensity, combined with danger, is extraordinary. Julieta and Xoan witness an accident while on the train, resulting in the death of young man.

In an interview conducted by Christine Champagne of Co.Create, Almodóvar said, "I remember I was completely hooked with the part on the train, what happens on the train. I was very surprised by that section in that story, and I found it particularly cinematic". He further said in the interview that for a long time he has wanted to emulate using a train ride similarly to Alfred Hitchcock's work in *Strangers On a Train, The Lady Vanishes* and *North By Northwest* (Champagne, 2016).

Julieta's background in classical Greek literature sets up the tragedy of her life. She teaches *The Odyssey*. Odysseus is shipwrecked, is lost at sea. The sea is a road to... where? The future? Odysseus meets Calypso, who offers eternal youth and immortality. He lingers awhile, but he leaves.

Xoan dies at sea. There were radio alerts that a storm was brewing, and all fishing and sailing vessels should return to port. There was no Calypso to grant Xoan immortality.

Thus perhaps there is parallel between the sexual intensity of the train ride, when Julieta and Xoan make love, traumatized by the accidental death they witnessed, and the potentially lethal anguished sea-faring voyage of Xoan as Odysseus, Xoan traumatized by the passion of female sexual jealousy, a death-driven voyage.

Ava, Xoan's sculptor friend, made the seated figure, the phallic male, bronze with a terra cotta glaze, and gave it to Julieta as a gift. She explains, "I try to make my sculptures compact, so the wind won't knock them over". Further, we learn that the gods made men from clay, and they are born naked and defenseless.

The wind knocked Xoan over. When his body was found, it was badly mutilated. Julieta identifies him by a tattoo. His ashes are united with the sea.

We discover that Julieta is shocked and disturbed by her own father's adulterous behavior. He has sex with Julieta's disabled mother's caretaker, the first triadic conflict.

Xoan has been Ava's lover. Another triadic conflict.

Antia blames her mother, and Ava, for her father's death. She believes a quarrel involving Julieta, Ava, and Xoan caused Xoan to escape to sea, despite the storm warning. Antia therefore believes that her mother caused her father's death, robbing Antia of a father. The ultimate triadic conflict.

After many years, Julieta eventually finds Antia, and tries to start a relationship with her again. Antia refuses.

After many plot twists, a resolution: Antia sends Julieta a letter, saying that her own nine year old son, named Xoan, drowned in a river. She says, "Now I understand what you have suffered when I disappeared".

The ultimate theme is longing and loss, passed on through the generations.

Is there an abiding theme that links these two Almodóvar films, *What Have I Done to Deserve This?*, and *Julieta*? Does the grounding of both films in the color red in the opening moments convey the eternal theme of human passion? Is the inner world of women more compelling than the inner world of men? Or, does Almodóvar see the desperate pathos of women's lives as most conducive to exploring and communicating the common human struggle?

Oscar Wilde wrote, "Women are meant to be loved, not to be understood"(p. 228). Or, perhaps, women need to know what they want. And, perhaps, there are no "women", only each individual woman. Does she want to be understood? Does she want to be loved? Does she want both? Neither? Perhaps we might ask, what do men want? Too broad a question? Then, what does Almodóvar want? What does he want us to resonate with when we watch his films? "Do we see or do we not see, that is the question." Perhaps the question is, what does each of us find of value when we encounter his films? Or, even more distilled, what does each of us find of value when we encounter a particular film of Almodóvar?

References

Allinson, Mark, (2001). *A Spanish Labyrinth: The Films of Pedro Almodóvar*, I.B. Tauris: London.

Almodóvar, P. (Director). (1984). *What Have I Done to Deserve This?* [Motion Picture]. *SA:* Teasuro.

____. *(Director).* (2016). *Julieta. [Motion Picture]. Spain:* El Deseo.

Champagne, Christine, (2016). "Behind the Script: How Pedro Almodóvar Turned Alice Munro Stories Into 'Julieta'", *Fast Company Newsletter*, 2/26/16 Master Class.

Olsen, Mark, "'Julieta' finds a new tone for that 'ultimate touch' of Filmmaker Pedro Almodóvar", January 17, 2017, the *Los Angeles Times*.

Wilde, Oscar, (1986). "The Sphinx Without a Secret: An Etching", *The Complete Illustrated Stories, Plays & Poems of Oscar Wilde*, Chancellor Press: London.

CHAPTER 6

Matador: Death in the Eclipse

Philip Matyszak

On the face of it, *Matador* (1986) is a standard 1980s detective story. It is an unsatisfactory one at that, because the detective does not do any detecting. All his evidence is spoon-fed to him by a troubled young man who inexplicably gets his information from visions. As well as our detective moving his case along with help from this extra-sensory human spycam, the plot involves an unlikely number of coincidences. Many issues raised in the plot are not followed up and the finale leaves many of the storylines dangling unresolved. Critics are quick to point out that the film lacks the smoothness and élan of Almodóvar's later productions. Even Almodóvar describes it as one of his less satisfactory efforts. It is something of a transition between the slapstick of his early productions and the smooth satire of his later films.

Yet *Matador* works. It works because the plot is merely a device by which Almodóvar can project a straight-faced but highly subversive look at existing social mores. Even the standard detective tropes become more explicable as the viewer comes to understand that the film is also a take-off of contemporary TV crime dramas – not because that is the purpose of the film, but because Almodóvar cannot come across an accepted convention without poking fun at it. The TV detective show with its one-dimensional characters and standardized format is mocked, but only as an incidental casualty of the overall movie.

A quick summary of the plot – such as it is.

A young man called Ángel is studying to be a matador. His tutor is a famous matador who retired from bullfighting after a bull won the particular bout which left him crippled. When the matador discovers that his student is a virgin, he questions Ángel's masculinity.

By way of demonstrating that he is all man, the student decides to rape his attractive neighbour – a model who (unlikely coincidence #1) just happens to be the matador's girlfriend. The rape, which takes place in an alleyway, is a brutal and sordid event, although the only injuries sustained are by the rapist whom the girl belts violently afterwards, and a cut sustained by the girl, who slips on the wet cobbles of the alleyway as she storms off. She turns to give the young man a parting glare, and he swoons away.

The next day Ángel is deeply troubled by his actions, which are partly explained when we meet his mother. She is a domineering woman who uses her narrow-minded religious fanaticism as a means of controlling social interactions. After watching her berate her son over a joyless dinner, his desire to go out and damage some-thing becomes more explicable, if not more excusable.

Since an anonymous rape will not provide the young man with the public validation he seeks, he proceeds to the police station and con-fesses his misdeeds, perhaps on the basis that prison is a satisfactory alternative to his home life. Regrettably his victim is singularly unhelp-ful when she is called to the police station. She refuses to press charges on the grounds that no rape occurred. Her attacker ejaculated on to her before he could get started. Afterwards he received a good telling off for his pains. As far as the girl is concerned, the matter is closed.

However, the detective is intrigued by the cut on the girlfriend's face. By what turns out to be another of those unlikely co-incidences, this resembles a cut found on the bodies in several recent unsolved murders. The detective shows the pictures of the corpses to the young man and asks what he knows of them. Yes, yes, agrees Ángel with considerable relief. I done it. I did all of it. I am a very serious and dangerous person. Please lock me up.

Enter our next protagonist. This is a tigerish and very self-consciously sexy lawyer who is prepared to defend her client for free, apparently as a reaction to the 'feminist lynch mobs' who are outraged by his behaviour. (We don't see or get any other details of this supposed public outrage. Indeed everyone is so matter-of-fact about the murders that we might as well be dealing with a moderate case of public littering.)

In the course of the lawyer's investigations, she and the matador meet and bond instantly. The matador intends to see his girlfriend at a fashion show, but leaves before the show starts to pursue the lawyer when he sees her among the guests. The lawyer resists the attraction, and the matador's advances, because she sees him as a has-been. Later we find that she revered him when he was a successful bullfighter, but now that he has stopped killing she has lost interest in him. Her interest is focused on Ángel, to whom she is drawn because she (initially) believes that he is the real deal – a hard-core killer.

It turns out that the lawyer has decided to dispose of the matador. Wearing an elaborate coiffure topped by a huge hairpin she lures him into a quiet nook. There, as they passionately kiss, she works free her hairpin and prepares - with evident relish – to stab him in the back. Not coincidentally the stroke with the long hairpin exactly mimics the *escotada* – the coup de grace by which the matador pushes his sword between the bull's shoulder blades into his heart.

The lawyer takes a moment too long savouring the moment of the kill. In that moment our matador divines the killer's purpose, and takes the hairpin from her. Rather than being outraged or frightened by her intent, he is more attracted to her than ever.

'When you're about to kill, don't hesitate', he tells her. 'It's a golden rule of bullfighting.' Later he adds, 'You and I are alike – obsessed by death.'

The matador discovers that the lawyer is herself responsible for some of the unsolved murders – those same murders to which her client has confessed. The matador knows who is responsible for the remaining killings, because he committed them. This gives him a bond with the lawyer which borders on a fixation.

When she asks him 'What do you want from me?' He answers concisely, 'Everything'.

Once the matador admits that he has continued to kill, and moved his focus from bulls to women, the lawyer loses all interest in her client and focuses on him. 'I have looked for you in all the men I've loved. I tried to imitate you when I killed them.' United by an interest in ritualized death, the pair become a couple.

Meanwhile the police detective is handed his next breakthrough in the case by the obliging Ángel. The detective has come to enquire how the young man was able to do one of his killings in the impossibly narrow time frame between leaving bullfighting classes and arriving home. An unrelated individual is brought into the room with a bleeding forehead. At once, just as he did when he saw the bloodied face of his 'rape' victim, the young man faints away. His mother contemptuously informs the detective that, like his father, the young man passes out at the sight of blood. How exactly this can be reconciled with Ángel's career as a prospective bullfighter is never explained, but it certainly exonerates him from what were somewhat bloody murders.

The matador's model girlfriend has been abandoned once the matador has become fixated on the lawyer. Set on a reconciliation, she persuades the matador's aged retainer to let her into the house, where she hears the two killers in discussion. She believes they are planning to flee from the law together, as the lawyer mentions sorting out the office, and he accuses her of constantly trying to 'postpone things'.

In fact the pair are set on a death pact, which they plan to enact in a country cottage at the moment of an eclipse. As one character puts it, 'When two heavenly bodies meet... they apparently extinguish the light from each other. But for a second they become bright in a new way, bright and burning'.

Warned by the omniscient Ángel, the detective and the (ex)-girlfriend pile into a car and race after the doomed lovers. They arrive at the cottage at the moment of the eclipse, too late to prevent the mutual murder. The detective looks at the two naked corpses entwined on the blood-red sheets and utters the movie's closing words.

'I have never seen anyone look so happy.'

Since we are agreed that the film is unsatisfactory as a detective movie, viewing the film becomes an exploration of what Almodóvar is trying to tell his audience. Is this simply an unlikely tale used as the scaffolding for a series of satirical jabs at life in contemporary Spain? Certainly there is much of that in the film. Religion, for example, or at least the mother's fanatical version of it, definitely gets a good kicking.

So does the fashion industry. In one wonderfully satirical scene the girlfriend/model is being made up to look like a grotesque corpse. This is to exploit her 'celebrity victim' status, as at this time she is believed to be the only survivor of an attack by the multiple murderer Ángel. At one point the producer of the fashion show sees a model shooting up with drugs, and irritably tells her, 'Not here, for heaven's sake. Do that in the toilets. That's what they're for.'

While good fun, such scenes are in fact distracting asides. In the end, so are the serious questions which the film raises about how we live and what we accept while doing so.

The first indication that Almodóvar is exploring the intensity of life on the edge is almost subliminal. The early part of the film shows mainly Ángel's house and the police station. At the police station the colours are muted pastels on Formica and painted chipboard. The predominant shades are pale blue and grey. The house in which Ángel lives is likewise dour and colourless. The only point where the colours become richer and the contrasts more pronounced is the rape scene in the alleyway.

As the film progresses, we note that deep, rich colours and pronounced contrasts are reserved for the clothing of the killers and the décor of their homes, and this contrasts markedly with the pallid world in which everyone else lives. Even the sky generally has a pale, high overcast until the final scenes when the lovers travel to their mutual murder in warm sunshine.

It is the transgressors, Almodóvar seems to suggest, who are more alive. For them life is simply more intense. The ever-present danger that they will be revealed as murderers and the anticipation of their next kill adds an extra dimension to their existences, giving them urgency and an appreciation of every transient moment. The days of our detective as he works his way toward his pension are by comparison mundane and quotidian.

In showing this Almodóvar does not endorse the lifestyle of the murderers, but he does not condemn it either. The murders and the murderers are displayed with complete neutrality. We see that the murderers live more intensely - and more briefly - as a result of their choices, but those choices are presented without judgement. The film cheerfully surrenders the director's pulpit and instead requires viewers to supply their own outrage, whether at sexism, murder or rape. (Note the casual comment of the model's mother as the young woman leaves the house to confront her lover. 'If you dress like that, no wonder you keep getting raped.')

Here, the straight-faced delivery of this and other outrageous lines works perfectly. The actors deliver them with such understated brio that people in the audience first take their words at face value, and then do a double-take as the implications sink in. Because the assembly of talent mustered for the film is high and the acting is so convincing, momentarily we accept that rape is a standard consequence of female beauty, that murder is an acceptable outlet for emotional or sexual stress, and discovering that one's boyfriend is a multiple killer is excellent news, because he can now be blackmailed back into a relationship.

It is not only the main protagonists who accept these unacceptable beliefs. When the model's mother is interviewed at the police station, she implies that Ángel's rape of her daughter is the daughter's fault - because the girl has already been raped 'four - or no, five times?' She looks at her daughter who nods confirmation. Everyone else grunts understandingly and they sympathize when the mother points out that having to discuss what has happened is just as distasteful as the event itself. It is around now that the audience is expected to stop nodding in sympathy as well.

At this point we are required to reject the cinema-goer's convention of at least temporarily agreeing with the director's premise. It is not the script that invites revulsion at the conduct of the protagonists. It is left for the viewer, who is compelled to break out of the conventional state of suspended disbelief and say 'Wait, no, hold on. This behaviour you are taking for granted … it is wrong!'

The audience goes into an Almodóvar movie expecting comedy, and this is indeed comedy, albeit about as black as humour can get. Yet as is often the case with comedy, the underlying point is dead serious. Almodóvar is saying 'Yes, this is surreal. It is incredible that the characters accept such transgressional behaviour so matter-of-factly. Yet in the world outside of the cinema, do we not do the same? We accept everyday sexism, shrug off environmental destruction as the price of progress, and turn off news of wars and famines on the television so we can go out for a beer. We accept the unacceptable every day without protest, so why are you astonished that the protagonists of this film do the same?'

While watching the film we might frown and shake our heads at the characters' behaviour. Perhaps later we might shake our heads at our own conduct. It's one of the ways that *Matador* works as a movie. It gets across a serious message about modern morality without being in the slightest sententious or preachy.

(In fact, the only time the film does get at all moralistic is when the lawyer is outraged at the lack of support Ángel gets from his religious mother. Even then the moment is rich in irony. 'I wouldn't ever take you as a client', the lawyer loftily informs the mother, and storms out of the house. We find ourselves united in sympathy with the seductress and multiple murderer and we unthinkingly accept her right to pass scathing judgement on a church-goer and law-abiding citizen.)

Thus our exploration of the film has already raised two thought-provoking issues. The first set of questions ask - Is life richer, and more fulfilling for those who live on the edge of losing life altogether? Does the predator live more intensely than the prey? Is an ordinary life a wasted life?

The second set of questions ask – have we been conditioned by society to accept the morally indefensible? Three generations ago many westerners wore clothing from cotton picked by slave labour, and drank coffee with sugar produced under horrific conditions in the West Indies. Like Almodóvar's characters, the people of that time accepted as normal what everyone else accepted as normal, independent of any objective moral repulsion. With what issues will future generations find it incredible that we could be so unthinkingly blind to the ethical considerations?

These points alone mean that *Matador* works as a film, and works as the best satire does – by holding a mirror up to our world, and by distortion and exaggeration causing us to see that world in a new way and question that which we have previously taken for granted.

Yet so far we have not approached the main premise of the film. This is the intersection of death, sex and power, which here is essentially what Almodóvar is all about. This, as we will see, is why the protagonist is a matador.

Death, sex and power are not interdependent. Individuals can and do interact with these different forces without the others getting involved. For example, when dealing with the tax man or a parking ticket in the courts we have a very clear idea of the power of the state, yet there is nothing remotely sexy about the experience, and the only risk of death is through boredom.

On the other hand, when the different factors of death, sex and power occur together they act for some – perhaps even most – individuals - as a powerful emotional multiplier. Today the interaction of power and submission in sex can be exhaustively examined by anyone with a computer and an internet connection (and in extreme cases a strong stomach also). The popularity of *Fifty Shades of Grey* as both a book and a film suggests that the topic of Bondage and Sado-Masochism is becoming almost respectable, and a set of handcuffs lined with fluffy pink fur are more likely to arouse knowing smirks than outrage. We are comfortable with sex and power.

Indeed, in a more diluted form the concept is not new. The average 'bodice-ripping' romance has for at least the last century shown a subordinate woman (a secretary, governess, employee or similar) attracted to a dominant male who usually owns a business, country estate, or whatever. Our hero is described as 'masterful' and 'harsh' and is initially brutal, unsympathetic or even cruel. Given that the heroine – and by proxy, female readers by the million – nevertheless ends by swooning into the hero's arms, we can take it for granted that, as Henry Kissinger once remarked, 'Power is the ultimate aphrodisiac'.

In *Matador* Almodóvar takes his usual more-than-somewhat skewed approach. The matador's youthful student is a virgin. The matador points out to his student that this makes his masculinity questionable. (Which is another of those assumptions that is left for the viewer to challenge. For the characters in the film the correlation between masculinity and sexual activity as a dominant is both explicit and taken for granted.) The student's response in interesting. Simple sex is not enough to prove true masculinity. He therefore makes no attempt to find himself a willing sexual partner – and there seems no reason why he could not, as he is a physically attractive young man with an amiable if very shy personality. Instead the lad opts to overpower and rape his neighbour – literally the nearest desirable woman. That is what a 'real man' does.

In the 1980s the expression 'toxic masculinity' did not exist. Yet this is exactly what Almodóvar is exploring here – especially the concept that a powerful male does not negotiate sex. He takes it, whether the object of his desires likes it or not. Again, everyone in the film acts as if this is standard and acceptable behaviour. Furthermore, once Ángel, our young man, is believed to be a rapist and killer, he immediately arouses the interest of not one, but two attractive women. In *Matador*, both genders buy into this over-the-top macho image. Power is sexy even if it is misused. In fact, especially if it is misused.

Almodóvar reduces the power balance between man and woman to one basic element – the difference in physical strength. At the fashion show, by giving the model make-up to look as if she has just been grotesquely molested, the designer not only accepts this concept but eagerly celebrates her female victimhood. Not co-incidentally, this

83

is the moment when the model's boyfriend, the matador, both literally and symbolically leaves her to seek more difficult prey. There is, after all, nothing arousing about exercising power over someone who can (apparently) be dominated even by the pathetic Ángel. While he does not yet know the lawyer is a killer, the matador knows that she is smart, sexy and confident. An attractive conquest.

So much for sex and power. Sex and death have an equally involved history. The term *femme fatale* was invented in the 1840s but the concept goes back much further. For an example, let us consider the vampire. The vampire is not just dangerous and powerful, but generally fatal to his – or her – victims. Even before the vampire (largely a Victorian invention) we have the succubus and incubus, male and female demons who suck out the victim's soul through sex. We find an early expression of the connection between death and sex in the story of a young man from Corinth who fell in love with a beautiful but mysterious woman. The pair were going to marry when a wise man intervened. He told the would-be groom:

'This blushing bride is a Lamia … For them, love and the delights of Aphrodite are a preliminary used to deceive those upon whose human flesh they later they wish to feast.' …

At this the spirit pretended to weep, and begged him not to harm her or reveal who she really was. But Apollonius was relentless, and kept pressing her until she admitted that she was an Empousa, one of that species [of proto-vampire]. She was preparing Menippos through pleasure, so that she might later devour his body. It was her custom to seek out young and beautiful bodies to feast upon, for their blood was pure and strong.

Philostratus *Life of Apollonius of Tyana* 4.25

That was written around AD 200, eighteen hundred years ago. Yet in *Matador* we find a female, the lawyer, who prepares her victims through pleasure, so that she might kill them. It was her custom to seek out young and beautiful bodies to feast upon, for their blood was pure and strong.

We shall come to the nexus involving death and power in a moment. Here though, we note the difference between the female who combines death and sex, and the male who combines sex and power. For the male rapist and the male killer, the important factor is that the victim knows full well what is happening but is powerless to prevent it. For the female killer, the death is the thing. With both the Lamia and the Lawyer's lovers, the male believes he is the one in control right up to the moment of his fatal disillusionment.

Which brings us to death and power. Or more particularly, to killing and power. The former does not always require the latter. Many a drunken driver is contemptible proof of this. Yet the ideas of death and power have always gone together. In ancient Rome the *fasces* of a Roman magistrate consisted of a bundle of rods and an axe. The axe was explicitly included in the package to symbolize the magistrate's power of life and death. The more important the magistrate, the more *fasces* his servants carried. In the city of Rome itself, where the power of magistrates was constrained, the axe was removed.

After all, most living things want to live. In many cases they want passionately so to do. Therefore taking a life is the ultimate act of power over that living thing. (It is also why, in most societies, the state reserves for itself the right to take human life. If the power to take a human life is passed to a non-state actor, then that actor possesses almost limitless coercive power over the person whose life he can take. Which also is why in states such as Iran this power is given to fathers over their daughters.)

Here again *Matador* joins the conversation. The film makes the point that killing is in itself pointless unless it is done as an expression of power. Otherwise one takes a life as a thief steals a purse - taking by stealth something to which one has no right. Such furtive haste expresses weakness.

To be done properly, the deed must be done with control. The perpetrator must be in charge, up to and including the climactic moment. The kill must be done in this way for the same reason that state executions are done with ritual. When the state kills somebody, every step is formalized, from giving the victim his last meal to the meeting with the priest, to the opportunity for last words. The effect of ritual is to show that those doing the killing are in charge. Everything proceeds at the measured pace the executioners have set, and the events move to their inevitable conclusion. A ritual killing is the ultimate combination of death and power.

The bullring is literally an arena in which the same interaction is played out. However, before we come to the bullring, and thus to *Matador*, it is worth stepping back to the precursor to the bullring – the arenas of the ancient civilization of Rome. Spain has a Latin culture, and much of the nation's tradition derives from many centuries of Romanization – and this includes the bullfight.

While we are mostly familiar in books and films with gladiatorial combat in the Roman arena, a more common event was the 'hunt'. Here, in a manner inexplicable to the modern observer, Romans would bring animals from the far corners of their world – crocodiles, bears, lions and giraffes – and kill them. There was a particular type of performer dedicated to such killings who was known as the *beastarius* – the precursor to the modern bullfighter. It was a precarious profession, for the humans did not win every bout. However even emperors joined in the fun – Domitian was fond of shooting animals with a bow from his imperial box.

When we ask what the Romans got out of what would today be considered a horrible spectacle, the answer is to do with a difference in perspective – and again the relationship between death and power. Today, we rightly regard nature as under threat. Humans encroach on animal habitats, and literally cut entire forests out from beneath the wild creatures that inhabit them. There will soon be more plastic than fish in our oceans. Under these circumstances the death of each wild animal is part of a greater tragedy, and the deliberate killing of say, a leopard, purely for the spectacle, is downright disgusting.

Yet to the Romans nature was not threatened, but threatening. They had a pretty good idea of the size of the world, and chauvinistically believed that theirs was the only civilized bit of it. In other words, the Roman world was perceived as a small island of civilization surrounded on every side by howling wilderness. There was enough nature for it to be inexhaustible. Even within the confines of the empire, humans were relatively rare. It is probable that the entirety of Rome's peoples, from the Thames to the Euphrates, numbered fewer than the population of modern England. Even within Italy, there were huge forests and trackless mountain ranges. Wolves, bears and other predators were not exhibits to be seen on reserves or in zoos, but a real threat for anyone outside the city walls.

The purpose of the beast hunt was to demonstrate the human control of forces that those same humans rather suspected that they did not control. The killing of a rhinoceros in the arena told the audience, 'See? We can travel to these faraway places. We can master these huge exotic beasts, and we have such power over them that we can slay them. Don't worry about nature. We are in charge.'

This urge for control - or at least the illusion of control - over perilous forces such as wild beasts is seen again in the execution of criminals. In the Roman arena thieves, bandits and murderers were not merely killed, but often killed with displays of sadistic invention in which the victims were forced to participate.

Again, what appears at first to be merely brutal pandering to the worst impulses of the crowd had a deeper meaning. Rome, like everywhere in the world until the early modern era, had no police force. The authorities did not enforce law and order, but only order. Law was up to the individual. Therefore, a populace which felt itself at the mercy of criminals found great reassurance in seeing those criminals dispatched. Not merely killed, but killed in a manner which demonstrated in the clearest terms that society was in control.

Before considering these impulses as being an aberration of an ancient civilization, let us consider the modern action movie. Here murderers, however ingenious, are invariably brought to book. Islamic terrorists and Russian spies die in a variety of gruesome ways, and the hero – usually and often explicitly an all-American kid – demonstrates yet again that the world is safe for law-abiding citizens. In other words, we seek exactly the same affirmation that the Romans sought, with the intimacy of the cinema compensating for the fact that the blood and viscera are not real. Even in *Matador,* the aberrant individuals eventually cancel each other out, leaving the world safe for civilization.

The matador in the bullring represents the same affirmation. The matador, elegant in his finery, represents civilized humanity while the bull reflects raw, savage power. Indeed, in the modern world any set of secret fears can be projected upon the bull for the matador to slay – with the added frisson of knowing that perhaps this time the bull might win.

Mark Twain, in his bitter condemnation of bullfighting, has one of his characters– a boorish Southerner—remark, 'Well, it is perfectly grand, perfectly beautiful. Burning a nigger don't begin [to compare].' What is significant here is that the comparison *is* made. Just as lynchings were a brutal expression of oppression over a people who were feared precisely because they were oppressed, so the bull in the bullring here becomes the physical manifestation of the southerner's secret dread. In modern Spain, the popularity of bullfighting is increasing among young women. It is not hard to imagine what the bull might represent to many of them.

In *Matador* Almodóvar makes explicit the connection between bullfighting, gender and death. Once he has stopped killing bulls, the matador kills only women. The lawyer who imitates him kills only men. In other words, for Almodóvar the bullfight is a metaphor for sexual dominance. It is a clear expression of the formula death = power = sex. It is not even that the film is subtle about it. The very start shows the matador sitting on the sofa masturbating furiously to images on the TV which show naked and dismembered women.

The bullfighters are explicitly sexualized. In one initially startling scene in the film, the detective goes to the bullring to check Ángel's alibi with the other trainee bullfighters. As the detective approaches the bullfighters, all we see of them on the screen as they go about their activities is shot after shot of their assorted genitalia clearly outlined against the tight fabric of their pants.

This is not the detective's perspective. As we have seen, our detective is a colourless, characterless individual who does not have a life, let alone a sex life. Rather this is Almodóvar stepping out of the plot for a moment to inform his audience, 'Here they are, the bullfighters. Basically a collection of lethal crotch-hats on legs.'

That much about matadors, and the perception of the bullfight needs to be clarified before the climactic moment of the film, which some commentators mistakenly refer to as the 'suicide pact' between the lawyer and the matador. Apart from anything else, the term is literally wrong. Suicide refers to killing oneself. In the film the two protagonists kill each other. More important is the matter of motive.

Suicide is a complex topic and it is hard to generalize about motivation. Perhaps the most accurate generalization is the callous statement that 'Suicide is the ultimate expression of self-criticism'. Every suicide reflects a personal decision that either individuals cannot cope with the world, or that the world is better off without them. Even a brief acquaintance with our protagonists shows that they do not meet these over-arching criteria. They are not only alive, but intensely so. Their lives have meaning. Nor, for a single moment do we see a trace of regret for their actions, let alone remorse.

However, both accept that the price for living more intensely is to live more briefly. Edna St V. Millay (dead at age 58) once wrote:

My candle burns at both ends
It will not last the night
But oh, my friends, and ah, my foes
It makes a lovely light.

Our protagonists are fully on board with that concept, though they would rather apply a blowtorch to each end of a stick of dynamite. They know that their chosen lifestyle is unsustainable, even without the spying model girlfriend and the psychic Ángel hastening their demise. So they keep ramping up the intensity.

Like her hero, the lawyer considers herself a matador. Both literally live to kill. Her preferred 'bull' is a powerful, virile male. His, a strong, sexually attractive woman whom he can totally master - with a ritualized killing as the final proof of that mastery. In short, the lawyer and the matador are a perfect match. Each represents the other's concept of the ultimate prey.

So the question is, what price are our killers prepared to pay for the taking of this greatest kill? We already know the answer, for it is explicit in the dialogue: 'What do you want from me?' 'Everything.'

The pact between the two is the opposite of a suicide pact. It is a consensual mutual murder. Each wants to make the perfect kill at any price, even if that price is their own life. After all, once each has made the ultimate kill, anything afterwards would be an anti-climax in any case.

So we proceed to the final bullfight, where each protagonist is the matador, and each the bull. While we see Ángel and the forces of law and order racing to prevent the scene in a disorganized rush, the Matador and the Lawyer proceed at a measured pace. He stops to buy her flowers, she prepares the cottage for their final encounter. Then an intimate meal by firelight is followed by passionate sex on blood-red sheets, and the final kill takes place with perfect timing at a moment climactic in every way.

Once we understand the protagonists, the final words of the film make perfect sense:

'I have never seen anyone look so happy.'

A final note – the title of the film is *Matador*. If the film were indeed about bulls and bullfighting, then Almodóvar would have titled the film with the more generalized Spanish word 'Torero' which means bull-fighter. Instead he has chosen a word derived from the Latin 'mactator' – which means 'slayer'. In bullfighting terminology a *matador de toros* is literally the 'slayer of bulls'. The title of the film correctly omits the last two words.

References

Almodóvar, P. (Director). (1986). *Matador* [Motion Picture]. Andrés Vincente Gómez, Cia Iberoamericana de TV S.A.

Epps, B & Kakoudaki, D. eds. (2009). *All about Almodóvar: A Passion for Cinema*. Minneapolis: University of Minnesota Press.

Evans, P. (1993). "Almodóvar's *Matador*. Genre, Subjectivity and desire". *Bulletin of Hispanic Studies* 70:3.

Pache, C. (2010). "Almodóvar's Female Odyssey" *The Classical Outlook*. 87(2):77–79.

Rossetti, A. & Kruger-Robbins, J. (1997). "Poetry and Film in Postmodern Spain: The Case of Pedro Almodóvar" *Anales de la literatura española contemporánea* 22:½, 165–179.

Twain, M.(1907). *A Horse's Tale*. www.gutenberg.org/ebooks.

CHAPTER 7

The Law According to Almodóvar

William Fried

Law of Desire (1987) begins with the film's credits, typewritten in a slapdash way and strewn with errors, on crumpled paper. The print is demarcated by an oval of light that serves to emphasize the wrinkles in the paper. It is as though the paper has been crushed and discarded, then retrieved and smoothed, as much as possible, to serve the purpose. These images foreshadow the central importance of a typewriter in the film, as an instrument of creation and destruction.

The *Law of Desire* is about Pablo Quintero, a film and theater director, and writer, and the people who desire and love him. In this essay, I will try to trace some of the sources and precursors of Almodóvar's inspiration for this film that may also be extrapolated to others. Some of my analysis will be focused on the phenomenon of narcissism in creative people, and the difficulties to which it often contributes. I will also direct attention to Almodóvar's treatment of problems inherent in the uses of language, narrative, and representation.

Almodóvar has certainly been influenced by Surrealist elements in the films of Luis Buñuel and, as I will show here, the works of Jean Cocteau, but these are ad hoc borrowings rather than essences. The liberties he takes with reality, as we ordinarily conceive it, are not for their own sake, or deliberately to subvert our take on the world, but to state and enrich the themes of his pictures. And these themes are always intelligible not in spite of, but because they are embodied in a visual idiom that is neither conventional nor self-explanatory. The dislocations, apparent non-sequiturs, abrupt changes of mood, and sometime clashes between the images and sounds, are all designed to support the underlying meanings. These may not be accessed without the modicum of effort required to understand all serious works of art, but there are pleasures and beguilements in the first viewing that, like the first reading of a good poem, beckon us onward and inward.

Before the title of the film is revealed, we are shown a vignette in which a young man is instructed to perform an act of masturbation by the voice of a movie director who is not seen until a few minutes have elapsed. The director tells the actor to remove all but his underpants, stand in front of a full length mirror, kiss the lips of his image in it, and grind his penis against its mirrored counterpart. He is then ordered to lie on the bed and touch his body sensually, wherever he likes.

Next, the director instructs the actor to pleasure himself but to imagine the director is doing it to him. He insists that the actor be excited, tells him to imagine that he, the director, is with him and that he wants to be fucked by the director. When the actor tries to look at him, he tells him not to, but to pretend that he, the director, is in bed with him. The actor protests that this was not in their agreement but the director cuts him off, saying "It's only a few words."

The director's assistant, standing very close to him, says "Fuck me" repeatedly. The director says "I want you to feel me inside." It is not clear whether he is saying this to the actor, his assistant, or both. The assistant is visibly aroused, almost beyond control. Someone (it is not clear who), says "Don't stop!". The director says "Tell me when you are going to come," and "Do you feel me inside of you?". The assistant gasps "Yes!" repeatedly, and seems to be reaching orgasm. Someone (actor, director, or assistant), says "I'm going to come," and someone replies, "I am, too." The camera pans on the director and his assistant. They are gasping as though they have just come. The film script is highly visible between them. The director commends the actor, gives him a wad of bills, and tells him he can leave after he showers. The actor counts the bills, kisses them, and puts them on the nightstand. The director bids his assistant "Freeze the image and 'The End.'" Thus, the film within the film ends.

The transition from excitement and pseudo-intimacy to business-like practicality, is abrupt. Where there was heat and urgency, there is now only a commercial transaction. A line from Yeats's "Leda and the Swan" (1983a) seems relevant: "... before the indifferent beak could let her drop?" refers to how Zeus, in the form of a swan, forcibly possessed Leda, and, after impregnating her in a violent paroxysm, just as abruptly released her. It is as though the scenario we have witnessed is, like all masturbation fantasies and their casts of characters, instantly forgotten after the moment of discharge, a disposable commodity that will be replaced by another, similar one, when excitement again rises above a critical threshold. Later, we learn that this scenario is the template for all of Pablo's erotic liaisons.

Immediately, a red curtain parts, revealing first, the words "FIN," also in red, against a backdrop of papers, one of which is a newspaper piece, likely a review of the film within a film called *The Paradigm of the Mussel*. Then, the face of Tina, Pablo's transgender sister, appears, as she emerges from the movie theater. She sees and embraces Pablo. Antonio, a young man who seems smitten with Pablo, enters left, keeping a distance from Tina and Pablo, and avoiding their gaze. The color is drained from the picture as the title of the film is scrawled in lurid pink; the "L" of the Spanish "La" (the), descends vertically and slashes right, describing an enclosure for the images of Antonio, Pablo, and Tina, the three principals. Beneath the slash, the word "DESEO" appears in stippled block letters. Significantly, this is the first of Almodóvar's films made under the imprint of his own production company, named "El Deseo," (desire). It has produced all of his subsequent films. Also, significantly, Almodóvar's brother, Augustín, his business partner and co-owner of "El Deseo," plays the role of the director's assistant in *The Paradigm of the Mussel*, and of Pablo's lawyer, later in the film.

Next, the words "Un film de Almodóvar" are printed at the bottom of the screen before the color is restored. Pablo remarks, "It looks like they're applauding," and Tina says "It's marvelous" before the two embrace. There follows a cut to the downstairs toilet, a mirrored room that Antonio reaches via a staircase. Because of the mirrors, it is difficult to determine Antonio's position in the room. Bypassing a row of urinals, he enters a cubicle in which the light fixture is reflected in the water of the commode, zips his fly open, and masturbates, while exclaiming "Fuck me," an echo of the voices of the director and his assistant in the film he has just seen. His expression is feral, mouth and teeth emphasized in a predatory rictus.

Much of the inspiration for this episode and the film of which it is a part derives from an early film by Jean Cocteau, author of the play *The Human Voice* (1928) directed by Pablo and starring Tina, that is shown later in the film. That silent film, *Blood of a Poet* (1930), opens with two printed statements by its author:

Blood of a Poet

Every poem is a coat of arms
It must be deciphered.
How much blood, how many tears
In exchange for these axes, these
muzzles, these unicorns, these
torches, these towers, these
martlets, these seedlings of stars,
And these fields of blue!

Free to choose the faces, the
shapes, the gestures, the tones, the
acts, the places that please him,
he composes with them a realistic
documentary of unreal events,
The musician will underline the
noises and the silences.

These lines could well represent Almodóvar's film credo or manifesto.

The phrase "a realistic documentary of unreal events" conjures

Marianne Moores's (1960) paradoxical "imaginary gardens with real toads in them." Both could easily serve as descriptions of the often phantasmagoric atmosphere of a psychoanalyst's consulting room.

Blood of a Poet opens with a shot of a huge, phallic, brick chimney collapsing spectacularly. Like all symbols, it is susceptible to myriad interpretations but, in view of what follows directly, it seems to be a representation of momentous events occurring in the environment surrounding the studio of the central character, an artist. That he has insulated himself from these events is conveyed when he tries the lock on his door to be sure it is secured. Both the costumes and appearance of the artist and the man to whom he eventually opens the door, suggest that the action is set at the time of the French Revolution, so that the collapsing chimney may delineate the fall of the *ancien régime*. But, the artist is so obsessed with his private experience that he can't spare any attention for what is going on in the world beyond him.

He draws a face on a translucent panel affixed to an easel. There is a rhythmic knocking sound as of someone's pounding on the door, or of drums or guns from beyond the studio. It heightens the sense of urgency that he is fighting off in order to be able to pursue the work that engages him. The lips of the face he has drawn begin to move. He tries to brush them away with the palm of his hand but is only partially successful, leaving a smudge of charcoal. Opening the studio door, he extends his hand to greet his visitor who, glancing down, is appalled to see the live lips on the palm of the artist's hand, and beats a hasty retreat. Ignorant of the cause of this behaviour, the artist tries to wash his hands in a basin of water where he now sees the mouth, air bubbles streaming from it through the water, as though it were gasping for breath. He pulls his hand from the water and, after several attempts to shake the mouth from his palm, is astonished to hear it speak, apparently asking him for air. He smashes a window pane and thrusts his hand through the frame. In a few seconds, he pulls it in again. The mouth seems to have revived. The action is suspended as the screen displays the printed message:

Emerging from a picture where the
naked hand had constructed it like
leprosy, the drowned mouth
seemed to expire in a small zone
of white light.

The artist evinces a new interest in it. After scrutinizing it very intently, he raises the mouth to his own lips while embracing his arm and himself. The kiss is followed by his placing the lips at his neck, and his nipples before moving his hand below the picture frame, to his lower body. There is a fade out, as he swoons into sleep. Before he awakens, another message appears on the screen, this one from Cocteau. First, in print, it reads "The sleeper seen up close, or the surprises of photography." Next, handwritten by Cocteau: "...or how I got caught in a trap by my own film."

The image that follows is of Cocteau's head, resembling a sculpture, lying on his left arm which is also supporting his right arm, the palm open and faintly imprinted with the image of the mouth.

This digression ends with a resumption of the main action: the artist awakens, looks again at the transformed palm of his hand, peers about stealthily, his gaze lighting on the statue of an armless, archaic female figure in a corner of his room. He claps the mouth embedded in the palm of his hand over the mouth of the statue and holds it there until the eyelids of the statue begin to flutter, and her voice is heard, saying, "It is already dangerous to wipe oneself against the furniture," and "Is it not mad to waken statues from their age-long sleep?" The artist's face reflects malicious exultation and relief when, glancing at his palm, he realizes that he has rid it of the mouth. The success of psychological disavowal is that it creates the illusion that one has jettisoned the unacceptable quality by (pun intended) palming it off on someone else.

He recoils from the statue for a moment as he hears her speak again. She asks, "Do you believe it's so simple to get rid of a wound, to close the mouth of a wound?" He grasps the sides of a full-length mirror; looking desperate and frightened he petitions her help. She replies, "You have one recourse: to enter the mirror and walk around inside it." "Mirrors cannot be entered," he objects. The statue rejoins, "My congratulations. You wrote that mirrors can be entered. And you don't believe it." He looks doubtful as he places a tentative hand on the surface of the mirror. She encourages him by reiterating, "Try! Always try!" several times. At last, he places his body before the mirror and plunges into it with a shout of alarm. It is seen to be made of water that splashes out as to the sides of a pool.

Narcissus, as he first appeared in Book III of Ovid's *Metamorphosis* (2000), commits suicide when, falling in love with his own reflection in water, he is overcome by longing. He chooses death because he can neither revert to a state of primary unity, nor remain transfixed by his own image. The only additional alternative to the dilemma of pathological self involvement is the one chosen by Cocteau's artist, who, by diving into the mirror, may be able to learn what he must, to unlock the riddle. In so doing, he uses the advice given by Stein to Lord Jim, the eponymous hero of Conrad's novel: "In the destructive element, immerse" (p. 229).

As will be seen, Pablo must follow a similar path after his shocking realization and acceptance of responsibility for the catastrophe wrought by his ruthless disregard for the distinctiveness and complexity of others. This change is shown in his smashing the typewriter with his crutch before Antonio's suicide, and, after it, hurling the instrument through the window from which it plunges into a dumpster on the street, the contents of which combust spontaneously. Horrified and chastened by Antonio's death, he cradles him lovingly as the altar built by Tina and Ada also bursts into flames. At a single stroke, the illusions and magical wishes of both siblings are consumed by the refining fire of tragedy.

I have taken this discussion of Cocteau's film to such length and detail because I believe that Almodóvar used it as a source of the ideas and some of the imagery of *Law of Desire*. First, there is the clear correspondence between the character of the artist and that of Pablo, the film director. Second, there are highly significant parallels between both auteurs, Cocteau and Almodóvar . Indeed the fictitious pair can be accurately seen as alter-egos for their creators, both of whom abrogate the boundary between their fictions and their lives.

Almodóvar's is a film about the dangers and pitfalls of artifice when it functions as a radically egocentric mode of behaviour. The actor in the *The Paradigm of the Mussel* is encouraged to play out a scenario that derives from the initial scenes of *Blood of a Poet*. Both involve onanistic acts, the use of a full-length mirror, and portrayals of narcissism. Cocteau himself appears in the form of a surrogate, a statue. Almodóvar counters this by casting his real brother, Augustín, as the director's assistant, and when the director urges "Do you feel me inside you?", the assistant pants, "Yes!" The three, director, actor, and assistant, achieve orgasm simultaneously, an invocation of excitement and elation, to foment the illusion of merger that affords Almodóvar a phantom presence in the scene.

Following Lewin (1950), I submit that the profusion of drugs, sex, music, and artifice in this work (and in many of Almodóvar's films) serves to create a hypomanic ambience in which fantasy, much of it unconscious, infiltrates and undermines causality, and convention. As a result, it is only the law of desire that coerces obedience, and takes precedence over almost all other imperatives. Almodóvar's genius is to wield a calculus that prevents the entropic dissolution and deterioration of his materials, by holding them in arcane, mobile, and intriguing configurations.

Among the operations by which the law of desire is implemented, fictions occupy a central place. The primary symbol of these fictions is the typewriter on which Pablo writes his scripts, letters, and other communications. Beginning with the typewritten credits, on rumpled paper, we are given evidence that there is something fundamentally tainted about this process. Each credit is surrounded by "the small zone of white light" that, in *Blood of a Poet,* is associated with leprosy. Thus, fictions may have the effect of a contagious disease that disfigures and wastes its victims. It may be introduced by a slight degree of dissembling, as when the director of *The Paradigm of the Mussel* overcomes his actor's objection to pretending he is in bed with him with the phrase, "It's only a few words," but, like any pathogen, it carries the threat of virulence.

The mouth that figures so prominently in the Cocteau work, is the organ from which language emerges. Thence, it can be either directly voiced, or transformed into script. The statue associates the mouth with a wound. She asks, "Do you believe it's so simple to...close the mouth of a wound?" Here, she is speaking as an emissary from classical antiquity, perhaps with a voice informed by the dread experience of a Medea or Antigone. If so, she is fatally familiar with the power of the mouth to wound and to express woundedness.

From Pablo's mind, the "few words" are reproduced by the typewriter whence they become the language of influence, the media for disseminating the director's sensibility and thought among the general public and specific individuals, his preferred method for feeding his insatiable hunger for something as elusive as it is exciting. The scenes that follow the end of the film within a film serve to establish Pablo's character. He is shown to be self-absorbed, charismatic, mercurial, manipulative, charming, and a magnet for the desire, envy, love, and affection of others. He is desired by Antonio, loved by Tina, Ada, and Juan, and lionized by the admirers of his films, including the doctor who tries to protect him from the police. He is restless, discontent, insatiable, faithless, and a person in whom love and desire are mutually exclusive.

Tina is his opposite. She has sacrificed almost everything for love: her sex and gender, her sexual organs, her family, and her relation to her lover (her biological father). She was prepared to sacrifice her life, as well. She is faithful unto death, willing to die for her faithless lover. The long relational hiatus from her abandonment by her father begins to be broken when she becomes infatuated with the faithless and ruthless Antonio, who uses her to get to Pablo. In stark contrast to Pablo's characteristic absorption in fantasy and artifice, Tina declares, repeatedly, that she can trust only her failures, memories, and losses: they are real, and constitute the cornerstone of her identity

Antonio is rapacious. Pablo is captivated by this rapaciousness because he believes it reflects pure, unconditional desire, and he needs, above all, to be certain that he is desired. Antonio murders Juan whom he perceives as a rival for Pablo's attentions. Juan loves Pablo but does not desire him. The law of desire is draconian: it demands complete obedience, submission. When Pablo explains that the letter Antonio has interpreted as a love note to Juan is a joke, Antonio declares, "Love is never a joke." There is no room for ambiguity, irony, or wit in Antonio's unsparing adherence to the law. Under its sway, his will becomes a juggernaut, single-minded and implacable. He murders Juan, sweeps aside all obstacles, and exploits anyone who can abet his ferocious envelopment of Pablo. His stratagem for complete control of Pablo echoes his mother's efforts to control him. He explains to Pablo, "My mother is German and she likes to spy,"; in a single stroke, a wry glance backward to World War II, and the hundreds of films of and about that period; and an inadvertent revelation of the source, in emulating his mother, of Antonio's invasive curiosity.

Pablo's sexual inclinations, as they are revealed in *The Paradigm of the Mussel,* include a wish to control the other, and force him to enact his wishes. When he cajoles his actor into feeling his presence within him, the act is not merely sexual, however; its intention is to project a part of Pablo's psyche into the mind of the actor, to coerce him to accept it, at least for a time, as the entire motive for his behaviour. His assistant, too, is bound by this obeisance to Pablo's demands. The phrase, "I want you to feel me inside of you," is illuminated by Pablo in one of the letters he writes to himself over Juan's signature. The passage reads, "I didn't leave Madrid to forget you because if I forgot you, like you said, I'd end up empty inside." Thus, it will be seen that Pablo's manipulation of others is predicated on the anxiety of being forgotten or expunged from their minds.

If the influence of *Blood of a Poet* can be detected in *Paradigm of the Mussel*, Cocteau's stamp is overt in the long segment based on his monodrama, *The Human Voice*. The play is directed by Pablo and stars Tina, with Ada, her ward, in a role added by Pablo. Comparing the two Cocteau contributions throws further light on the contrasts and similarities between Pablo and Tina. Where Pablo's life and career are founded on the ruthless manipulation of others, Tina's history is that of a serial victim. Presumably seduced by her father, then persuaded by him or for him, to change from male to female, and later abandoned by him, she defines herself by her losses and failures. Prior to these events, she was sexually abused by a priest in whose church choir she sang.

Ada is the child of a transsexual friend of Tina's. She has been left in Tina's care while her mother pursues a modeling career. Tina and Ada are deeply devoted to each other. The child is also in love with Pablo. Calling the child whose position between Pablo and Tina "Ada" is a borrowing from the novel, titled *Ada* (1969) by Vladimir Nabokov, about the sexual affair between Ada and her brother, Van. Tina and Pablo may not be lovers, but their style with each other is unquestionably erotic. Moreover, if Tina had remained a boy, the probability of an intimate link between her and Pablo would have been strong.

Ada brings love to the relationship between Pablo and Tina. This function is nowhere more apparent than in the scene in which the three are strolling on a deserted street after the performance. Ada rides piggyback on Pablo, and after they all pass under the arc of water from the hose of a street cleaner, Tina complaining of the heat, asks the man to drench her. She is very pleased by the cooling effect. The name "Ada" is also suggestive of ardor, as Nabokov overtly indicates in the full title of his novel, *Ada, or Ardor: A Family* Chronicle. Tina's ardor, inspired by the role she has just played, as well as by her dangerously strong connection to Pablo, requires cooling. There is a sense in which Ada syphons enough ardor from the siblings to make their relationship safe from incest. Pablo refers to Tina's soaking as hydrotherapy, but it can also be thought of as baptism in view of her passionate, if idiosyncratic, espousal of religious faith.

Tina is thus typecast in *The Human Voice* as the quintessential rejected lover. The play is an agonizing depiction of a woman's vain attempts to metabolize an inevitable loss. The element added to the play by Almodóvar through the agency of Pablo, his cinematic counterpart, is Ada's lip synching of the heart rending Jacques Brel song "Ne Me Quitte Pas," ("Don't Leave Me") (1959). She stands on a dolly with casters that are fitted to tracks that run the width of the stage and allow her to be moved laterally. Behind her, Tina, as the protagonist, enacts a spectrum of desperate gestures. *The Human Voice* stands in opposition to the duplicitous typewriter as a medium of emotional truth. It is Tina's intrinsic mode of expression where typing is Pablo's. Her clear, piercing mezzo startles as she suddenly sings the song being played on the church organ by the priest who abused her. It is a plea to the Virgin to hear and soothe her suffering. In the scene that follows, Ada plays it on the harmonica (also called a mouth organ) given her as a gift by Pablo.

There are other echoes of film and theater history in the movie. Pablo's surname, Quintero, is almost certainly a reference to José Quintero, the Panamanian director credited with the founding of Off Broadway theater in New York City. One of the innumerable plays he produced in the theater he co-founded, Circle in the Square, was *The Human Voice*. Quintero's father, who formally disavowed him, hoped that he would be a girl because he already had sons. He was an indifferent student in high school, and was noted only for his talent in decorating altars. He was also gay. Late in his life, his larynx was surgically removed to treat his throat cancer. Afterward, he was unable to speak.

Almodóvar's movie explores the question of narcissism in the personality of the artist. It refers, thematically, to the innumerable examples, well known, and documented, of artists of every kind, who have used and sacrificed the people in their lives on the altar of their métier, as though the work, talent, or gift were a license to do so. There is also the matter of how others may be willing, even eager, to give themselves to the artist in exchange for a variety of subjectively conceived rewards ranging from aggrandizement by association, to a masochistic need for self-immolation. The artist may be admired, envied, loved, worshipped, fetishized, mystified, or the object of any other species of human obsession. As a character, Pablo embodies qualities that are endearing, exciting, elusive, and commendable. But the behaviour that seems most alluring to his acolytes consists of such contraries as warmth alternating with coldness, and the remoteness that he simultaneously cultivates and deplores.

The film's conclusion, in which Pablo gives up his art in an attack of conscience after attaining insight into its destructive consequences, would be unconvincing even if we yearned to believe it. Almodóvar spares us the willing suspension, however, by ending the film without presenting evidence of Pablo's ability to persist in this resolution.

Another pervasive concern is Pablo's uses of art for the purposes of exploitation and deception. The *Law of Desire* broaches the limitations of language itself to adequately represent human experience, and the inevitable elisions, cruxes, and lacunae where falsehood, betrayal, and faithlessness can infiltrate a text to render it treacherous. Narcissism is shown to be untenable by its solipsistic nature, implemented not by dialogue so much as by directive and pretense. Yet, the more authentic relations between human beings, because they are mediated by language, are subject to their own sources of pain, misunderstanding, and corruption. Those aspects of life, people, or movies that cannot be represented in language include inaccessible reaches of the mind, unbearable truths, and the bewildering manifold of experience. For knowledge of them we must search between lines, absorb silences, and brood over negative space.

References

Almodóvar, P. (Director). 1987. *Law of Desire. [Motion Picture].* El Deseo, Laurenfilm. Cinevista (Distributors) (USA).

Brel, J. (1959). *Ne Me Quitte Pas.* Accessed at www.lyricstranslate.com/en/ne-me-quitte-pas-dont-leave-me.html-5

Cocteau, J. (Director) (1930). *Blood of a Poet* (film). Accessed at www.openculture.com/2012/11/jean_cocteaus_avante-garde_film_from_1930_ithe_blood_of_a_poeti.html

Cocteau, J. (1928). *The Human Voice.* Accessed at video.search.yahoo.com

Conrad, J. (1900). *Lord Jim.* Edinburgh and London: William Blackwood and Sons.

Klein, A.S. (Trans.) (2000). *Ovid's Metamorphosis.* Accessed at http://ovid.lib.virginia.edu/trans/Ovhome.htm

Lewin, B.D. (1950). *The Psychoanalysis of Elation.* New York: W.W. Norton.

Moore, M. (1960). Poetry. In: L. Untermeyer, Ed., *Modern American Poetry, Mid-Century Edition.* New York: Harcourt Brace

Nabokov, V. (1969). *Ada or Ardor, A Family Chronicle.* New York: McGraw Hill and Co. 370–371.

Yeats, W.B. (1983a). The Second Coming. In: R. Finneran (Ed.): *The Poems: A New Edition* (pp.187–188): New York: Macmillan.

CHAPTER 8

Desperately Seeking Ivan or, Healing the Vertical Split in *Women on the Verge of a Nervous Breakdown*

Jeffrey Stern

For readers who haven't seen the film or haven't seen it recently, here are the central dramatis personae:

Pepa, a television actress near 40 who also dubs films and is newly pregnant. She has lived for an unspecified number of years with Ivan, also an actor who dubs films. A week before the action takes place Ivan leaves Pepa and the new penthouse they had very recently moved into. Ivan is in his early 50s and has a son named Carlos whom he almost never sees and about whom he has never told Pepa. Carlos is in his early twenties and engaged to Marisa. They are looking for an apartment and are sent to Pepa's because she has decided to sublet it since Ivan will no longer be living there with her. Carlos was raised by his grandparents because his mother, Lucia, has lived in a psychiatric hospital for all but the past 12 months of his life. Lucia was Ivan's lover and became pregnant with Carlos. Ivan left her before Carlos was born and Lucia had a psychotic break. Candela is an actress and model and Pepa's friend and colleague. She looks to be in her mid- to late twenties and has become romantically entangled with a Shiite terrorist. Paulina Morales is a lawyer who represents Lucia but becomes involved with Ivan. There is also a blond taxi driver whose name we never learn.

Critics, not to mention Almodóvar himself (Evans, p. 30), have compared *Women on the Verge of a Nervous Breakdown* (1987) to

Shakespeare's *A Midsummer Night's Dream*, due to its magical drugged gazpacho, Arcadian setting, and pairs of lovers. But in *A Midsummer Night's Dream* the drug with which Puck anoints the lovers' eyes only temporarily disrupts the romantic couplings. At the end of the day, that is, night, the original groupings are all restored: and so Puck says:

> Jack shall have Jill,
> Nought shall go ill,
> The man shall have his mare again,
> and all shall be well. (MND: 3.2.477–479)

This is not how *Women on the Verge of a Nervous Breakdown* ends: Pepa's gazpacho never reunites her with Ivan; the spell it casts over Marisa destroys her attachment to Carlos (and more happily, her sense of herself as a virgin) and entwines Carlos with Candela. Pepa and Marisa end the drama uncoupled. If "naught shall go ill" it is not because any man in the film has his "mare" again.

There is, however, a deeper connection to *A Midsummer Night's Dream*, easily overlooked, but nonetheless I think vital. Oberon goes to war with Titania because one of her vestals becomes pregnant and dies in childbirth. Titania adopts the changeling boy whom Oberon desires for a "henchman", but when Titania refuses to render him up, Oberon is enraged, and to punish her anoints her eyes with love juice to make her love the ass Bottom. Pepa needs no special love juice to love the ass Ivan. But his flight from her may indeed have to do with her pregnancy.

Following the opening credits Pepa's voice is heard while we look at the architect's doll house sized model of her new apartment (a reference to Ibsen?) saying "the whole world is crumbling." Why is not clear. But she says she has sought to save it, and chiefly to save her also crumbling relation to Ivan, which is why Noah-like she has moved them into this ark of a penthouse and filled it with two of every kind of creature (this is of course not literally true; she has some hens, ducks, rabbits, and doves), and why she has become pregnant.

Although it's time to get up Pepa can't hear the four alarm clocks she's set to awaken her for work. She needs the clocks because since Ivan's departure she's had to knock herself out with pills to get to sleep. So she's late. But on her way to the studio she makes a stop at her ob-gyn's office because she's late in that sense too. After the doctor confirms that she's pregnant she tries to reach Ivan, believing that when he knows about it he will come back to her.

It's more likely, however, that his suspicion at some level that she's pregnant is why he left. He's been gone a week and she has already taken the pregnancy test we see her learning the results of, meaning that she is probably at least a week or two past her period when Ivan departs. Moreover he is well aware of the fact that Pepa's plan at 40 (give or take) to move into a new apartment and repopulate her world like Noah, suggests that she sees her and their restoration in terms of a baby. Which is exactly what he doesn't want. This, presumably, is why when he leaves Pepa he takes up with Paulina Morales, a "feminist" lawyer also around 40 and unlikely to want to set her career back with a child and why he left a pregnant lover once before. Twenty some-odd years previously he was with Lucia but abandoned her when he learned she was pregnant. She had a nervous breakdown that landed her in the psychiatric hospital where she lived for all but the past 12 months of her son Carlos's life, a life that Ivan has completely concealed from Pepa, although they have been together for years. Lucia's fate might be thought a limit case for Pepa if losing Ivan takes her beyond the verge of a nervous breakdown and into a catastrophic psychotic depression.

Such a fate destroys the heroine of Jean Cocteau's play *The Human Voice* (1930), the tragic source of Almodóvar's screwball comedy, or to put it another way, the depressive core that lies beneath and behind the film's mania and represents a constant if veiled and suppressed threat to it in Pepa's thoughts of overdosing, Candela's near fatal leap from Pepa's balcony, and Lucia's plot to murder Ivan.

Like the plot then of *A Midsummer Night's Dream*, the crisis that sets the plot of *Women on the Verge of a Nervous Breakdown* in motion might be thought a crisis of the Lacanian Real (Muller and Richardson, 1982). By which I mean it is a crisis generated by time in the form of Pepa's biological clock. Until this moment of necessity and opportunity, she has, it seems, kept at arm's length her awareness of the need to make a radical change if she is ever to be happy. Becoming pregnant perturbs the comparative (if crumbling) stability of her world and life and brings about what she thinks of as her own Noah's flood with its promise of transformation.

Ivan and Pepa play phone tag because despite his protestations to the contrary – "I'd like to talk…I miss you!" – he wants to get away from her – "listen, put my stuff in a suitcase, I'm going on a trip tomorrow," – not to reconnect. Pepa hears his sugary words but doesn't believe them: "You're such a liar" she says to the machine, "damn asshole!"

Awash in self destructive misery she replaces her gray business suit with a tomato colored housecoat. Slicing tomatoes for gazpacho she nicks a finger, then takes a "morphidol", having convinced her friend the pharmacist to give her a supply without a prescription. She opens the package and seems to consider swallowing all of them before dumping the handful into the gazpacho. Then she grabs some hangers of Ivan's clothes from the closet and angrily kicks the bag he has asked her to pack for him across the bedroom. Deciding to have a cigarette and then thinking she shouldn't smoke she throws the lighted match and box of wooden matches on the bed accidentally setting it on fire. Although she watches transfixed as it burns it's not clear she realizes that her accident may not be wholly accidental, that she is at least partly ready to see her relation with Ivan go up in smoke.

After putting out the blaze with the garden hose from her balcony, Pepa angrily throws some of Ivan's things into his suitcase with a roll of wet carpeting, torn up photos, a pair of shoes, a plastic "stupid!" flower he'd given her and a duck: "Who gives a duck as a present?!" But she doesn't take the suitcase down stairs to leave for Ivan with the super. Despite her rage she still wants him to come up to the apartment to get it so that she can give him the gazpacho—"[he]

used to love the way I mixed it"—laced with the morphidol, hoping that drugging him will somehow result in his wanting not to leave again. "I didn't want to kill him, just to make him stay."

Pepa then gets herself dressed and heads off to Ivan's studio hoping to catch him. The fact that she is desperately seeking him, however, in no way means that she is unaware of his failings. In her dream she pictures him as an aging and fatuous lothario, ridiculously spritzing his throat before uttering romantic clichés—"My life without you makes no sense! I can't live without you! I need you! I want you! I love you!"—to a line of women (including a nun) from around the world dressed in silly national costumes—as if for a Miss Universe pageant. She tells Carlos that Ivan has been cheating on her and lying about his feelings: "He never says anything, never admits anything," and that he is a coward who "never reproaches anyone." But such knowledge doesn't make her think she might be better off without him.

Kohut (Goldberg, 1999) would say she is "vertically split": meaning that she keeps her awareness of Ivan's failings and her rage in the face of them from impacting her ("reality ego") sense that she couldn't live without him. Rehearsing a scene from (Nicholas Ray's) *Johnny Guitar* (1954) in the dubbing studio Pepa hears Ivan's voice coming from Sterling Hayden's lips: "Lie to me!" the voice says, "Tell me without me you couldn't live!" "I couldn't live if I didn't have you," she replies. "Say you care," Ivan's voice continues, "as much as I do". "I care for you as much as you care for me," Pepa says and then faints. She faints because it would be lying to say she couldn't live without Ivan, then the truth is she could, and if she cares for him as much as he cares for her, she may not love him at all. These thoughts are too distressing to contemplate so she blacks out. Her ability to disavow her rage is sent up in the television commercial she does for "Ecce Omo" laundry detergent in which she white washes the clothes her slasher son wears committing his crimes. "No trace of any blood stains!" one cop marvels, "Or any guts either!" adds his partner.

But why does Pepa believe she can't live without Ivan? In her dream he speaks to the women through a silver microphone that makes a fetish of his voice. Joye Weisel-Barth (2013) argues that fetishes counteract an underlying "sense of lifelessness" following "an overwhelming loss that is unmourned and unmentalized" "The creation of a fetish reflects temporal, affective, and cognitive dislocation" and points to a self's "last-ditch effort to avert total psychic disintegration." The idea that Pepa has traumatically lost something squares with her saying that the world before she moved into the penthouse was crumbling and with the images in the opening credits of women in fragments and "Soy Infeliz" (sung by Lola Beltran) on the soundtrack. But why might her world be crumbling and what might she have lost? In *Johnny Guitar* Ivan—who looks to be a dozen or so years older than Pepa—is the voice of the romantic hero, the noble man of action from a bygone era, a role he has doubtless played in many films. This suggests that what Pepa's world may have lost is the romantic ideal of patriarchy Franco's Spain professed in which women were taught they needed strong men to protect and guide them. Of course Ivan—"the terrible" as one critic called him (Forbes, 1989)—is neither strong nor noble, nor was Franco's Spain to be sure, but Ivan is the father of the child she is carrying and his disembodied voice electronically dislocated into the mouths of many heroes may offer Pepa an illusion of a desperately desired—if always already imaginary—masculine ideal. It's of course ironic that the film Ivan and Pepa are at work on is *Johnny Guitar* because Sterling Hayden's Johnny doesn't in the end save Joan Crawford's—that is Pepa's—Vienna. Vienna saves Johnny—and not from a man, but from a gun slinging woman (Mercedes McCambridge) like Vienna herself. In the end, of course, Pepa, having finally accepted her own strength and the idea that she doesn't need Ivan, will similarly save him at the airport from the gun slinging Lucia.

The idea that the crumbling of Pepa's sense of world and self is connected to "overwhelming loss that is "unmourned and unmentalized" hints at something deeper than her culture's loss of heroic masculinity. Given that the event that sets the film in motion is the pregnancy that comes so late in Pepa's life, it seems this "unmourned and unmentalized" loss may have to do with mothering, which makes sense given that the patriarchal culture of Franco's Spain taught all women, all mothers, to see themselves as deficient. Hence the inevitability that such women will place their self-esteem and emotional equilibrium in the hands of weak and deceitful men—themselves victims of the inadequate parenting that is the legacy of patriarchy—and find themselves on the verge of a nervous breakdown.

Pepa never speaks of her parents, but we may get a sense of the mothering she might have endured in the response to her of Christina, the receptionist and controlling maternal presence at the dubbing studio. Christina is flirty with Ivan. Ivan: "Will you please call these two numbers?" Christina: "I can only call one of the numbers one at a time!" But when Pepa asks her if Ivan called for her, Christina tells her to forget about Ivan over an open mic as if Face Book shaming her in an era before the internet. It is good advice but unempathically rendered and Pepa isn't listening. After she faints, Christina tells her she's acting like a fool: "I told you this would happen!" She knows the kind of man Ivan is and can't understand why Pepa can't figure it out and leave him: "She won't learn, she'll never learn! Not her!" With her sharp, abrasive, know-it-all style, Christina is a mother whose advice Pepa may need but can't use. She offers her single moment of empathy—"Hey, Pepa, please forgive me, I'd no idea you fainted!"—to the air as Pepa walks out.

The only actual mother in the film is Lucia's. Dressed in the same tomato and white colors Pepa wears when making gazpacho, Portera asks Lucia why she wears clothes that are out of date. Lucia—who has lived in an institution for the better part of two decades—says doing so makes her feel that time has stood still, to which Portera mutters bitterly and in a manner not far from Christina's that she's sorry to inform that it hasn't. It's hard not to think that Lucia's fatal attraction to the faithless Ivan and the fragility of her psyche have much to do with her mother's coldness.

The mother-figure whose responsiveness to Pepa does help to set her free from Ivan is the Mambo taxi driver. Pepa walks to Ivan's studio where she runs into Lucia who is also looking for him. Lucia jumps into a cab and drives off despite Pepa's efforts to detain her. The instant Pepa raises her hand for another the Mambo taxi is there. "Follow that car," Pepa says. "I thought this only happened in the movies!" the driver (whom one reviewer mistook for Almodóvar himself [Levy, 2014]) excitedly replies. The cab is equipped with whatever Pepa might fancy or need: music, magazines, newspapers, tissues, Coke, cigarettes, and gin, and everything is "on the house."

Mambo plays on the sound system but the driver tells Pepa he's got "all kinds of music. I've got heavy metal, easy listening, I've even got classical! Salsa? Techno pop? Jazz?" but Pepa says "mambo" [so close to mamma!] "is fine", which bonds them. "I love the mambo," he says happily. " It's what goes best with the car's décor!" More than fine, with its warm infectious rhythms mambo is exactly what she needs. Recognizing her the driver says, "Say, aren't you on tv? You're the mother of the mutilator! You're really funny!" and asks for an autograph for his girlfriend, Begonia, "with a very personal inscription!" Rather than being annoyed, Pepa brightens noticeably at this display of mirroring interest (Kohut, 1971).

Kenneth Newman argues that for Winnicott the child's imaginative and creative coming into being hinges on the willingness of the mother to respond to its so-called "omnipotent gesture": "the child's libidinal appetites create the need for [a need gratifying] object — and through the proper maternal adaptation the object is there to be found" (Newman, 1996). This seems to describe the Mambo driver to a T. Whenever Pepa is ready to learn something about Ivan that she needs to know in order to heal the split within her but hasn't wanted to know – that he has a son with Lucia, that he is involved with Paulina Morales, that he really shouldn't be part of her future – he is there to provide a literal vehicle to move her along, even as Puck in *A Midsummer Night's Dream* and Ariel in *The Tempest* magically appear whenever summoned to carry out their masters' grand designs. Like them the Mambo driver ultimately represents an attenuated part of Pepa's (grandiose) self (Kohut, 1971) that the developmental imperative of her pregnancy calls into being.

Whereas after seeing Christina Pepa bought "morphidol" in case she wanted to commit suicide, after being with the Mambo driver she begins to change. In her first maternal moment she embraces her hens and ducks and gives them Ivan's "suit valet": "Ladies, here's something to hang onto! You can perch on it and shit on it as much as you like!" Later she speaks similarly to the plants and rabbits: "Poor little things, you're all shook up, aren't you. You're gonna miss me when I leave. I'll take you with me, I'm not the kind to forget you and leave you behind."

Having thus far had eyes wide shut—the result of the split—she decides she wants to know the truth. She begins to pace; we see her at shoe level going back and forth—thought is action—until she gets an idea. Opening the phone book she discovers that Lucia's address is the address of the woman Ivan called from the dubbing studio. She leaves another message for Ivan telling him that she's coming to look for him, which probably guarantees that he won't be there. And of course he isn't, but she walks back and forth through the night between his apartment and Lucia's. She's become a detective—a truth seeker—as is clear when she sees "Miss Torso" (from Hitchcock's *Rear Window*) dancing in a window near Lucia's. Her hard day's night is rewarded when Lucia throws Carlos's suitcase out the window and it crashes against the phone booth Pepa is in, breaking open and exposing a framed photo of Ivan and Carlos with the inscription "your Dad who doesn't deserve you, Ivan."

Pepa blames her ignorance of Carlos's existence entirely on Ivan. She tells Carlos his father is impossibly withholding and that she only learns important things about him by accident. But it's hard not to think she has been complicit in her ignorance: that she hasn't wanted to know what she hasn't known, but that now she does. Because finding out that the father of the child she is carrying is already a father is something very much to her purposes.

Or at least she thinks it is. Presumably she imagines the fact that Ivan is Carlos's father makes it more likely that he will want to parent their child with her. But he has not done that with Carlos, whom he never wanted. Why isn't clear, but given how narcissistic and needy he

is, it seems reasonable to think he felt he didn't have the internal resources to give to a child. Pepa's dream suggests that Ivan needs a
continuous supply of feminine admiration to shore him up. Communicating (disingenuously) with women only through his silver
microphone even as he communicates (dishonestly) with Pepa—only
through her answering machine, Ivan the voice actor epitomizes the
false self (Newman 1996). Winnicott sees the false self as a
characterological solution to the problem of a mother's failing to
cherish her child and respond to the full panoply of its needs. Instead,
the false self mother responds to her child's needs selectively and only
to the extent they gratify her own. The sons of such mothers grow up
lacking a strong sense of self and learn not to trust women. Instead
they learn to seduce and manipulate them in order to keep from being
traumatically seduced and manipulated by them. Vienna in *Johnny
Guitar* is a former prostitute. Johnny leaves her when she wants them
to marry: "He couldn't see himself being tied down to a home," because he cannot imagine she won't betray him: "How many men have
you forgotten?"; and perhaps because like Ivan he knows he isn't capable of responding to the needs of children. Johnny returns to Vienna
after five years, when she is too old to have a family. (Joan Crawford
was 47 when the film was shot.) But Johnny continues to believe
nonetheless that the only way he can imagine she loves him is if he
orders her to lie to him and pretends to believe her. "Lie to me. Tell me
all these years you've waited for me… Tell me you still love me like I
love you."

Almodóvar seems to be arguing that under patriarchy women
cannot be good (enough) mothers nor their sons good (enough)
husbands or fathers. Ivan might be said to be trapped in a system
that makes him both victimizer and victim. This is the reason that
despite his dreadfulness he remains ever so slightly sympathetic in
his message to Carlos on their photograph or when apologizing to
Pepa for his faithlessness – "I want you to know that the years we
have spent together have been the best years of my life"—or to Paulina Morales for his weakness, or when addressing Lucia tenderly even
after she tries to shoot him.

When Pepa returns to the green world of her apartment, fate seems to require her to begin acting the role of mother. This of course doesn't come easily or particularly naturally to her, but I think it follows from the fact that she has chosen to be pregnant and has been tenderly responded to by the Mambo taxi driver.

When she walks in she checks her machine to see if Ivan has called. He hasn't, but Candela has over and over. Furious, Pepa rips the phone cord from the wall and throws her tomato colored phone through the glass partition leading to the balcony. She will tell Carlos she did it to keep from strangling herself with the cord (like the woman in *The Human Voice*).

The doorbell rings and Pepa rushes to answer, thinking it's Ivan. But of course it's Candela needing a place to hide out, as well as soothing and advice. Pepa is hardly gracious: "you're a real pain in the ass!" she says, but when Candela says she'll leave, Pepa invites her in, then runs out to report the broken phone to the phone company.

When Pepa returns she discovers Carlos and Marisa who have come to see the apartment. It could be argued that only the madcap conventions of screwball comedy would allow Ivan's son to consider sub-letting the apartment that had been his father's the first morning it's available, and indeed even before his father's possessions are gone. But if a patient were to tell this story the therapist would assume the coincidence was more apparent than real: that the son would have wanted to be where his father had been and would have consciously or unconsciously made it his business to get there. Given that Lucia tells Pepa she knows the location of the new apartment Carlos might easily have come across the address at home, especially given the fact that he's a relentless snoop. "I wouldn't trust your stepson one bit" Candela tells Pepa, after she returns from her visit to Paulina Morales' office: "He's been spying all afternoon, all afternoon!"

Pepa is thrilled when she finds Carlos in her apartment mere hours after discovering his existence. "I was almost your stepmom!" she tells him as she pulls her hair back, then touches his cheek, takes hold of his hand, walks with him arm in arm, touches his shoulder, then his hair. There is definitely a gleam in her eye although it seems more Oedipal than Kohutian. Later she will ask him to come into her dressing area and zip her up, her back naked and her breasts visible under her sheer lingerie. Nevertheless, despite the erotized nature of her warmth—or perhaps because of it—her responsiveness does the Kohutian trick of enhancing his sense of self and bringing him to life. It's easy to see why having Lucia for a mother, her bitter mother Portera for a grandmother, and the absent Ivan for a father, Carlos has languished, and, unlike his silver-tongued father, stutters. He tells Pepa his grandparents kept Ivan from seeing him, but it's doubtful they'd have succeeded had Ivan not readily complied. Indeed it's the sort of story grandparents might invent to spare a grandchild's feelings.,

When they arrive at Pepa's apartment Carlos is completely dominated by Marisa. Although he likes the apartment—"it's marvelous if you ask me"—she's having none of it: "Carlos, it's not very good. It's too high, too expensive, not a real house." Noticing Pepa's attraction to him, Marisa tells her to back off: "He's mine. We're getting married!" But despite Marisa's insistence that they leave, Carlos takes off his coat when Pepa asks him to fix her broken phone and insists on trying. Pepa can't believe Carlos doesn't know where Ivan is and rarely sees him, and he can't believe his father never once mentioned him to Pepa. Their shared hurt bonds them.

When Candela tries to jump from Pepa's balcony they save her together, and when Pepa, badly shaken, berates her for not being tough enough to cope with adversity, Carlos unexpectedly silences her: "Pepa please, now's not the time!" Pepa is startled by his unexpected show of strength and inadvertently calls him Ivan, an unexpected Freudian slip.

Marisa is also startled and unnerved by his attention to Candela. "Carlos," she says anxiously, "love me?" But he turns away coldly, seeming not to. Hurt and distressed Marisa opens the refrigerator, finds the spiked gazpacho, drinks it, and falls into a trance-like sleep.

Pepa's greeting, "Oh, it's you, you're a real pain" does not go over well with Candela: "I've called you a thousand times! I won't be spoken to like that! I'll leave here this very moment!" Nor does Pepa's shunting her aside to lavish her attention on Carlos in her hour of need. Candela is frantic having learned from television that her terrorist boyfriend and his accomplices have been apprehended by the police and having assumed they will arrest her as part of the conspiracy. She needs her parents but they aren't an option: "I can't go to my folks, it's bad enough I'm an actress!" But Pepa—who doubtless knows only too well what it's like to be told to wait by women catering to men—insists she be patient. "I just found out the man I've been living with has a son! Shouldn't that come first?" "But I'm in a terrible mess myself!" Candela tells her urgently. But Pepa, not used to thinking like a mom, ignores her. So Candela, frantic, impulsive and despairing, drops over the side of the balcony. Because this is a comedy she manages to catch herself before she gets free of the railing and Pepa and Carlos are able to haul her back up. This of course gets Pepa's attention, which was no doubt its' principal intent.

Like Lucia, Candela represents another dream or through the looking glass aspect of Pepa. She is fragile and depressed, but because much younger than Pepa, more dangerously impulsive. Which is why she attaches herself to a foreigner whose name she doesn't know even after they "screwed all weekend". When she hears this and sees the goosebumps Candela gets just thinking about the guy, Pepa assumes that she is driven by lust. "It's a shame sex is so important at your age!" she says without irony. But as with her own attachment to Ivan its more likely that what Candela ultimately craves is an attachment to a fetishized (and thus idealizable) self-object (Kohut 1971). "If he's a terrorist, living in constant danger, he gives more of himself than a regular guy!" she tells Pepa. But of course this is ridiculous, as Candela is eventually forced to recognize: "He wasn't really in love with me! It was all just a lotta junk because he was just using me for him!"

Unlike Pepa, who splits off thoughts and feelings that conflict with her desire, Candela has no vertical split because her desire is conflict free. Things for her are as they seem, so she doesn't hesitate to act on her impulses, nor does she separate them from feelings that might challenge them, because she seems not to have feelings that challenge them. She is like a child who believes what grownups tell her and doesn't learn from her experience: "Men are always trying to take advantage, and by the time I realize what's going on its always too late for me… Look what happened to me now with those terrorists! They took advantage of me! I certainly didn't deserve that!" But if Candela had had a "good enough" mother she would doubtless have learned that a girl who spends a weekend in bed with a Middle Eastern stranger whose name she doesn't bother to learn deserves the terrorist she wakes up with. Indeed the result for Pepa of allowing Ivan to remain in many ways a stranger to her over the years is that eventually even he begins to seem like a sort of terrorist himself.

> Paulina: Maybe someone lied to you.
> Pepa: Yes. I've been lied to.
> Paulina: By a terrorist?
> Pepa: You could call him that.

Candela's particular form of feminine cluelessness is the subject of the tv commercial for condoms she is in with Pepa dubbing her voice. Candela plays a bride whose groom is asked by the priest if he "will be faithful for richer or for poorer, in sickness and in health, till death do you part?" "Yes, I,—guess so," he says, looking trapped. When Candela's character—who is utterly oblivious to her intended's tone and demeanor—is asked she answers, "why wouldn't I?". The priest then tells her she can never trust any man. "Even my husband?" she asks. "No," he says, "you can't be too careful," and drops a condom onto her bouquet.

Doubtless Candela's impulsiveness, blindness and desperate need for male attention has everything to do with the lack of maternal responsiveness we see in her interactions with Pepa prior to her suicide attempt. But after the rescue Pepa begins to relate to Candela in a manner that seems to enhance rather than undermine her emotional growth.

Listening carefully to Candela's story, Pepa, on the advice of Carlos, takes it upon herself to get her a lawyer, but Paulina Morales proves to be more a threat to Candela's safety than its defender. She tells Pepa Candela has committed a crime and needs to go to jail. Paulina may be a "feminist" but she is no sister. Lucia hires her to sue Ivan but she not only fails to get any money from him, she ends up in his bed. Pepa then comes up with a plan to take Candela out of town for a week until things blow over. After starting slowly she is beginning to live up to her quintessential maternal responsibility of protecting her child's safety.

The upshot is that Candela decides she wants to be just like her. Thus when Pepa returns from Paulina Morales' office Candela has taken off her childish blue and white halter and mini skirt and put on one of Pepa's elegant black dresses. She's also gelled her hair and combed it back and taken off her manic pixie dream girl espresso maker earrings. The scene is shot with Candela and then Pepa in front of a mirror suggesting Candela's effort to make herself into Pepa's image. This is in obvious contrast with the cold and critical mothering that Lucia gets from Portera. Rather than wanting to be like her and to dress like her, Lucia insists on wearing clothes her mother can't stand.

When the police come to investigate Carlos's call regarding the terrorists, Pepa suggests they play "Stratego" in order to look as unsuspicious as possible. The idea that Pepa wants Candela to begin to think – to be strategic rather than merely impulsive – is the point. Lucia says that Carlos's forsaking of Marisa for Candela indicates that he is as faithless as his father. But he may be drawn to Candela because she is in effect the child of Pepa even as Candela may be drawn to Carlos for the same reason.

At the end of *A Midsummer Night's Dream* Oberon's love juice reconnects the lovers with their proper partners. At the end of *Women on the Verge of a Nervous Breakdown* Lucia throws gazpacho into Pepa's eyes to blind her so that she can escape to the airport to kill Ivan. She sees murder as the only way to forget him. When he forsook her decades ago she was able to accomplish this by becoming psychotic. "At the hospital I forgot Ivan." Unlike Pepa's vertical split wherein attempts to isolate her knowledge of Ivan's faults from the emotions that would compel her to leave him take place within the realm of consciousness Lucia's split is horizontal, the unendurable knowledge of Ivan's rejection blotted entirely from her mind by a sealed repression barrier. But the price Lucia must pay for thus foreclosing all knowledge of Ivan is the foreclosure of all knowledge connecting to Ivan: which is to say the foreclosure of Lucia's reality: "Actually I forgot about everything."

But Lucia tells Pepa that a year ago while watching television she heard Ivan's voice coming from the lips of another actor professing love to a woman exactly as he had professed his love to her once upon a time. The shock woke her from her limbo, retraumatizing her, and she decided that to forget him again she'd have to kill him (a short sighted plan because even if she succeeds she is likely to hear his voice again on tv the same way. But Lucia clearly isn't thinking that far ahead…)

Pepa avoids abandonment by Ivan for years by not becoming pregnant, but when he leaves her she nearly decompensates like Lucia as we've seen. She can't sleep without pills and considers both suicide and murder, although she manages to remain on the verge of a nervous breakdown and refrain.

What sustains her is the split that while allowing her to experience Ivan's faithlessness and the pain of his abandoning her allows her at the same time to keep these thoughts at arm's length – ("what do you think, I didn't know he was seeing someone else? 'Course I did. I put up with it!") – and imagine he'll come back to her. Unlike Lucia, she doesn't obliterate the truth until it comes flooding back to make her crazy all over again; rather helped by the mirroring Mambo driver and her self-self-object relations with Candela and Carlos the split within her becomes increasingly unnecessary, allowing her to become strong enough to accept Ivan's true nature and the pain of loss.

With eyes burning Pepa looks for a cab and of course the Mambo driver is there to again follow Lucia, who this time is on Enrique's motorcycle. The perfect maternal self-object, he has remembered to stock the cab with eye drops which he didn't have when Pepa asked for them on the ride to Paulina Morales' office because she was crying: "You're marvelous!" she tells him. After Pepa saves Ivan she faints as she had in the dubbing studio when she heard his voice saying what she couldn't bear to hear: "Lie to me. Say without me you couldn't live." She fainted then because the words coming from Sterling Hayden's Johnny Guitar suggested truth she couldn't accept: perhaps he doesn't love her; perhaps she doesn't love him. When she awakens this time he holds her in his arms. It would be easy to imagine that all will be well between them going forward. But Pepa no longer needs to split what she knows to be true from what she desires. With eyes wide open, she tells Ivan goodbye.

The split in Ivan is unaffected by his experience. He cheats on Pepa, lies to her and conceals his history from her even as he avoids his responsibilities to Carlos as a father. Only when he is in effect caught red handed is he chastened. "Pepa, I'm so ashamed of myself. I behaved very badly. Please forgive me." This is because only when he is caught red handed does his split collapse forcing him to think about the ways he has hurt those who love him. At all other times he is able to separate his sense of himself as a "good" person from his knowledge that to live as he wishes to he must behave in a manner that he finds morally reprehensible (Goldberg, 1999).

When Pepa comes home Marisa wakes up. In *A Midsummer Night's* Dream she would be compelled to "madly dote" on the first creature she saw. It's Pepa. Is that what we are to imagine happening after the projector runs out of film? Who knows? Pepa does touch her face and tell her that she has beautiful skin. So it isn't beyond imagining. But what is in front of us is tenderness. Marisa went to sleep an angry and petulant child and awakens transformed. She tells Pepa she feels wonderful but says Pepa looks tired. Pepa then tells her that she's pregnant. Marisa is the first person she's told, perhaps because she's finally able to fully embrace the idea herself, perhaps too because Marisa suddenly seems daughter-like. When Marisa stands up she is shocked to see Carlos entwined with Candela and gasps, but Pepa immediately succeeds in soothing her. We never see

Marisa's mother, but it's hard to imagine her connecting with her as warmly as she connects with Pepa at this moment. She then tells Pepa her midsummer day's dream: which is that she is somehow no longer a virgin. Pepa assumes she's been raped, but Marisa assures her that it only took place in her imagination. In Pepa's safe maternal and gazpacho-magical world Marisa has had her first orgasm, and this has given rise to a newly empowered sense of self.

Whereas the film opened to "Soy Infeliz" with images of women—mannequins—in fragments with enormous flowers, clothes and jewelry concealing and at the same time revealing their state of lack, it ends to the strains of "Teatro", a song in which a woman (the singer La Lupe) angrily condemns her two-faced lover. Were this Shakespeare's *Twelfth Night*, Feste would say: "And thus the whirligig of time brings in his revenges" (Act 5, Scene 1, pp. 358–359).

On the screen we see two women each uncoupled from her man—"Jack shall [*not*] have Jill!—but each complete within herself—and all shall be well" (Act 3, Scene 2, p. 477)—talking warmly and smiling as the night comes on.

References

Almodóvar, P. (Director). (1987). *Women on the Verge of a Nervous Breakdown* [Motion Picture]. El Deseo, S.A.

Cocteau, J. (1996). *The Human Voice*. Trans. Anthony Wood. United Kingdom: Samuel French.

Evans, P.W. (2009). *Women on the Verge of a Nervous Breakdown*. London: British Film Institute.

Forbes, Jill. (1989) Ivan the Terrible: *Women on the Verge of a Nervous Breakdown*. Sight and Sound: 58:135.

Goldberg, A. (1999). *Being of Two Minds: The Vertical Split in Psychoanalysis and Psychotherapy*. Hillsdale: The Analytic Press.

Kohut, H. (1971). *The Analysis of the Self*. Madison: International Universities Press.

Levy, E. (2010). *Women on the Verge of Nervous Breakdown: Almodóvar's First Masterpiece,* Website EL: Emanuel Levy Cinema 24/7.

Muller, J.P. & Richardson, W.J. (1982). *A Reader's Guide to Ecrits.* New York: International Universities Press.

Newman, K.M. (1996). Winnicott Goes to the Movies: The False Self in *"Ordinary People." Psychoanalytic Quarterly*, 65: 787–807.

Ray, Nicholas. (Director)(1954). *Johnny Guitar* [Motion Picture]. USA: Republic Pictures.

Shakespeare, W. (2007). *The RSC Shakespeare: William Shakespeare Complete Works. J.* Bate and E. Rasmussen, eds. New York: Modern Library.

Weisel-Barth, J. (2013). Review of Pedro Almodóvar's "The Skin I Live in." *International Journal of Psychoanalytic Self Psychology* 8:111–114.

CHAPTER 9

Tie Me Up! Tie Me Down! Abduction, Violence, Lust, Drugs, Pornography and True Love

Herbert H. Stein

Tie Me Up! Tie Me Down! The title suggests something possibly erotic, even pornographic, sadomasochistic. The basic plot supports that. A man gets out of a mental hospital, stalks a porn star, steals her keys, breaks into her apartment, knocks her out and ties her to the bed. No wonder the film was X-rated when it came to the States! Actually, it was probably properly rated for that time given the nudity and sex scenes.[1]

But, in fact, it is the opposite, or, perhaps, an upside down version of that X-rated plot. If I were going to pigeon-hole *Tie Me Up! Tie Me Down!*(1989), I think I would link it to the screwball comedies of the 1930's and 40's. Two beautiful people in a crazy caper that ends in true love.

The two would be lovers are Ricky (Antonio Banderas), a 23-year-old orphan who has lived most of his life as an inmate in a mental hospital, and Marina (Victoria Abril), a porn star and recently recovering opioid addict who is the star of a film described as a "horror film spinoff".

---

[1] Aspects of this basic theme reappear in later Almodóvar films, notably *The Skin I Live In,* in which a man holds a woman captive in bed, and *Talk to Her,* in which a male nurse cares for a semi-comatose woman patient lying helplessly in bed.

When we first meet Ricky, he is told that the director wants to see him. The director, a middle-aged woman, tells Ricky that "The judge has decided there's no reason to keep you here. He thinks you're ready to rejoin society as of today."[2]

He responds enthusiastically, "Great."

"You won't have to run away anymore. You're free, Ricky. Though being free also means being alone."

At this point, she breaks into tears. *She has strong feelings for this young man.*

"I won't be there to protect you anymore. ... You'll be responsible for your own actions, like any other citizen."

Ricky appears unfazed and unmoved by her attention.

"Don't worry. I'll manage."

"What will you do?"

"Get a job, start a family, like any normal person."

"You're not a normal person."

"The judge says I am."

"What does he know?"

After a pause and a change in focus so that we now see them facing one another she hands him an envelope, explaining as he looks at it that it's 50,000 pesetas. She then explains,

"It's for the drawings ... and for the mad, passionate moments you gave me."

Suddenly, our awareness shifts as we realize that the director is not a concerned, caring parental figure, but a woman being abandoned by her lover. Ricky is the object of her erotic desire.

When she turns away from him and says, "Now go away and never come back", we see her not as a protective caretaker, but a spurned lover.

We see her staring out the window for a moment, then saying, "I said to leave".

He approaches her and says, "I want to thank you for everything first," and begins to kiss her, first on the cheek and then on the lips as

---

[2] Quotations are taken from the English subtitles.

she slowly, but passionately, responds.

Marina is also the erotic object of a director, in her case the director of the film she is making. Naturally, as a porn star, she is used to being the object of erotic desire, but we see it expressed throughout the film by the director, Maximo.

Maximo is an elderly man in an electric wheelchair who seems dedicated to two things, making films and sexuality. Soon after we first see him, he says, "Since I've been confined to this chair, I've felt hornier than ever. My wife says I'm regressing back to childhood. She may be right". At one point in the film we see him watching a pornographic film in his home while his wife tries to pull him away from the television.

So when we see him staring admiringly at Marina as she gets ready to shoot her scene, we know that there is a strong erotic component to that admiration, not unlike the same type of affection that we saw from the hospital director towards Ricky. The one scene we see from the film they are making parallels this, as Marina's character must fight off a monster with no face who wants to take her with him to the land of the dead. Maximo continues to ogle Marina and pursue her (ostensibly to work on his film) throughout the movie.

But Maximo is not alone in his eroticism. Other characters repeatedly talk about wanting to "get laid" and their frustration in that desire. In fact, the film suggests an entire society absorbed in erotic fantasy and desire. When Ricky and Marina go looking for a pharmacist late at night, they knock on the door, disturbing the woman pharmacist who is in the middle of having sex with a younger man. At one point we see a television advertisement for an investment company that suggests the Spanish are absorbed with sex in contrast to the Germans, wearing swastikas, who take care of their financial future.

Which gets us back to my original point, that this film is an upside down version of the X-rated, sadomasochistic thriller that the title and basic plot suggest. What turns it on its head is the fact that Ricky, the proposed sadist, and Marina, his erotic victim, are the two people in the film who do not appear to be primarily motivated by sex. They are not sexually frustrated because they are the two beautiful people in the film, the objects of sexual interest.

When Ricky kidnaps Marina in her own apartment, we see some disturbing violence. He pushes his way into her door, having stolen her key at the movie set. When he tells her not to scream and she screams in response, he punches her, knocking her out and allegedly breaking her tooth. Later she throws a glass of water at him, smashing it on his head. It is after that that he grabs her and they stand close together in an embrace.

She seems to soften after her initial alarm and anger and says, "So you want to fuck me? Go on. Get it over with."

He answers, "Relax. We'll fuck when the time is right."

He is not after her for sex, and she has no strong need to avoid him sexually. In fact, it is this point that gives the lie to the suggestion that this is primarily a film about lust. Ricky does not kidnap Marina out of sexual desire. He explains to her what he wants, sitting below her, almost kneeling.

"I tried to talk to you, but you wouldn't let me, so I had to kidnap you so you could get to know me. I'm sure you'll fall in love with me, just as I'm in love with you. I'm 23 years old, I have 50,000 pesetas, and I'm all alone in the world. I'll try to be a good husband to you and a good father for your kids."

He goes on to explain that he had met her by chance at a bar and they had gone back to her place to have sex. He is surprised that she doesn't remember. In fact, we assume that this was not an unusual event in her life.

He adds, "I promised to come back and protect you".

She responds by throwing something at him and shouting that "lots of men have said that!"

Marina assumes that men want her for sex, and only sex.

These are two people who can easily be "loved" for their attractiveness and eroticism. She appears to be resigned to that, unbelieving that anything else is possible. He is seeking love, marriage, family. But why Marina?

Later in the film, he will tell us that after meeting her the last time he escaped from the hospital, he decided to stop faking mental illness in order to have a place to live, leading to his release. We come to see that he is not mentally ill in the usual sense. He has sociopathic tendencies. We see him steal. We see him use brute force to subdue Marina at the start of the kidnapping. But he is not psychotic.

Yet, he is certainly odd in his ambitions and his manner of pursuing them. Obviously his plan to kidnap a woman to allow her to love him is a plot device that gets our attention. But why is he so desperate, and why Marina?

One answer to that last question is easily suggested by the plot. Like him, she is alone. She has friends, a family, a sister with whom she is close; but she can't find anyone to love her as a husband and father of her children because all men see her as a "porn star and a junkie".

She is the other kind of woman, lonely in stardom, admired for her beauty and eroticism, but incapable of being loved by a man. But that does not fully explain why he chose her.

And it does not explain how she will come to fall in love with him. (Sorry for the spoiler.) Almodóvar makes us wait for that, and when it comes, we don't quite see it at first, although he has given us a clue much earlier in the film.

We are first led through a series of machinations that are fueled by his need to help her deal with the pain he caused her when he punched her in the jaw and supposedly broke her tooth. In a crazy set of scenes, he takes her out late at night handcuffed to him to visit the doctor who detoxed her from drugs in order to get a prescription for strong pain medication. If that sounds a little incongruous, let me add (for those of you who have not seen the film) that the doctor——a young woman herself with two small children——at one point offers Ricky a joint, which he turns down.

As it turns out, they can't use the prescription she gives them and have to go to the drug dealers in the street. This is probably appropriate, since Marina over the next couple of days appears to be driven by her drug cravings under the guise of pain. It is this drug seeking that eventually leads them to true love. (I did say screwball comedy.)

Ricky begins to go out to get the drugs, leaving Marina tied up in the room. On one of these forays, he is beaten and left lying on the street by a drug dealer he had earlier stolen from, and her two male accomplices. When he returns to Marina, who has managed to undo her ropes, but hasn't gotten out of the locked apartment, he is bloodied and shoeless. It is then that she begins to fall in love with him. After she helps him clean himself up and tends to his wounds, they make passionate and extended love, after which she says to him, "Now I remember you".

What has happened here? We have a clue from a small scene early in the film that I barely took note of the first time I saw *Tie Me Up! Tie Me Down!* I don't think most viewers would take note of it at the time with no context with which to understand its significance.

It comes when Ricky is beginning to stalk Marina as she is leaving the film studio to go home. He has gotten into her dressing room and stolen her keys and a few other items. She is walking outside to go to a car that is waiting to take her home. On the way, she passes a man with a horse cart. Marina looks at the horse, pets it, asks its name and then reaches to look at its left front hoof. She's told us earlier that she used to work as a horse trainer in the circus.

Marina tells the man with the cart, "She's got a corn".

We see Ricky, watching the scene from above, give a little smile.

Marina tells the man, "You better un-shoe her".

"Who'll pull the cart?"

"If you don't, gangrene will set in. Make a plaster of bran and vinegar, put it in some burlap, and wrap her hoof. Take it off 24 hours later and clean it with iodine. When it dries, she'll be fine. Right?"

She turns to the horse, telling her, "Don't let them treat you bad," and adds to the owner, "She really could die".

He thanks her and she says goodbye to go to the waiting car. We hear him telling his young assistant, "The young lady's right. You see?"

When seen the first time, this little scene appears to be incidental to the main story. It is only much later, when Ricky's injuries from the beating seem to have softened Marina and won her love, that it's importance becomes clearer.

Apparently, Marina is moved to help those in need, in pain, or in trouble. In effect, she can offer Ricky the maternal caring that the hospital director initially appeared to be offering.

With this insight, we are prepared to understand the film's moving happy ending.

When seeing a patient in analytic therapy, most clinicians take some time initially to get a history. A film is more like a patient who insists on telling it in her own time, in her own way. In *Tie Me Up*, we must wait for the history that will help us understand it all.

The morning after they have made love and she has remembered Ricky, Marina wakes up to find him in another room sitting in his briefs over a drawing table.

He explains, "I drew you a map of my life".

"Show me."

"Imagine my life's a subway line. First stop: orphaned at three."

The picture shows a drawing of a little boy leaning over a coffin, crying. Above the picture in blue capital letters is the word GRANADILLA.

He goes on, "Orphanage. Mental Hospital at 16. What a career. I learned a lot of trades there. Locksmith was my favorite——breaking in and out. So I'd escape now and then, but I always went back."

She asks, "Why?"

"I had nowhere to go and the director lady liked me."

She immediately intuits that relationship, obviously drawing from her own experience.

"Ah, that's why you're such a good lay."

"With them it was different."

"Were there lots of directors?"

"No, only one director. The others were nurses."

"Now I understand. Go on."

"Last year I escaped and met you. That stop changed my life. You were all I could think of, and thinking took up all my time, so I stopped acting crazy. A judge came along, gave me a test, and said I was fine. They let me go. End of the line."

Here we see a picture of a woman sleeping in bed, with the caption in red, "MARINA".

"You."

She responds, "Me."

Although he does not explain what it was about her that so attracted him, he has explained to us that he deliberately found his way out of the hospital because he felt he no longer needed it for shelter and basic care and was ready to pursue the rest of his life.

We next see them in happy domesticity in bathrobes while she makes breakfast and sends him to set the table. Seated over the breakfast table, he points to a map conveniently serving as a table-cloth.

"Here's Granadilla, my home town. Not far from Plasencia. I'll steal a car tonight and we're off."

She objects to going there in a stolen car.

"Then we'll go by train or bus, but we're going."

He asks about her pain.

"My whole body hurts."

"Then we'll go tomorrow."

Having won the love of the woman he is pursuing, the end of that subway line he had drawn, he now desperately wants to take her back down the line to his birthplace, Granadilla, pictured in his drawing as a boy crying over a coffin. We have another clue to what he is seeking.

Sometimes in the course of an analysis, we come to a point at which things become clearer as the evidence points to an overarching fantasy. In this case, we begin to understand that nearly all the action of the film is motivated by a fantasy that a lost mother, a lost source of love, can be found again in someone new. Psychoanalysts might call this a "transference", as features of someone from the past are transferred to someone in the present. Whatever we wish to call it, we can see at this point in the film that Marina satisfies a fantasy of the return of Ricky's lost mother.

And sometimes when we come to such a realization, we also begin to understand something that came earlier that seemed peripheral or trivial at the time. We saw an example of that with the awareness of the significance of Marina's encounter with the horse.

We now have perhaps another such retrograde understanding available. I'm referring to the violence at the beginning of Ricky's abduction of Marina. He grabs her around the throat as he pushes through the doors, then head butts her, then punches her in the jaw, knocking her unconscious. It's very disturbing to watch, and I think affected some of the reviews of the film. Without diminishing its disturbing quality, we may at least have a better sense now of how it fits into the film's overriding fantasy.

A mother who abandons her small child, even through no fault of her own, may well be the object of frustration and anger. In the fabric of the film, Marina's otherwise reasonable resistance to a break-in can be understood as a renewed refusal to show the love and caring that has been so long wished for. We can speculate that Ricky releases 20 years of anger and frustration at having been abandoned.

But the film does ultimately offer some hope.

Ricky and Marina become separated when she is discovered by her sister while Ricky is out stealing a car to go to Granadilla. He sets off on his own while Marina convinces her sister that she loves Ricky and wants to marry him.

When Ricky gets to Granadilla we see a deserted, long-abandoned mountain village. Seeing him alone without Marina amidst the deadness of Granadilla reinforces our sense of his loss and grief.[3] He looks at a faded picture showing a man and woman with a small boy standing outside a doorway to a home.

It is suddenly clear that Ricky is looking to re-find the long lost loving family that he left behind. As we put together the pieces of the puzzle, we realize that he was somehow touched by Marina's genuine caring and her ability to know how to take care of a wounded child, the qualities that we observed when she encountered the horse with the damaged hoof.

The hospital director told Ricky that "being free also means being

---

[3] My thanks to Merle Molofsky for pointing my attention to the significance of Granadilla, whose inhabitants were forced out for the construction of a dam, something I assume a Spanish audience was much more aware of than an international audience.

alone". Ricky told Marina, "I'm 23 years old, I have 50,000 pesetas, and I'm all alone in the world".

Ricky sees Marina as the cure for his loneliness, someone who can love him and care for him out of pure caring and concern.

After telling her that he's all alone in the world, he added, "I'll try to be a good husband to you and a good father for your kids".

He envisions having children with her. *Knowing his history, we can easily imagine him wanting his children to have a mother who will care for them.*

The fantasy that underlies the film is now almost complete. Two people looking for love in a world in which people want to use them for their sexual pleasure can find that love in each other. An orphaned boy has a chance to re-find his mother. There is one missing piece, and that comes with the end of the film.

Marina convinces her sister, Lola, to drive her to Granadilla to find Ricky. They meet him there and we see them in the car driving back with Ricky in the back seat, Lola and Marina up front. There is music playing and Ricky is singing along with them as they go. The little orphan boy has found a family, and I for one was surprised to find tears in my eyes.

I'll add a brief addendum. Many viewers must wonder how a sociopath who steals without hesitation, uses force and whatever means to achieve his ends can go on to a happy life as a well behaved member of society. If this were a documentary, they'd be correct to ask that question.

But Almodóvar is not attempting to recreate life exactly as it is and we don't go to his films seeking that. He is an impressionist, to borrow from another art form, and his films are designed to make us feel through a mix of reality and fantasy. The sense of family and wholeness at the end of the film is at the heart of that fantasy; but, so is the stealing and sociopathy. We respond appropriately, and to what is at the heart of the matter, a story of two people who find complete love elusive, but ultimately achieve it together.

References

Almodóvar, P. (Director). 1989. *Tie Me Up! Tie Me Down!*. [Motion Picture].
S.A.: El Deseo.

CHAPTER 10

Free Associating while Riding in a Red Convertible with Almodóvar: *High Heels* & *Volver*

Nancy R. Goodman

Throughout the two films, *High Heels* (1991) and *Volver* (2006), Pedro Almodóvar mixes the real and the imagined. This magical realism is similar to what psychoanalysts consider psychic reality, the inner life of the mind that is; a continuously flowing mix of reality and unconscious fantasy. Free associating to symbols in dreams, imagery, and narratives opens a view to the dramas of the unconscious, the conflicts, wishes, and terrible fears. Almodóvar gives us copious material for associating and uncovering the joy of letting the mind discover and play with wild, humorous, and scary material. There is the serious and the terribly funny in these films and Almodóvar's use of color, facial expressions, landscapes, music and stories of relationships automatically commands a free associative process without even trying. There is always more than one thing going on in our psyches and in these films. For example when Penelope Cruz (in the role of Raimunda) is driving to La Mancha, they pass fields of turbines awakening in one's mind windmills from *The Man of La Mancha*; and, Pedro Almodóvar is from La Mancha, Spain. This is the working of the mind to discover links in all directions, past and present and future. Throughout, he links one image with another; one time period to another; one moment to others. Symbols resound, creating connections and resonating with forbidden knowledge of murder, incest, sadomasochism, and the power of the fetish.

The cinematography of these two films is vibrant, creating a need to blink, sigh, and to almost moan while pondering the question of what is real. Each film directs the viewer to travel down paths of the tragic, horrifying, passionate, traumatic, and sadomasochistic. These tremendously serious topics are then intermingled in Technicolor distractions, haunting music of tango rhythms, and slapstick comedy. Intense affects are present in varying forms, styles, and costumes.

Imagining a road trip with Almodóvar and with psychoanalytic thinking

I choose to imagine my free associative process taking place as I ride in a red convertible. The color red is found throughout both films in the portrayal of love, trauma, sex, and hatred. With the top down, I take in the terrain that is sometimes straightforward and understandable and sometimes mysteriously configured with uncertainty about where one is headed and what could appear around a curve in the road. With the wind blowing in my face, it is often difficult to get a clear view as my hair sweeps across my eyes. To accompany me and to help sort out unconscious events in *High Heels* and *Volver*, I have thrown an array of psychoanalytic writings onto the back seat. I have chosen topics of trauma, perversion, the primal scene, incest, the fetish, soul murder, narcissism, and sado–masochism. With the help of Pedro Almodóvar and his special visual effects, I have added some features to my vehicle: the indelible red shiny paint, white leather interior, and multiple mirrors mounted in the car. Where does one look, which mirror reflects what is true? It is difficult to know what is a reflection, or even what I will call a double reflection; that is, a reflection of a reflection obscuring the exact nature of the scene unfolding before one's eyes.

Watching the films of Pedro Almodóvar brings one into a world in which more than one event and one perception is simultaneously taking place. This is similar to the way conscious and unconscious are found in unconscious fantasy (Arlow, 1969; Ellman and Goodman; 2017; Isaacs, 1938; Klein, 1930; Steiner, 2003). The placement of mirrors in my red convertible plays off of the visual effects in both films in which reflections are used to convey confusion and uncertainty about where to focus and how to be sure about what is being seen. This is the layering of the mind psychoanalysts expect to discover in analytic process and what I see as the process of finding unconscious fantasy on the stages of the inner theatre (Goodman, 2017). The idea of reflection is a prominent feature of the psychoanalytic process in which the dramas of the mind are taking place within a frame of analyst and patient watching what is happening in narratives and interactions of transference and countertransference configurations.

The array of feelings found on Almodóvar's film screens include confusion, eroticism, sadness, rage, hatred, love, loneliness, and a good measure of downright hilarity. The films are female in multiple dimensions, including beautiful women as the main characters, young and old, family (pairs of mothers and daughters with grandmothers, and aunts), and neighborhoods of women who dance together and commit crimes together. A more dangerous world is depicted for men, who end up dead, usually in their beds, killed by the women they traumatized, raped, betrayed, and abandoned. It is regularly uncertain who is the father of children, and only women get to know for sure they are the biological parent.

The female of Almodóvar

High Heels and *Volver* are about females; individual female yearnings, humiliations, and relationships with men and children and among women. Women are powerful, sexy, sad, and mad. The women portrayed are complex, beautiful, troubled, erotic, and murderous. Women are presented as keepers of life and death as they claim passions, competitions, envy, and hatred, and do so with a Latin style of dress and gesture. They are mothers, not always such good mothers, who are disappearing when their daughters need them. The women have men in their lives and their beds. Most often, the men are betrayers and molesters, including incestuous predators to their daughters or stepdaughters. Women are depicted as both terribly alone and embedded in social networks of other women and family. The body of woman: breasts, genitals, lips (with plenty of red lipstick), and the blood of menstruation are present and alluring as well as dangerous to men.

There are mothers who abandon daughters and appear unreal wrapped up in their narcissism, and who disappear and reappear as ghostly apparitions. Past traumas are transmitting across generations so that daughters unwittingly, that is unconsciously, re-enact the same disturbing events of the previous generation. The psychic life of daughters is threatened with having an internal mother figure of absence, the "no one" who does not notice nor actively witness leaving desperation concerning how to care for oneself and if it is even possible.

The importance of the scene

Like the way the unconscious appears in psychoanalytic sessions, Almodóvar moves from scene to scene bringing about a revelatory process in which fragments of psychic realities accumulate, leading into dramatic events. Psychoanalysts consider scenes to be the basic organizers of the unconscious mind. Scenes are discovered in the narrative of the sessions and in the processes of enactments between analyst and analysand as on the stages of an internal theater (Goodman, 2017). Almodóvar creates scenes that fold into each other, building depth of story amidst often chaotic, sad, and desperate situations. He functions as a psychoanalyst and he presents the films as analytic process, making the audience find ways to fit it all together. In other words, he makes his audience into psychoanalysts, even if they do not realize it. As a psychoanalyst, I found these two films compelling and related to major psychoanalytic ideas. In this way, each film contains lessons about the mind.

The Film stories and psychoanalytic lessons

HIGH HEELS: NOW I SEE IT NOW I DON'T

In 1905, Sigmund Freud showed how there can be deep psychic meaning in the content of jokes. Something seems funny and at the same time signifies truths of the unconscious, forbidden wishes and deep anxieties. There are delightful farcical scenes in *High Heels*. We immediately find a combination of the fetish (high heels, earrings, a transvestite) and of childhood longings for mother. The Spanish title actually translates as distant heels and we learn that this refers to a child listening for mother's return and hearing mother's leaving, especially when there is a mother who is psychically and painfully removed and thus distant.

The film opens with Rebeca as a sophisticated woman waiting in an airport. Her face signals sadness, a searching waiting quality conveyed with her big beautiful eyes. She is in an elegant suit and looks like she has been waiting for a long time. Almodóvar creates an impression of time and space that is compelling, such as seen in many airports, where there are glass windows allowing views of other glass windows in a dizzying array of images, making it seem that one is flying even before taking off. The entire film is about seeing and what happens when looking creates confusion, anxiety, and desire.

Rebeca is waiting for her mother, Becky, a torch singer, who has been in Mexico, away from Madrid for 15 years. Almodóvar uses the technique of flashbacks to show what in her past has led to the emotions of her lonely waiting. Rebeca is shown as a little girl with her mother and stepfather, Alberto, at a marketplace. The little girl gets her mother's attention, asking her mother to buy her the pair of earrings she wants. They are hoops like her mother has, and for a moment the little girl looks triumphant. She has what her mother loves and she has her mother's eyes on her.

Becky then turns to flirting with Alberto, taking her eyes off of Rebeca, who has walked away searching for an earring that she already has lost. Soon Rebeca is surrounded by a group of men who tease her and appear predatory. She gets mad and pushes them away when her mother and her mother's husband find her and enter a game involving bargaining how much the men would have to pay to buy her. Everyone is laughing with the exception of Rebeca, who appears scared and humiliated, and who turns and runs off again. Here is the major motif; a mother's narcissism blinds her to her child, creating anguish, emptiness, and sadomasochism in the child. Her mother tells Alberto that he has again traumatized Rebeca with the ugly threat of being sold. It is agonizing to see how her mother was also enjoying the sadism and once again showed no protection for the little girl.

Rebeca has a wish to go to Mexico with her mother who will be performing there, and who has said that the little girl has to stay home with her stepfather. Rebeca switches his upper and downer pills, resulting in his falling asleep at the wheel and dying in a car crash. Rebeca has killed her stepfather hoping to then be able to be with her mother. In the sadomasochistic pair, she has become the sadist who then has to live with guilt and shame. Also, the little girl has become the masochist, trying to live in an embrace with her mother. The plan fails as Becky says she will go alone and Rebeca must stay with her biological father.

The film progresses, showing the many ways that Rebeca tries to be with her mother: copying her style, including her wearing of extravagant earrings, choosing a career with an audience as a news-caster, choosing a husband, Manuel, who once was a lover of her mother, and being a follower of a transvestite named Letal (the name "Letal" translates to "Lethal" in English), whose cabaret act is mirror-ing the singing and style of her mother. Rebeca is forming a merged sense of herself in the trappings of her mother. Rebeca can be close to an imitation Becky and in fact Becky is herself an imitation moth-er. For the full impact of the name Letal for the English reader I take the liberty to use Lethal. Lethal is a perfect representation of the illusory, having it all, female body and male body all at once and mother and not mother at the same time.

The transvestite is a caricature of the mother: blond wig, outrageous earrings, red lipstick, a figure to kill for and able to perfectly lip sync the sultry lyrics of a song titled "Piensa en Mí", "Think of Me", which is Becky's signature haunting song. We again have a mirror theme of multiple images all at once. Rebeca's husband is flirting with his former lover, her mother; and Lethal looks and sounds like her mother. Everything is unusual and difficult to hold onto. (Is this a take off on the kind of shock children can feel when noting sexual difference for the first time?) The very entertaining performance is accompanied by viewing Becky's facial features as she watches herself being pimped by such excellent impersonation. At one point the mother asks if Lethal is mocking or honoring her. Aha, this is the question. Is woman and sexual desire for her so overwhelming that the image must be obscured? After the performance, Lethal sits with them at the table, eventually inviting Rebeca to help him change his costume, and she readily follows him/her to the dressing room. Before they leave the table the husband, mother's former lover, glances at Lethal's crotch – is it a male or female genital or both?

TRANSVESTITE AS PERFECT FETISH FOR CREATION OF POTENCY

After all of this comes what has to be one of the best sex scenes in film. It is erotic and funny. This scene demonstrates the power of the transvestite as the magic of a perversion, the phallic woman, the woman with a penis, a combination of male and female and mother and father together. In my thinking, the name Lethal (imagine Almodóvar dreaming up this name) links to unconscious fantasies about the destructive power of the female genital in all of it's imagined scary forms, such as the Medusa. For my patients, both male and female, the image of the powerful mother and her sexy and frightening genital has been portrayed in such forms as the spider, the witch, the great hairy grizzly bear, and the gorilla.

What makes this sex scene in Lethal's dressing room not just pornographic is the hilarity of the seduction. Rebeca discovers Lethal's erection under his female padding, and with a look of great puzzlement on Rebeca's face, Lethal proceeds to arouse and pleasure her. The seduction first appears forceful and then a scene full of excitement, like a confusing lethal primal scene. Somehow, she is swinging from a horizontal bar as her clothes fall off and Lethal has his face in her crotch, leading later to penetration. She is trying not to have an orgasm, biting on her fingers, explaining that she has been on a sex diet for months. Lethal, the male-female fetish, is unafraid of her body and of her sexual response as he gives her pleasure and an orgasm.

Almodóvar demonstrates that fetish can be a powerful aphrodisiac for females as well as for males. This is not a well recognized psychoanalytic understanding of women and fetish, and yet is so well demonstrated in Almodóvar's sex scene. It is my hypothesis that the arousal felt when seeing mother's and father's genitalia and the resultant fantasies of sexual desire are forces at work in creating the fetish. That is, knowing and not knowing of desire itself is created with the unconscious hope to thwart imagined superego punishments, castration and female genital anxieties. Better to have sex with Lethal than to have sex resulting in a lethal outcome. Naming the transvestite Lethal is pure brilliance, a potent force linked to death that is able to counter fears about females and the terrifying seductive female genital. The fears, arousals, and fantasies about sex difference and the primal scene are obscured with the transvestite offering the opportunity to have sex with male and female combined.

MURDER MYSTERY

A who-done-it mystery/comedy ensues when Rebeca's husband is murdered. The handsome judge (sunglasses and groomed moustache) has three suspects, Rebeca, Becky, and the sign language translator for the deaf who pairs with Rebeca on the television news program. He interviews all three together and each confesses their sexual relationship with the same man, Manuel, and denies being the murderer. Rebeca looks more and more forlorn, and, in a hilarious scene, ends up eventually confessing on her news show with all descriptions, sexual and the shooting, being represented in sign language. The judge is sure she is innocent and sets out to prove that. We later find out about the multiple identities of the judge, who has disguises for enrolling in different guises as his informants so that he is actually his own informant.

Rebeca's time in prison is presented as a musical with dancing and singing as in *West Side Story*. There is also a huge confrontation between Rebeca and Becky in which Rebeca screams that she has spent her life trying to be like her mother in every way — the masochistic solution of denying autonomy. Rebeca has a fantasy that she can transform her mother through a kind of timeless identification as if looking in a mirror waiting for the mother to appear. While in prison Rebeca discovers through photos of a friend's boyfriend's penis with a mole on it that Lethal, the transvestite, must have another identity. She also discovers that she is pregnant from her encounter with Lethal.

At the very end of the film, Rebeca and mother are repairing their relationship as Becky lies dying in the basement apartment with the windows that look onto the sidewalk where you see a woman (maybe a transvestite) in high heels walking by. Becky puts her fingerprints on the gun that Rebeca brings her after she has confessed that she, Becky, is the murderer. She also advises her daughter to learn to "solve your problems with men in a different way". The confession, although false, rings true to my psychoanalytic ear, knowing the soul murder crime of Becky, the narcissist, to her daughter Rebeca.

THE TERROR OF ABSENCE AND DESIRE: NEED FOR A FETISH

I put forward the hypothesis that the entire film is about the need for the fetish, the need for something that fills perception of absence — the absence of mother and the absence of the penis. When there is desire and absence, the psyche experiences loss and terror and intense need. Creating the image of a fetish provides something to hold on to that uses the illusion of knowing and not knowing to disavow the unbearable.

Freud's original idea (1927) is that the awareness of the female genital ignites such castration fear in the male that his psyche creates a substitute, such as the foot or a piece of clothing, that then allows for arousal and diminishes dread. Contemporary psychoanalytic thinking extends this idea in many directions. The fear of difference, all differences combined with narcissistic vulnerabilities (Bach, 1994; Bass, 2000; Basseches, Ellman, & Goodman, 2013) can bring about fear of annihilation/castration, leading to the need for a fetishized idea, perception, or sadomasochistic object relationship. When there is enacted sadomasochism, the psyche is showing attachment to this internal object relationship representation, a fetishized image to keep away annihilation terror. The narcissistic mother who is threatening to the growing autonomy of the developing child is one of those impingements that can lead the developing psyche of the child to form a fantasy representation of togetherness based on sadomasochism and illusion in attempts to try to keep the terror of separateness at a distance.

VOLVER: LIKE A SOAP OPERA "AS THE PAST TURNS AND RETURNS"

The Spanish word *volver* is translated as "to return" in English, and there is much that returns in the film including incest and dead mothers. As in the first scene of *High Heels*, the first scene in *Volver* sets up what is repeated throughout the film. The main characters of the film are bantering with each other and attending to a ritual of cleaning and polishing granite and marble tombstones in ad cemetery in La Mancha. They speak of the wind which begins to blow, reminding them of the way fire spreads. The members of this cleaning crew are all female characters who are related or have grown up as neighbors. We discover that the mother and father of two adult sisters died in their beds when a fire spread in their home, killing them. These are their graves. A close friend, who is obviously ill with cancer, comments that she too may soon be in the grave she watches over. She wonders where her mother is and hopes she will re-appear. She disappeared at the same time as the terrible flames consumed the sleeping couple.

The graveyard scene leads into a moment of forbidden sexual tension between father and daughter. Raimunda returns home to find her husband, Paco, drinking beer and watching television. Paula, the 14-year-old daughter, throws herself onto a chair, looking at her cell phone with one leg over the arm of the chair thus opening her legs in their pink tights. Paco glances at her crotch. Raimunda tells her daughter to close her legs. As he drinks more beer, Paco announces he has been laid off from work. Raimunda, who has been working at the laundry washing, drying, and folding clothes, berates him, threatening that there will no longer be money to pay for the television soccer games. She also yells at the daughter to put away her cell phone and go to her room. Paco too goes to his room and, passing his daughter's room, sees her undressing through a crack in the door and ogles her breasts. Then husband and wife are in bed and Raimunda rejects Paco's advances even when he says, "I will do all the work". The cold reception leads him to masturbate next to her.

INCEST AND MURDER

The next day, Paula is waiting in the rain for her mother to return from work. As Raimunda climbs down the steps of the bus, she sees her daughter wet from the rain and looking horribly distressed. She asks her what is happening and where is her father. Paula says that her father is in the kitchen. Raimunda discovers him on the floor with blood pooling over the floor. Paula explains that he came on to her, saying he was not her father and putting his arms around her. She explains that she pushed him away and he then unzipped his pants. Paula then took a knife and threatened him to scare him. She is crying explaining that he did not believe her and jumped at her. "I stabbed him. I killed him." Raimunda immediately tells Paula to remember that she, Raimunda, killed him. Paula nods in agreement; yes, the story is that Raimunda is the killer. This is a scene that has been taken from Raimunda's unconscious theater of the mind to be enacted in the next generation, by her daughter.

BLOOD

The scene of blood surrounding the dead body lying on the kitchen floor becomes farcical. Raimunda's work is in the laundry and we have already seen her shining tombstones. Here she is using ordinary props to mop up what cannot be cleaned — incest and murder. We see a kitchen paper towel slowly soak up blood, making a geometric pattern from the weave of the paper. She wipes and cleans and rinses and there is more and more blood. Then there is a knock at the door, and she answers. Her neighbor is giving her the keys to the restaurant next door while he will be away. There is a blood smear on her neck. He asks if she is all right and she responds with saying that the mark of blood on her neck is a woman problem. This is a reference to menstruation, the flow of blood from women that some men and women may unconsciously consider evidence of castration or of castrating powers. This is likely also the root of Almodóvar's love of marking his films with things red.

As the cover-up of the murder takes place, Almodóvar continues to use humor. Raimunda has to get rid of not only the blood but of the body. She roles it up in a rug and stores it in the freezer of the restaurant she now is managing. She convinces women in the neighborhood, including a prostitute, to join together in moving the freezer. The man's body is frozen, entombed, and secreted away. Eventually, she gets the prostitute to accompany her to bury the freezer down by the river and to swear to secrecy. The freezer is a symbol of what women can do to phallic power when they are furious about possible rape of their daughters. Men need to fear women's revenge and solidarity.

I think Almodóvar needs to make murderous women less serious as he turns to humor, trying to disavow the terror about all that blood. He is providing mastery over what may scare men the most— the repetition of female seductive and murderous powers and the envy felt at their fertility and generativity. Almodóvar marks his women with blood and death and cleaning. This is woman, "no importa", nothing to worry about; except, this is precisely what the psyche worries about. Does the bleeding mother pose danger to men and to small children who can all envy her for her capacity for reproduction and creation?

The trauma of incest across generations

Later when Paula wants to know who her biological father is, Raimunda says she will explain later. More layers of the scenes of fathers who are not fathers, of incest and murder come to light in the rest of the film. Raimunda was incested by her father and impregnated by him. These are also dramas of the unconscious mind in which incestuous desires can be discovered along with envy and guilt. However, when the incest taboo is broken, it is traumatic in multiple ways, with daughters being raped in body and soul, especially when a mother is blind to what is taking place. Almodóvar provides the twist for psychoanalytic theory—that women hold the boundary of the law against incest by murder of the perpetrator.

There is a sub-theme in the story of Raimunda's mother who supposedly died in a fire. This is symbolic of the mother who has not protected her daughter, and has been a passive bystander to her daughter's sex abuse from her father, the mother's husband. She murders her husband, and his lover, because she discovers his infidelity, not because she finds out about the incest. She then becomes a phantom, taking care of the old neighbor, and even when she reappears and helps her other daughter in her at-home hair salon, there is uncertainty if she is real. Can a mother who shows soul blindness to incest of her daughter be allowed to be fully alive? Relationships with mothers reveal what André Green (1993) would call the dead mother, the mother who does not see her child and does not register that her child is in pain and in need. Eventually two mysteries are solved: the identity of Paula's biological father, and why their friend's mother disappeared at the time of the bedroom fire. She was the other woman.

Psychoanalytic understanding can be brought to concepts concerning intergenerational trauma. A horrible story of the incest and impregnation of Raimunda by her father is a secret. The dead place in the mind (Goodman, 2012) of not knowing gets exquisitely revisited in variation by her daughter demonstrating how a traumatic scene from the past gets into the psyche of the next generation. Paula uses a knife to attack her almost rapist stepfather, resulting in death of the perpetrator. The daughter and child of the raped woman is the one revenging the crime of the past. The past then becomes known in the present, what psychoanalysts would call *nachtraglichkeit*. In the process of psychoanalytic treatment, the back and forth of the transference/countertransference dialogue, we often discover to be enactments of the past which have been embedded in the unconscious, especially when related to traumas of the past (Ellman and Goodman, 2017).

Concluding remarks on the psychoanalytic road trip with Almodóvar

The road trip of associating with Almodóvar while riding through the sceneries of these two films is coming to an end. Each film has offered vivid portrayals of women caught in dramas with their men, their mothers, and their daughters. *High Heels* shows the importance of early abandonment and the type of unconscious fantasies that can develop along with the ways the fetish, particularly the phallic mother, fills space of fear and terror of traumatic affects including desire itself. *Volver* brings together death and life instincts in secrets of incest and retaliation and the way unconscious knowledge from one generation gets revealed in the following generation.

There is a deep psychic pain when a baby or young child experiences being out of mother's mind; that is, having a mother who denies her child's being and need of her. Fantasies about oneself as a criminal can result, turning aggression against the self with masochistic retreats and partnerships with sadists. In *High Heels* Rebeca's expressive facial features show over and over again the sadness, yearning, and masochistic helplessness, from the scene of waiting in the airport to the scene of being interviewed by the judge. The film elaborates on the basic wish, the desire for her mother and desire in general. Furthermore, Rebeca's hatred of her mother has her murdering the mother's husbands and lovers. There is a repetitive waiting for the distant high heels to appear and bring a loving mother. And while Rebeca is waiting, some men have to be murdered.

The story in *Volver* grows out of the trauma that occurred when Raimunda's mother does not see that her husband is sexually molesting her daughter. Mother not seeing is mother not having the child in mind. The not knowing is a kind of perpetration, leaving the incest victim with internal fantasies of the double wounds of being betrayed by both parents. The potential repetition in this film of Raimunda's daughter being raped by her stepfather is interrupted. Paula's murderousness and fatal stabbing of her stepfather is a culmination of transgenerational trauma and rage. The past *vuelva*, returns. What is in the unconscious concerning trauma and fantasy requires reflection and symbolic meaning to stop repetitions.

The Crotch: genital difference and excitement

In both films the crotch, male and female, causes trouble and brings about pleasure. Almodóvar seems to be wondering if the desire to look at the genitals of the opposite sex leads inevitably to molestation and castration/death. These films are representing a kind of psychoanalytic nightmare in which the superego gets to play out revenge because the arousal of seeing and feeling desire must be countered by annihilation or rape. As Almodóvar is working out how we live with unconscious fantasies about sexual desire and sexual difference, he creates scenes of pure silliness to keep our attention. Glances at the crotch, however, seem to lead directly to incest, rape, and murder. A terrible perverse primal scene is enacted over and over and someone gets killed. Can male and female exist together or is there just too much mayhem? These are serious matters, and Almodóvar writes and produces scenes drawing our attention and making us laugh and cry and want more. As Almodóvar plays with fire, he circles around longings and lust and seems to get somewhere by depicting the resilience of women, even if they have taken the law into their own hands.

As I put up the top of my red convertible preparing for the end of the road trip, I notice how shiny the red paint is in the sunshine. I will never see the color red again without tuning into the stream of fantasies produced by Almodóvar in his exploration of the wonders of woman: blood, lipstick, cars, earrings, hair, clothing, and of course red high heels.

References

Almodóvar, P. (1991). *High Heels*. [Motion Picture]. Spain: El Deseo and Ciby 2000.

———(2006). *Volver*. [Motion Picture]. Spain: El Deseo and TVE Canal Plus.

Arlow, J. (1969). Fantasy, memory and reality testing. *Psychoanalytic Quarterly*, *38*: 28–51.

Bach, S. (1994). *The Language of Perversion and the Language of Love*. Northvale, NJ: Jason Aronson.

Bass, A. (2000). *Difference and Disavowal: The Trauma of Eros*. Stanford: Stanford University Press.

Basseches, H. B., Ellman, P. L., & Goodman, N. R. (2013). *Battling the Life and Death Forces of Sadomasochism: Clinical Perspectives*. London: Karnac.

Ellman, P., & Goodman, N. (2017). *Finding Unconscious Fantasy in Narrative, Trauma and Body Pain: A Clinical Guide*. London: Routledge.

Freud, S. (1905). Jokes and their relation to the unconscious. *Standard Edition* 8:1–247.

———(1927). Fetishism. *Standard Edition 21*:147–158.

Goodman, N.R. (2012). The power of witnessing. In: N. R. Goodman & M. Meyers (Eds.), *The Power of Witnessing: Reflections, Reverberations, and*

Traces of the Holocaust—Trauma, Psychoanalysis, and the Living Mind (pp. 3–26). New York: Routledge.

———(2017). The "Finding theater" A schema for finding unconscious fantasy. In P.L. Ellman & N. R. Goodman (Eds.), *Finding Unconscious Fantasy in Narrative, Trauma, and Body Pain: A clinical book*, pp. 22–34. London: Routledge.

———& M. Meyers (Eds.), *The Power of Witnessing: Reflections, Reverberations, and Traces of the Holocaust—Trauma, Psychoanalysis, and the Living Mind* (pp. 3–26). New York: Routledge.

Green, A. (1993). *The dead mother: The work of Andre Green.* (Jean Kogan, Ed.). London: Routledge.

Isaacs, S. (1938). The nature and function of phantasy. *International Journal Psychoanalysis 29*:72–97.

Klein, M. (1930). The importance of symbol formation in the development of the ego. *International Journal of Psychoanalysis 11*:24–39.

Shengold, L. (1989). *Soul murder: The effects of childhood abuse and deprivation.* New York: Ballantine Books.

Steiner, R. (Ed.) (2003). *Unconscious phantasy.* London: Karnac Books Press.

CHAPTER 11

The Secret of Almodóvar's Flower:
Michael Eigen's *Toxic Nourishment*

Selma Duckler

Dorothy Parker's "A Lovely Leave" is a 1943 short story about a woman who destroys her relationship with her husband while he is on leave from the army. When he calls to tell her he has a leave, she begs for a few minutes of tender phone conversation. He explains to her that others are waiting to use the phone. She can hear the background clamor of voices. He assures her he will see her soon and hangs up. Feeling that he chose to respond to the rising voices and not to her, she drops the phone angrily. "Then she told herself to stop her nonsense. If you looked for things to make you feel hurt and wretched and unnecessary, you were certain to find them, more easily each time, so easily, soon, that you did not even realize you had gone out searching."[1] Parker portrays a woman who understands she seeks rejection, but despite this insight, cannot alter her self-destructiveness.

Pedro Almodóvar's reinterpretation of Parker's story, *The Flower of My Secret* (1995), gives this heroine a life and history, a new presence, and a name: Leo. We meet her mother and sister, who provide a picture of Leo's conflicted past: a best friend who is having an affair

---

[1] "A Lovely Leave," Dorothy Parker, in Complete Stories. (1943, republished 1995, Penguin).

with her husband; a maid, torn between loyalty to her son and to Leo; her employer; and Leo's editor, who values the money she makes from Leo's romance novels over Leo's psycho-emotional needs. Over the course of the film, Leo does meet a man who offers love, but he's not seen as more desirable than her self-centered husband to whom Leo devotes endless amounts of energy in bouts of panic, anger and feelings of rejection.

Like Parker, Almodóvar doesn't excuse, condemn or ridicule his characters. Almodóvar remains empathetic to Leo through the self-destructive struggles she inflicts upon herself.

The Flower of My Secret ushered in a new phase of Almodóvar's career. Until this point, the director's films were largely known for their spectacle—fantasies of murder, suicide, sex, prostitutes, junkies and drag queens. Although the characters were always presented with respect, the sensational quality of their stories was a signature of the popular director's style. *The Flower of My Secret* was the first of Almodóvar's work to not focus on outcasts, but it is precisely the lack of lurid overtones, I believe, that brings more clearly into focus some of the themes throughout Almodóvar's oeuvre – the psychological world of those people who must live with and love others who also harm. When asked about this shift towards more quotidian topics, Almodóvar responded, "[*Flower*] is more austere, sober and cohesive".[2] In this essay, I'm going to look at *Flower* by utilizing Michael Eigen's ideas of toxic nourishment to bring to light central psychological themes. Eigen's work on toxic nourishment provides a good lens through which to understand and illuminate Almodóvar's films because Eigen's idea—that the psychological nourishment that women give to others in their body and soul carry toxins that not only harm the recipient but also provide life-giving sustenance. It helps us understand Leo's complexities. Michael Eigen dedicates his book, *Toxic Nourishment*, to "all who live through the unlivable. To

---

[2] *Almodóvar on Almodóvar*, edited by F. Strauss. (1994, Faber and Faber) p. 207.

the life no poison can kill".[3] No better words fit Pedro Almodóvar, whose concern for women embraces this particularly difficult situation with humor, accuracy, compassion and courage.

An example of Almodóvar's sensitivity to, and concern for, women, can be found in the moment when Leo's mother says to her, "You are like a cow without a bell". When Almodóvar was asked about this scene, he explains, "I thought of making it the title of the film. It sounds great in Spanish but it's only used in La Mancha, where it's very common. To be like a cow without its bell means being lost, without anyone taking any notice of you."[4]

I understand this type of feeling of being "lost, without anyone taking any notice of you" to be the "unlivable" life Eigen refers to for those who have had to endure toxic nourishment. Almodóvar also gives evidence that he understands this feeling in his characters. He chose to abandon his studio for this film and shoot it on location in Madrid and in a town similar to La Mancha, where he grew up. "Shooting on location was above all an aesthetic and visual decision. *Flower of my Secret* reflects my conception of neorealism . . . When I talk of reality, I think of something which exists, which one can show as well as transform—a representation. Reality interests me in so far as it is something which can be represented and used as an element to build a fiction. It's true that the emotions one provokes in this way are linked to an irrefutable reality—to our own existence, our own sensibility—but for me a film will always be representation, which always means artifice. When one talks of reality, one also talks of manipulation".[5]

This "manipulation" is an essential part of his filmmaker's "reality" and expresses an important element of the world of toxic nourishment. Children who are born to parents where the toxicity and nourishment are mixed together often feel manipulated by the parent's narcissistic needs and, in turn, are only able to navigate the

---

[3] Eigen, Michael. Toxic Nourishment. (1999, Karnac) p.v.

[4] *Almodóvar on Almodóvar*, edited by F. Strauss (1994, Faber and Faber), p. 156.

[5] *Almodóvar on Almodóvar*, edited by F. Strauss (1003, Faber and Faber), p. 157.

environment by manipulating the toxic parent's narcissism. "One of the great secrets of trauma," Eigen explains, "is that it trades in radiance. Not simply that radiance and black hole mirror, filter, mix with each other, which they do. Pain and something beatific inextricably fuse, creating a more intense, endurable bond than either alone. One becomes bonded to one's own deranged structures, self as one knows it, as well as to warps of others. . . ."

Eigen points out that Freud identified helplessness when encountering destructive forces that could not be understood or assimilated. Eigen cites Blake, who "recognized Satan's radiance". Further, Eigen recognizes what he calls "heavenly and hellish ecstasies". Eigen realizes that radiance does not only mean goodness, as what he calls "demonic glows" can "captivate, enthrall"[6]

Almodóvar started going to films when he was about 10 and was entranced by how films communicated this destructive force he could not "fathom". The films, Almodóvar explains, "touched me profoundly. None of these films spoke about my life, yet I felt strangely close to the world they described...I'd say to myself, 'This film speaks to me' which was rather an exaggeration since I was still a child. But the film was about ennui and . . . I knew all about that... . Maybe it has something to do with my gay sensibility, but it was sincere. I remember *Bonjour Tristesse* and feeling totally nihilistic. By then I'd already rejected religious education. From the start I knew the priests had nothing to say to me. I recognized myself in *Cat on a Hot Tin Roof*, the church considered the apotheosis of sins. I'd say to myself: 'I belong to the world of sin, of degeneracy' I was twelve years old and if someone asked me "What are you? I'd reply: 'A nihilist.'"[7]

Almodóvar was born in La Mancha in l949. Franco died in 1975 and the law making homosexuality illegal was overturned in 1979. Homosexuals were considered psychopaths. One could be imprisoned or killed. Being gay was considered to be against religion,

---

[6] *Emotional Storm*, Eigen, Michael (Wesleyan University Press) p. 70–71.
[7] *Almodóvar on Almodóvar* edited by F. Strauss (1994, Faber and Faber), p. 3.

morals, society, people. It was in this setting — where one's natural impulses could easily be seen as psychopathic, criminal, dangerous — that Almodóvar became the cinematic artist he is. The courage to be himself is reflected in his empathy for his characters, who so often struggle to be true to themselves.

Eigen's concept of toxic nourishment is useful in understanding that social and family milieus can offer nourishment and poison. In a sense, we all are liable to nourish others with "social and psychic poisons". He points out that all lives are touched by "fusions of trauma and nourishment". He offers hope that understanding, awakening, can "shine through injury".

We can try to envision the unfolding of *The Flower of My Secret*, the "blossoming" of the enclosed secret in the flower, as a realization of Eigen's understanding that in our creation of culture and social structures, all of us are toxic.[8]

Flower opens with two earnest, serious young men in physician's white coats, explaining to a grieving mother that her comatose son is dead. They want her to donate his organs to their Organ Donor Center. They try to achieve a manner of care, concern, and empathy to the sobbing, disbelieving mother, but they never relinquish their goal of getting the organs donated.

There is a sense that the grief is being exploited to gain the donor's organs. This experience of sorrow being manipulated by the other is an essential part of Eigen's idea of toxic nourishment. The film conveys a feeling of betrayal by someone who is believed and trusted.

Almodóvar presents two levels. There is the level of character in which Leo feels pain intertwined with nourishment in receiving love from her husband. Her vulnerability makes feelings of betrayal all the more profound. The second level is one of narrative, where we, as viewers, are given a taste of betrayal, since after we see a woman sobbing, the camera dollies back to reveal a long table with students learning how to get organs in times of tragedy. We have been watching a television enactment. We have been duped, and for a moment

---

[8] Eigen, Michael. *Toxic Nourishment.*(1999, Karnac)), p. 225.

we don't understand. When the three actors come to sit and discuss their performance (Was it good? Will it reach their goal?), we are left with a disturbing sense of distrust. Our experience, like that of Leo's, is now not to be trusted. We cannot trust that our feeling is a good guide. Trust and protection causing pain is further developed in the first part of the movie regarding ill-fitting boots. The camera scans Madrid neighborhoods; children are at play and the camera comes up to an open window. On the sill are geraniums. We see a woman asleep in the bed. On the table next to her are pictures of a man and woman kissing, pictures of love. There is a box of ginseng tea to calm nerves. The camera goes down to the floor where books are stacked. Pages are open and circled in pencil with notes in the margin. Morning arrives; the sleeping woman is now awake and dressed in a red sweater, and is typing at her desk. She is typing a letter to Paco, her husband. She thinks of him all the time. Can he remember he gave her boots a few years back? Every day, she wears something he has given her. Today she is wearing the boots; they are too tight. She smiles as she thinks of him. She says they are oppressive (like her marriage, her life?). She can't get them off. She swivels her chair and struggles to get the boots off. She pulls and pulls and gives up. She dials her maid, who is on her day off. Bianca and her son, Antonio, are flamenco dancers, and are in a dance studio where he is dancing while she and friends clap hands, flamenco palmas. We are treated to an interlude of brilliant dancing. They don't hear the phone ringing.

This scene is like a dream, and portrays Leo's repressed feelings. The phone ringing, yet not heard while people are dancing, evokes a child crying out her need and loneliness. The couple dancing, her mother and father engaged in their private pleasure, are tuned out so they don't hear their child, alone and in distress. The boots are to keep her warm and dry but they are just a substitute for actual love. The boots fail, and she cries out. But her parents, and later her husband, abandon her, and she goes begging for someone to release her from the painful boots. She is too helpless to remove the boots herself but needs someone to do it for her, which keeps her dependent, unable to move forward. She meets a man who tries but she fears he will hurt her and escapes him. Finally, she finds a good mother substitute who easily removes them. This woman's toxicity is interwoven with her kind help but Leo is used to that.

Michael Eigen explains this paradox with how concept that emotional toxins and nourishment can be commingled to the point that they are perceived as one, they cannot be distinguished from one another. Nourishment cannot be obtained without toxins. Thus the feeling of reality seems inseparable from toxins, from toxic nourishment.[9]

The movie elaborates the dream. Leo is outside. A drug addict comes up to her and asks for money. She pushes him away but then says: "I will give you 5000 pesos if you can get my boots off". It's a deal. She sits on a concrete ledge and he pulls. The boots don't come off. She shows him how to pull. It hurts but he continues to pull. She says she will give him the money anyhow but stop! She will fall off the ledge.

It starts to rain. She gives him the money and runs into a coffee shop to order coffee with cognac and to use the phone. She calls the National Transplant Association to talk to her friend Betty but is told Betty is giving a training seminar and won't be available till late. She hangs up and we see the TV program continue.

Now they are trying to get the bereaved mother to sign an authorization form for the boy's organs. The mother becomes defensive. She says, "They told me in the waiting room this would happen". They plead that her son's organs will help five people live. She relents a bit. "To whom will it go?" "Whoever needs them" is the reply. "I don't want it to go to an Arab," she says. They stiffen a bit and tell her that they can't say to whom it will go. "Will it stay in Madrid?" "We can't say." They tell her that 80% of the families consent. It makes them feel better. They give her an emotional look. "They are here to console her." They should have said that first and they stumble over the name of their organization. This exposes their real goal and the actors walk out of the studio. The actress worries that she overacted.

---

[9] Eigen, Michael. *Toxic Nourishment*. (1999, Karnac), p. 1.

They take seats and are asked how they felt doing this. The scene has important symbolic content. Almodóvar used the same situation in *All About My Mother*, a subsequent film that won him the Golden Globe award.

Michael Eigen's ideas help to clarify the latent content of this dream as it relates to early childhood development. He discusses the situation of babies' feeling free of outside judgment, relying only on their own "sensation-feeling states", a form of "Primary Normal". He points out that some people do not have this sort of freedom, people "for whom the emotional flow itself, including body sensations", are unpleasant. Their self-states may be compromised. "Aliveness is repudiated and repugnant, through and through."[10]

One area that we see the compromise of the "emotional flow itself" is in Leo's creativity. On the one hand, Leo's creativity—symbolized in her writing—is her livelihood, her fame, her identity. It is what I take to be her "flower" that the title of the film refers to. But, on the other hand, the secret of this flower is the poison. The popularity of her writing (and presumably her persona) is based on its flight from reality. She is a sentimental romance novelist who helps her readers avoid reality. The poison is her jealousy, her vulnerability to rejection, her fragility and bottomless needs, (her "secret"). It is this poison that, as Eigen puts it, makes being and self "taste sour" together. Leo is a competent, accomplished author who keeps herself fragile and dependent on others for sustenance. She owns resource and capability but, at the same time is brittle, easily destroyed, and expects to be rejected at every turn. This is the dilemma of toxic nourishment that Eigen beautifully describes in the souring of "being" and "self".

One typical way in which people attempt to survive from toxic nourishment is to split the self in order to navigate this conflict. We see this in the film in which Leo, who writes under the pseudonym Amanda Gris, has split herself into a successful, sweet, and sentimental persona set in stark contrast to a more hidden, discarded or

---

[10] Eigen, Michael. *Toxic Nourishment*. (Karnac, 1999) pp. 98–99.

repressed self, represented by a story she writes but throws away. *Cold Storage* is homicidal, psychotic, full of hostility, pain and suffering.

I understand Leo's throwing away her manuscript as symbolizing the conflict she suffers from. She is aware of this hostile, psychotic part of her identity, and it cannot be denied.

The boots, a gift from Paco that do not fit her, are also a symbol of a painful reality that she knows about and denies. She does not fit easily in with the external world and cannot accept it or find the right fit, but must constantly struggle to try to change herself in ways that are, in reality, impossible. This denial of reality and the obedience Leo accepts to make external reality fit her internal needs is dramatized in a scene where Leo, sitting outside the seminar in her rain-soaked clothes, enters as the students leave. Seeing her friend in an all-too familiar state, Betty says sharply, "What are you doing here?" Leo explains she has had a terrible day. She needs her boots taken off. It is her maid's day off and she couldn't get in touch with her. Betty has a look of exasperation. Leo asks her not to look like that. She has no one, she states, in a voice of self-pity.

Betty says, "You can't go on like this. You can't be so fragile. A lot of people have marital problems. You aren't the only one". She tells Leo to sit down and she pulls the boots off neatly. Leo tells her they were a gift from Paco.

No one seems to relieve Leo of her discomfort except for Betty. Later that night at dinner, Leo is drinking and says everything upsets her, so she can't handle anything, except when drinking. Betty has been talking to her about meeting a new editor. Leo says she can't just walk in on him. Betty says promise me you will go to meet him. Leo asks, "Did you tell him who I am?" No, Betty assures her, she did not. Betty respects and understands Leo's vulnerabilities. This makes the betrayal of her trust by her affair with Leo's husband all the more devastating for Leo.

Leo goes to her editor, Alicia, who has made a fortune publishing the popular Amanda Gris. Have they received her new novel? Yes, they have. It is not an Amanda Gris novel. Why has she sent it? Leo says this is the way she wants to write from now on, about reality. Alicia goes over the new novel. A man has raped his daughter and the daughter killed him. The mother hides the body in the freezer in the restaurant next door, to save her daughter.

Alicia, the editor, gets mad. Who will the reader identify with? The mother is a junkie and into black men. Amanda Gris is very successful. Alicia says their books are published to help people to escape reality. Reality isn't what people want. Reality is for newspapers and reality should be banned. "Let me remind you of your contract," Alicia explains. "You write five romance novels a year. They all end happily. The novels do not have a social conscience and no politics. Suggested sex but not direct. Illegitimate children are ok. No violence. In return your name will be kept a secret, no interviews or publicity."

The contract was indeed, an accurate picture of what Leo wanted. But it also symbolizes something about the state of Leo's psychic structure. Leo's successes had to be moderated for her toxic mother so that Leo didn't own them. The fantasy she built of herself was that she had no authentic thought or feeling. She was not responsible for Amanda Gris. Amanda Gris didn't write about reality because Amanda Gris was not a real person. This was the only way she could allow herself success. This was the price she had to pay to be alive. She had to forsake herself to stay alive. The person she hid was Leo. The real Leo was well hidden from the world and from herself. But a part of her was starved for recognition. When the desire to have an aliveness, to live who she was, became so demanding that she couldn't deny it, she used her strongest resource, writing, and wrote her reality, pain and suffering. Pain and suffering seemed to be her destiny, for all the years she had lived a deadened life.

The next morning Leo talks to Bianca, her maid. She throws the manuscript for the story in the wastebasket. The doorbell rings. She jumps. Bianca says it's just her son. Antonio tells his mother that he has been offered a large sum of money for them to do a dance performance. Bianca says she is too old, she hasn't danced in a long while and her kidneys are a problem. She doesn't trust her son's business arrangement, disbelieving a producer would give them such a large sum of money. Antonio says he will take care of it and she replies that's what bothers her. She tells him to take the garbage out. When he does, he also takes the tossed manuscript and keeps it.

It is not clear whether Leo knows Antonio has been stealing from her or not, suggesting that Leo unconsciously lets people take advantage of her as she needs to feel important even though she willingly lets them abuse her. She seems to rely on the exploiter/abuser because the relationship gives her a feeling of security (the sweet scent of the flower) so Leo turns a blind eye to their exploitation of her (her secret). Antonio and Bianca also live on toxic nourishment, each from the other. Both are creative artists, dependent on each other for their creativity to flourish, which it does as long as they have the poison that each of them needs. Antonio demands that his mother must do what is past her physical time to do and puts her in an inappropriate, incestuous role. In the romantic, exotic dance, he wants her to make him appear strong, virile, demanding, dominating, and powerful, to fulfill his idea of the overpowering macho male. When the dance is over and the applause ends, they go back to mother/son roles of mutual dependency.

There are moments, however, where there appears to be a way out of the toxic nourishing dynamic. For instance, when Leo meets Ángel, the editor whom she visits at the bequest of Betty, she explains to Ángel that she is a writer and she would like to write for him. He asks what she has published. She says she is unpublished, but she brought some manuscripts. He asks her what writers she likes, and she says she likes women writers. He asks, do you like Amanda Gris? No, she says, I don't like her. I write about pain and suffering, and Amanda Gris doesn't write about reality. Ángel says Amanda Gris is the height of femininity and he likes her. He says Leo appears not to like writing that is sweet and sentimental. "Yes." She tells him, she would like to use a pseudonym if she writes for him. He offers her a book by Amanda Gris and says write what you just said about this. She says I can't bear Amanda Gris. Fine, he says. We will have one article for Amanda Gris and one against. You will have the one against. No, she says. I don't want to write negatively. I have too much in my life that is negative already. She gets up and leaves in a huff. But Ángel likes her. When she walks out, he says to himself, "You are such an asshole".

In this scene, Leo is confronted with someone who, unlike her husband, is very sensitive to her feelings. In fact, he immediately and correctly (but unconsciously) associates her with her alter ego, Amanda Gris, instinctively seeing the connection. This alerts her to how intuitively he knows something of her. This is both stimulating and frightening. He sees her but he also sees through her subterfuge. Anxiously she attacks Amanda Gris, but also defends her by refusing to write negatively about her, and then runs off. Ángel does not know why and is angry at himself because he takes her departure to be a result of his clumsiness. She is being offered love, which she wants and fears. She has limited acceptance ability and yet she is drawn to him. He sends out a lifeline but her fears prevent her from receiving it. The contact between Leo and Ángel is, in fact, the basis for the anger that Leo has during her husband's leave, their fight and their breakup. Ángel is an unseen and unspoken part of Leo's new ability to express some of her real feelings of hurt and anger at her husband.

The doorbell rings. She runs excitedly to the door. It is Paco. She doesn't let him in the door. She pushes up against him and kisses him passionately. He tries to talk but she just kisses him with more passion. He says, "Let me shut the door at least. Is Bianca here?"

"No, I want to be alone with you. I gave her time off."

"I have to iron some shirts," Paco blandly states. Leo is hurt and stunned. "I can do it for you." He goes into the kitchen and smiles. "Paella!" She says. "I made it for you". No response. She confesses, "Well, Bianca made it. I added some rice". He takes a taste. "It's cold." "I'll put it in the microwave." He says, "I don't like it reheated" She stiffens with a rising anger. "I didn't know when you were coming. If you had the delicacy to let me know—", and she stops her anger. She starts to kiss him again, trying to manage the waves of hate and love toward him. "We'll fuck and fuck and then rest awhile and then we'll fuck again," she says. Paco says, "I have to take a shower. And we have to talk". He goes into the bathroom, and gets into a steamy shower. She looks through the shower enclosure, watching him. He puts his towel over his head and face and starts to rub with the towel. She grabs it and rubs it down on his body. When the towel gets to his genitals, she puts her mouth on the towel and kisses and he pulls away. She jokes about feeling horny and grabbing any man. He doesn't respond to her joking. She says she has the feeling he is avoiding her. He repeats, "We have to talk". "What do we have to talk about? For God's' sake tell me what we have to talk about", she pleads.

"I don't want any yelling or tears."

"What is it?" "My leave is changed to two hours. I have to be back. The conflict has worsened. I am a soldier and I have a duty." "You're a husband", She screams furiously. "Don't you have a duty to me? You can't just park me like a car." "I am trying to save lives", Paco rationalizes. "There are people who are starving and line up for food. There is no heat, no electricity, no food, people are being killed and dying." She screams at him, "You son of a bitch. Why did you volunteer for the peace-keeping corps? You could have stayed with the group you were with. You joined and went away to avoid the war here at home. You have been separating from me. You could have stayed to work out our problems, but you ran away. You are using the poor Bosnians as a pretext". Crying, she takes a picture of him and smashes it on the floor. "I hate you," she screams. "And I will hate you forever. You owe me the rest of your two hours." He says, "I couldn't stay with you for 24 hours". As he leaves she asks, "Is there any hope for our relationship?" He answers flatly, "No".

She goes to the medicine cabinet and takes out her sleeping pills and begins to swallow them. She hears the phone. Her mother is calling her. She falls on the bed into a sleep. When she opens her eyes, she hears another message from her mother. Leo pulls herself up and starts to vomit. She goes into the bathroom, into the tub with her clothes on and douses herself with water.

Paco has not loved Leo for a long time if indeed, he ever did. The truth that he doesn't love her is becoming harder to stifle. She feels she is fighting for her life, but that is not entirely true. She was successful writing about love and being wanted, needed. It fulfilled her needs and her readers' fantasies. The stories made it seem true. Her present need to write stories of pain and suffering showed her conflicts were becoming more conscious and she has to deal with that. She decided to handle it in the way she knew, to write about it. She turned her hostility into a murder in a manuscript but threw it away. Now in her anger, she forgot her success as Amanda Gris and turned the murder inward on herself. In her present state of pain, she thought she couldn't live without Paco's abuse. She couldn't allow herself to see how successful she had come to be and that it was her strengths that were promoting conflicts. She was healthier than she believed so she didn't take enough pills to kill herself, and when she awoke, her mother's voice on the phone reminded her she had lived with abuse long before she met Paco and could survive. She dressed and left the apartment. She wanted to murder Paco, but all she could really kill was herself. But which part was to be killed? The successful persona or the psychotic homicidal angry part?

Towards the end of the movie, we get a glimpse of the early origin of the psychological struggle. Leo is being driven by Ángel to the village, with her mother, Jacinta. When Leo left her apartment, she unexpectedly ran into Ángel, who saw how distressed she was and took her to his place to recover. Her mother's message had been to go back to her village and Leo decided to go back with her. Jacinta is eating, and tries to get Leo to eat, but she won't. Jacinta recalls that Leo was 10 lbs. at birth but didn't eat well. Jacinta's mother told her to take the infant outside into the freezing weather. She did, and the infant, after almost freezing, nursed frantically with great fear. "Do you remember that, Leo?" "No, how could I?" Jacinta's talk attacks Leo because she won't eat her food, so Jacinta reminds her when she didn't conform to expectations as an infant her response was to physically abuse the infant in the bitter cold and evoke a reaction. An infant born at 10 lbs. is a good-sized infant. Jacinta, who probably had a fear of death with her own toxic nutrition, is advised by her mother to take the infant warmed by the breast and mother's body into freezing temperature to panic it with a death threat. It worked. Leo nursed to satisfy her mother because of her fear of dying. It was her first experience of toxic nutrition and marked her life. When she decided to write about pain and suffering, her manuscript was a murder where the body was hidden in a freezer, a direct return to her fear of death in frigid weather. This also helps us understand why Leo panicked if there were a threat of separation. Her relationships were with people she saw as mothers. They rejected and hurt her, or so it seemed to her, and she fought to keep the dynamic as she felt she couldn't stay alive without the toxic hostility.

When they arrive in La Mancha, Leo gets out of the car but falls in a faint. Ángel carries her in and places her in bed. Her worried mother comes over to ask her what is wrong. "I'm going crazy, Mom." Leo's world collapsed, and she is dealing with a fragmented self.

"No, not you, your sister yes, like all the others, but not you." Throughout the movie, in scenes with Leo's sister Rosa, Jacinta is hostile, terrible, and demeaning to Rosa. But Leo did not escape. She was the same mother to both of them, just overtly hostile to one and radiating repressed hostility towards the other.

"What is it? Paco?"

"Yes."

Jacinta says, "You are like a cow without a bell, wandering without direction. When that happens, you have to go back to the place you were born. Oh, what an effort it was to raise you."

To go back to your birth suggests it cannot be changed and threatens Leo if she tries. But Ángel's loving help works and Leo gets better.

She gets a phone call from Alicia, her editor, thanking her for the last two Amanda Gris stories. They are wonderful, the best she has ever done. Leo is perplexed as she hasn't written any but she doesn't say that. Alicia also mentions a film that is being made of "Cold Storage". Did Leo sell the story? No, Leo says, she just shoved it in a drawer. "Somebody maybe stole it." Leo calls Ángel and tells him. He says, thank god you didn't say you didn't write them. I did, and I sent them in. Ángel says he always wanted to be a romance writer. He likes writing Amanda Gris romance novels. The viewer now can recognize the "obvious", Ángel's "secret flower", that Ángel knew Leo was Amanda Gris when they first met.

Before Almodóvar started to develop movies, he wrote under a female pseudonym, Patty Diphusa. Almodóvar explains his reasoning. "When the time comes for me to write and direct, women attract me much more. I've always liked feminine sensitivity and when I create a character it's much easier for me to do a feminine one and I manage to shape it in a more solid and interesting way . . . women hold a greater mystery inside, they have more nuances and a sensitivity that is more authentic . . . I see more possibilities in a feminine role."[11]

Leo comes back to Madrid and goes with Ángel to Bianca and Antonio's performance. The dance is a drama of hate, love, conflict, and is the toxic nutrition between mother and son.

They go to Ángel's place and she realizes he is in love with her. He asks her to stay with him but she leaves and goes home. Antonio comes over. Can he stay with her? She says no but has a drink with him. He confesses that he stole jewelry from her. He also stole a script and sent it to a friend who is in the movies and it is being filmed. He and his mother owe her so much. She says, "How many fucks will it take to absolve him from his debt?" He says his mother is very upset and loves her. She says she loves Bianca too and the money could not have gone to a better purpose than their dance performance. She needs to learn how to live without Paco and how to live without liquor.

On New Year's Eve she goes to visit Ángel, who is alone drinking in front of his fireplace. "It is New Year's Eve and I need human contact", he says. Will she kiss him? They kiss tenderly, and the movie ends. Ángel offers love, understanding and acknowledgement of who she is and her needs. He gave her strength to respond to Paco

---

[11] Llaurado, Anna. "Pedro Almodóvar: Interviews." In Pedro Almodóvar Interviews (University Press of Mississippi: Jackson, 2004), pp. 57–8.

for his abusive behaviour and not to accept his insults. He is a new life source, but is she strong enough to accept and use that love? Can she live with diminished toxicity? Is this Almodóvar's hope for everyone? Eigen articulates the possibility of joy in the following way.

Raw joy is a bull in a china shop—and I love it. But little by little I learn to trust the joy that passes through the ache of awareness. The joy another can say "yes" to.... I am smiling: sweet aching heart and wild joy couple, not entirely wild, far from tame. Something I can say yes to also.[12]

References

Almodóvar, P. (Director). (1995). *The Flower of My Secret*. Sony Pictures Classics.

———(1994). *Almodóvar on Almodóvar*, ed. F. Strauss. London: Faber and Faber.

Eigen, M. (2005). Emotional Storm. Middletown: Wesleyan University Press.

———(1999). *Toxic Nourishment*. London: Karnac.

Llaurado, A. (2004). Pedro Almodóvar: Interviews. In: *Pedro Almodóvar Interviews*. Jackson: University Press of Mississippi.

Parker, D. (1943). A Lovely Leave. In: *Complete Stories*. New York: Penguin, 1995.

---

[12] Eigen, Michael. Toxic Nourishment. (Karnac, London, 1999) p. 215.

CHAPTER 12

Live Flesh and the Trembling
of Sexual Desire and Fear

Adriana Prengler

*"…Twenty years ago I took my revenge on Franco by not acknowledging
his existence, as if he had never existed. Today I think I can't forget that
period, which is still relatively recent. That's why there are two births in
the film: the first in a city besieged by fear, and the second in a city full of
people and happiness, that has forgotten fear…"* —Pedro Almodóvar

The film *Live Flesh*, released in October 1997, is a dramatic love story
that begins in Francisco Franco's dictatorial Spain and is based on
the 1986 novel with the same name (*Live Flesh*), by Ruth Rendell, a
British author who writes of the passionate circumstances in psychological murder mysteries.

Rendell's novel *Live Flesh* tells the story of a man named Victor,
who is sent to prison for shooting and crippling a police officer. He
claims that his action was unintentional, and in some way provoked
by the victim. In the novel, there are veiled reasons for this event that
the reader only comes to discover later in the story. In Almodóvar's
film we also discover an "unintentional" crime with a plot of reasons
that are gradually revealed through the course of the film, as it inter-
twines the lives of the characters.

Almodóvar's *Live Flesh* begins one night in Madrid, just after
Christmas 1970. Under Franco's dictatorship, Spain was submerged
in fear, political repression and loneliness. Earlier that day, Franco

175

declared martial law throughout the country. That night, in a dark and desolate Madrid, Isabel, a young prostitute, gives birth to her baby on a bus while passing in front of the Puerto de Alcalá, a central monument that stands as a symbol of Madrid. She names her baby "Victor", as if to predict that someday, not too far off, he will see victory in the long-awaited freedom that will come when Franco's dictatorship falls, a victory that prophesies a victory in his internal world, as well.

Centro, the madam at the brothel where Victor's mother, Isabel, was working, assists Victor's delivery on the bus and proclaims that the new born baby could not wait to get to the hospital. He had not chosen the best moment to be born. "You couldn't wait!", she jokes. This comment announces his "strength and decisive personality" but also his "impatient impulsive acting out" that will later get him in trouble. Victor could not wait to be born, he was in the wrong place at the wrong time from the moment of his birth.

Because he was born in a public bus, the city government proclaims him "Son of the City". On the TV news, the newborn was predicted to have a future "on wheels" and was "generously" provided with a free pass for bus trips for the rest of his life.

Victor becomes the "Son of the City" without much hope. He's coming from a low socio-economic level with an uneducated mother and an unknown father. He is immersed in the feelings of oppression, loneliness and lack of freedoms under this paternal totalitarian regime. How much "victory" could he expect under these circumstances?

Democracy has been crushed along with the freedom of expression. Victor, with less than a future "on wheels", will be granted nothing more than fertile ground for acting out, transgressions and a desperate need of secrecy. He is the son of a social and political tragedy.

The scene changes and baby Victor, now a teenager, has just had his first sexual experience — a fortuitous and unfortunate act with a beautiful young drug addict named Elena, with whom he has the illusion of falling in love, idealizing the encounter. They have agreed to a second date, but when the day arrives he calls and Elena doesn't show the slightest interest in him. She dismisses Victor, but he can't accept the rejection and insists on following through with their date.

Victor goes to his date with Elena on the bus. He rides in circles passing her apartment without getting off the bus, as if he sought support in the memory of his mother delivering him. To get into Elena's home, he enters in place of the drug dealer she was expecting, taking someone else's place, a stolen place.

He cannot tolerate the frustration of her rejection and insists on following through with the date by transgressing the limits and invading her home. She is saying "No!", but he cannot listen to her. He only knows that he wants to be with her and he would do any-thing to fulfill his wish, regardless of what she wants. He is again in the wrong place at the wrong time.

Victor is starving for love and the desire to occupy a place in the mind of someone. He feels a bond with Elena after only a casual and ephemeral encounter and seems to establish a relationship with her only in his mind, struggling for the bond of love that never fully existed for him.

The reality principle is being over-ridden by an irrational search for pleasure, an uncontrollable desire to be with her. In this moment, he has no access to the common sense and reality testing required to leave her home when she demands that he go. His ability for sound judgement is suspended, and he is incapable of tolerating the frustra-tion of her rejection. He cannot wait, the gratification of his desire cannot be postponed.

Despite Elena's rejection, Victor remains in her home, in his need to "penetrate" her space in some way, concretely or symbolically.

Elena mocks him about their first sexual encounter, saying: "Eres un baboso, ni siquiera me la metiste" ("You're a slobberer, you didn't even put it in me"). Her words are burned into his mind as a humiliat-ing castration and as a reconfirmation of having no place in the mind or body of someone else. He had not been wished for by his own mother, and now also not by Elena. Her words are a terrible narcissistic wound, a deep pain experienced as a castration and a new rejection, and he will not rest until he finds a place and a desire in her mind, to recover not only his masculine dignity but also his right to exist.

Elena threatens him with her father's gun and demands that he leaves. But he stays and his nightmare begins. They struggle, the gun is triggered accidentally, without injuring either of them. A neighbor hears the shot and calls the police.

Two policemen arrive, Sancho and David. Sancho is an unstable and violent alcoholic who suspects his wife Clara of infidelity, and David is Sancho's younger partner and occasionally the secret lover of Clara.

A violent scene is precipitated by Sancho, in Elena's apartment, and it ends up leaving David shot in the spine, disabled and confined to a wheelchair for the rest of his life. Victor is accused of a shooting that he never intended. He gets a six-year prison sentence. From his cell, Victor watches the Para-Olympic Games and recognizes David as one of the wheelchair-bound athletes, and Elena, who is now David's wife, cheering among the other spectators. This stirs Victor's desire to seek revenge on both of them after his release.

In Victor's eyes, David was the one who had "everything", a good job, strength, power, and now he has Elena. His anger grows inside him and he works hard in jail, to become stronger and educated in preparation for his revenge after getting his freedom.

Four years later, Victor is released from jail. His mother has died in the meantime, leaving him some money from her work as a prostitute, and a house in an area scheduled for demolition. In this home he finds a toy soldier left there from when he was a child, a reminder that he will have to fight like a soldier and win the victory, employing all possible weapons.

The first thing Victor does, after his release from prison, is to visit his mother's grave. By chance, Elena is there at her father's funeral and Victor takes advantage of the opportunity to approach her, offering his insincere condolences.

That same day he also meets Clara, Sancho's wife, and soon they get involved in an erotic relationship. He asks Clara to be his sexual teacher, and she gradually falls in love with him, while his only goal was to learn how to be the best lover possible in order to seduce Elena and take revenge on her.

Clara, when meeting Victor at the cemetery, admits that she "is lost", she doesn't know where her car is. "I have no sense of direction" she says. She is disoriented, but not only in physical space. She does not know what she wants. She is trying to orient herself in search of love and attention. She has been submissive to Sancho in a masochistic way, not defending herself when Sancho gets abusively angry or hits her. She only gets bruised, treating herself as an object of others. She also becomes Victor's object, who takes her as a sexual object to learn how to be a lover in an asymmetric love relation. She is an expert in sex. Perhaps in some ways Clara represents his mother, Isabel, another sexual "expert".

Victor wants Clara to teach him how to be the best lover in the world, but perhaps Clara also represents the unconditional mother who feeds him, takes care of him, and accepts him no matter what he does or who he is. Clara is devoted to "teaching" him and giving him a unique place in her mind, instead of being just one more of the thousand men that his mother had.

He told Clara that he has 150,000 pesetas and that he did not steal them. They are his inheritance. It was a way to inform her that he had a mother, that his mother thought of him. He is recognizing his need for a mother, a role which Clara assumes later in an incestuous-like way.

And what does Clara want from him? Clara assures him: "I do not ask you to love me", but she begs him not to leave her. She is in despair when Victor does leave her. She looks at Victor's picture when he was a child with his mother and exclaims, "My boy", as if she were his mother. She displaces onto Victor her unfulfilled maternal longings for the son she never had, in a confusing incestuous-like relation.

Victor finds out that Elena works in an orphanage, and offers his services there as a volunteer. Continuing to act out his repetition compulsion, he invades Elena's space at the children's orphanage. He is consciously in search of revenge, but maybe more unconsciously, seeking a place among the orphans, where he also belongs. And perhaps he is searching more for love than for revenge.

Victor is involved in triangular relationships. From his tragic date with Elena, he has saved a triangular shaped piece of cardboard onto which he has written Elena's phone number. Victor is in the middle of two triangles: one with Clara and Sancho and another with Elena and David.

His involvement in triangular relationships could be seen as a symptom that is covering an unconscious desire to be the winner this time, with the secret hope of finally defeating the symbolic father, the father regime, the fatherland that oppressed and abandoned him and his mother. But it is also all the men who took his mother's attention away from him, those that excluded him, again and again, as a function of her work as a prostitute.

But this time he will be the conqueror in the Clara-Sancho-Victor triangle and in the triangle of Elena-David-Víctor. That is, he will become "victorious", as predicted by his name.

David, for his part, is trying to defend his place with his wife, but at the same time he also has secret reasons to feel guilty, and maybe he was unconsciously looking for his own punishment. Years ago, when he and Sancho arrived at Elena's house as police officers, David sensed the danger and alerted Sancho of the need to call for reinforcements before entering Elena's house. But Sancho ignored him, and David followed Sancho in this irrational decision to initiate the police action without protection, while exposed to the rage of Sancho against him. This may represent a slip that unconsciously led David to look for some kind of self-punishment, a castrating disability to pay for his guilt of betraying Sancho for having an affair with his wife, Clara. David is now confined to a wheelchair, unable to access a complete sexuality, not only at that time with Clara, but also now, with his own wife, Elena.

Elena, on the other hand, is not protected from her own sense of guilt and self-punishment. Although, in the beginning and at first glance during the tragic event at her apartment, she finds David enormously attractive and they exchanged very erotic glances. She ends up being his wife, confined to a life with him, without the kind of sexuality that she would have wished for, but trying to repair the bloody event in her father's apartment, while waiting desperately for the drug dealer, a situation in which she also feels responsible, and even more so after learning Victor's story about who was really responsible for shooting David.

Sancho is addicted to alcohol and also to his wife, Clara. He cannot live without her but hits her and asks for forgiveness. They maintain a sado-masochistic relationship in which he takes her as an object, and abuses her. His narcissistic way of relating to the other does not allow him to tolerate anything other than the satisfaction of his own needs. He tells her, "As long as I still love you, you will not separate from me". He cannot express his hate and frustration other than acting with violence and oppression. He is a living metaphor for the Franco regime, filled with oppression and intolerance of the other. He is the powerful dictator in his home who gets drunk with his own illusions of power and brutishly submits another to his will.

Both Franco and Sancho know that the way to remain in power, to command others without limits, is to exclude the other, annul their will, devalue them, subjugate them into dependence; Sancho at the family level, Franco at the social political level.

But in his heart Sancho knows, as any dictatorial regime knows, that subjugated, oppressed and frightened people will sooner or later rebel.

Sancho knows that Clara, his subjugated love object, is not loyal to him. He has the strong suspicion that she was sleeping with David in the past and is certain that she is now with Victor. Sancho felt castrated by David and when struggling with the gun in Victor's hand Sancho placed his finger over Victor's and pulled the trigger, taking revenge on David by shooting him in the spine, foreclosing his potency in retaliation for sleeping with his wife. Sancho shot David and now he is planning to kill Victor, as if destroying the rival would bring his wife back to him.

Clara is now deeply involved with Victor and desperate to run away from Sancho. To separate from Victor is to die anyway, so she sacrifices her life to keep Victor alive. She protected him, supported him financially, took care of him, and now will die for him. But he needs now to separate from her, to become a man and look for his own woman, not shared with a third.

According to Piera Aulagnier (1980, pp. 166–184), every passion demands the presence of two actors (at least!) to allow a drama or a comedy to be represented. The body plays an essential role, both to grant pleasure and suffering. Clara had a passionate relationship with Victor. For Aulagnier, in the passionate relationship the chosen object, in this case, Victor, recognizes in the other, Clara, nothing more than one source of pleasure, creating an asymmetric relationship. Clara depends exclusively on Victor, who has become more than a source of pleasure, a necessity for her to live, and the exclusive source of all pleasures. In her mind, he is the only one who could give her pleasure and joy. In this situation, the possibility of thinking is not effective, similar to what Victor had felt when he met Elena. The pleasure becomes suffering.

Clara seeks her own death to calm the drive that definitively and totally will allow her to end her suffering and her demand for the love that Victor cannot provide to her. She has nothing left to lose.

We don't know what was in the mind of Almodóvar, but we play with interpretations and create ideas that may or may not be in the mind of the director who created the movie. Of all the multiple interpretive possibilities, my reading is that when Victor breaks up with Clara, sends Clara out of his life, he is also ready to let go of his own mother, his first object of love who was lost long ago. Accepting the loss of those whom we have already lost frees up psychic space, and releases the painful feelings of abandonment and dependence, rendering us more available for a healthier and less dependent relationship. Victor can now end his triangular relationships and gain access to a more mature, dyadic, intimate and integrated love with Elena.

In the last scene, we see Victor and Elena about to deliver their baby, in a similar situation as when Victor was born, but this time in a taxi, instead of a bus, during the day instead of at night; in light, not darkness; with joy, not desperation; with hope instead of despair. Spain has changed. The streets are now full of people, and there is a feeling of freedom and joy. Prostitution, though it still exists, as it does almost everywhere, no longer exists as a metaphor of the re-pressed desire that needs to be satisfied in a secret and forbidden way. Nothing is the same, not only in the external reality but also in the inner world. There is a political and social change, resulting in a corresponding psychological transformation in the minds of the inhabitants. The first scene and last scene of the film offer the viewer before and after images. The opening scene of political and psychic repression has given way to political and psychic freedom.

Victor's son is also being born on wheels. He jokes, telling his son to be patient, just as Doña Centro, who helped to deliver him, had joked for him to be patient when he was born. Maybe his son will be more patient and will use his mind in a more mature way, with more control of his actions, since he will have all the possibilities that Victor didn't. This son will not need to be the son of a dictatorial regime. He has a mother and a father, Elena and Victor, who will take care of him. He already has a place in their mind, and so maybe he will not need to be so impatient in looking to find that place. We hope he will be able to postpone the demand for an immediate pleasure to guarantee a fuller pleasure at a later date (Freud, 1911/1980).

The film is like an analytical process searching for the patient's truth. There is nobody totally bad or good, but each one suffers and is driven unconsciously to satisfy his or her desire, seeking for a space in the mind of the other, guided by love, hate, guilt, passion and aggression.

In psychoanalysis we look for the truth, with all the consequences that it may bring. We try to make what is unconscious, conscious, to find our own truth and be able to manage our lives and avoid impul-sive actions. *Live Flesh* invites us to wonder what drives each character into action, what drives each one of their emotions and what the thoughts and feelings are behind their actions.

As psychoanalysts, we privilege the internal world in its engage-ment with the external world, but *Live Flesh* draws us into the mutual reflection of internal reality and external reality on the threshold of "trembling flesh", which is a more accurate translation of the original Spanish title of the film—*Carne Trémula*. The flesh trembles, not only in erotic desire but also in fear or when the freedom is threatened.

We can imagine the political transformation in Spain that Almodóvar alludes to, taking place during Victor's life from his birth in dictatorship, through the fall of Franco and into freedom, but those years may not be enough to transform the structure of a mind raised in a dictatorial system.

My personal experience of political oppression allows me to identify closely with Almodóvar's words presented at the beginning of this chapter. He says, *"I can't forget that period"*… but represents at the end of his film a city . . . *"that has forgotten fear". (P.238)* I suppose the city is carrying on, but it is hard for me to believe that after so many years of living under political oppression (from Victor's birth until the birth of Victor's baby), the fear is forgotten. Gutiérrez-Albilla (2018) in his rich discussion of particular Almodóvar films shows how the auteur/director reflects the traces of the global trauma that leaves its mark on us. The impact of the trauma as trace reflects my own experience from having lived under a dictatorship. In my view, the experience of the repression from a dictatorial regime structures and shapes the mind in such a way that it is difficult to make it disappear during one's life or even within the first generation of descendants. Moses, the prophet, led the Jews through the desert for 40 years, so new generations could be born with a "free mind", free from all the years of slavery. The fear stays inside the mind for decades.

I lived my childhood and adolescence under an authoritarian regime in Argentina. In the early 1970s I left with my family when I was a teenager. Shortly after our departure Argentina's Dirty War began in which members of my extended family and friends were imprisoned, tortured and killed for thinking differently. Their crime was dreaming of freedom. I emigrated to my second home, Venezuela, a country that taught me the unknown feelings of freedom and democracy, but after three decades I experienced the tragedy of watching Venezuela's democracy fall before my very eyes. Suddenly Venezuela, my second home, was taken over by a dictatorial regime and had become a foreign place inside my own home.

In 2010 I emigrated, once again in search of freedom and democracy. I came to the United States, a beacon of freedom and a model of democracy to the world. And yet now, in 2018, as I write, we see how democratic space is collapsing and authoritarian tendencies with intolerance to differences are taking root right here in the US. I sincerely hope that we, as did Victor, can come out victorious from these times of troubles, and transform the threat of defeat into the promise of victory.

References

Almodóvar, P. (2017). *The Pedro Almodóvar Archives.* P. 238. Editors Duncan and Peiró. Kohn, Germany: Taschen.

—— (Director). 1997. Live Flesh. Ciby 2000, El Deseo, SA:France Cinema.

Aulagnier, P. (1980). *Los Destinos del Placer. Alienación, amor, pasión.* Madrid, Spain: Petrel.

Freud, S. (1911/1980). *Formulaciones sobre los dos principios del acaecer psíquico.* Buenos Aires, Argentina: Amorrortu.

Gutiérrez-Albilla, J.D. (2017–2018). *Aesthetics, Ethics and Trauma in the Cinema of Pedro Almodóvar.* Edinburgh: University of Edinburgh Press.

Rendell, R. (1986). *Live Flesh.* London: Pantheon Books.

CHAPTER 13

All About My Mother

Arlene Kramer Richards

Watching *All About My Mother* on a rainy Mother's Day in New York, I am moved to tears at every unfolding of secrets and mysteries. Like life, the movie shocks again and again. And like life, the cycles continue. Beginning in the middle, it moves to the end and then to the beginning. What happens?

In the first scene we are introduced to a medical apparatus for sustaining life, an intravenous drip, then to another apparatus for determining the moment of death, an electroencephalograph. A nurse says that she will inform the transplant authority. A life is over, another life can be saved from the organs of the corpse. So this is a story of death and rebirth.

The second scene shows the nurse Manuela with her son Esteban who calls her to see a movie, *All About Eve*. Manuela finishes preparing a salad that they will eat together while watching the movie. The movie they watch is about one woman taking the place, career, and life away from another woman whom the first woman envies. This will be one of the themes of this film Manuela and her son are living. It will function like the "play within the play" in Shakespeare's *Hamlet*. The death of the older woman is the price of life for the one who envies and eventually replaces her. Esteban tells Manuela that he wants to write about her, establishing the movie as the story he writes.

We see Manuela in a video playing a woman being told that her husband is dead and asked to donate his organs to save someone's life. The video is being used to train hospital workers to get families to agree to organ transplants. So we learn that Manuela can be an actress as well as a nurse. Her younger actress self has been replaced by her new self as a mother and a nurse. She has gone from being inauthentic to being an authentic protector of life, even of life after death.

Manuela gives her son a copy of a Truman Capote book for his birthday. At his insistence she reads aloud to him from the preface. Capote writes about his becoming a writer as a child. He calls it being chained to a demanding master. Esteban says it shows he is not the only one to chain himself to writing as a child. If Esteban is the writer of the movie, Manuela is his mother and the movie is all about her.

By the next scene Esteban is writing in a café. He sees his mother waiting for him in front of a huge poster of a woman's face. The poster and his mother are interchangeable. Then they and we are in a theater seeing the final scene of a production of *Streetcar Named Desire*. Stella leaves Kowalski with her infant in her arms after he has had her sister Blanche committed to a mental hospital. Blanche is the star of the play, the woman whose face was on the poster, but the heroine is Stella because she is the mother who defies her abusive husband and protects her son.

After the play Esteban's request for an autograph is refused by the star named Huma. He runs after her taxi and is killed on the street. Manuela, ironically, is asked for his organs. She consents but becomes obsessed with the man who receives Esteban's heart.

She travels from Madrid back to Barcelona to find Esteban's father. She looks in a place where prostitutes meet customers, sees one being beaten up, rescues her, and finds that she is an old friend, Agrado, a transsexual, but one who has not had his/her penis removed. Her name means that she tries to please everyone. She was a friend of Manuela and her husband eighteen years before, but has not heard from Manuela since then. Manuela is looking for her husband, to tell him about their son. He is now Lola, a transsexual like Agrado, who has kept his/her penis, but Agrado has not heard from Lola since she stole everything of value from Agrado's apartment.

Agrado is especially sad at losing the statue of the Virgin Mary that her mother had given her when she left home.

Since it is unlikely that men looking for a prostitute would find her attractive, because her face is swollen and bruised from the beating she took, Agrado agrees to try to get a job. She and Manuela go to a convent where the nuns help prostitutes. Rosa, a beautiful young nun, takes Manuela to her mother to try to convince her to hire Manuela as a cook. Her mother refuses indignantly. She will not have a prostitute in her home. Ironically, she herself is an art forger specializing in Chagall. This is a false mother with a false self. She lives with a demented husband and their dog. She relies on the dog to take her husband for walks and lead him home. Agrado takes a job cleaning staircases. At least it is an honest living in contrast to Rosa's mother's forgery.

Manuela goes to see Huma playing in *Streetcar*. She helps Huma find her co-star, the woman who plays Stella in the play. Huma tells her she always depends on the kindness of strangers. She is repeating her last line in the play. She tells Manuela that she started smoking to identify with Bette Davis, the star of *All about Eve*. She took the name Huma because it means smoke. She is addicted to her co-star who is addicted to heroin. Manuela finds and returns her to Huma but is left in the street to find her own way home.

Next morning Rosa comes to Manuela to ask her to rent her a room because she needs a place to stay while pregnant with Lola's baby. Manuela agrees to accompany her to the doctor, but refuses to let her stay in her apartment. Meanwhile Manuela gets a job working as assistant to Huma, reports that her co-star is too bombed on drugs to play Stella that day, and replaces her as Stella for that one day. We see the scene where Kowalski gives Blanche a bus ticket home, causing Stella to cry; Stella goes into labor. The audience applauds enthusiastically.

Nina and Huma confront Manuela the next day. Nina says that she is like Eve in All About Eve, scheming to steal her part and her life. Huma asks why Manuela wanted to see her in the first place. Manuela tells her she is the mother of the boy who wanted her autograph so much that her ran after her cab, was run down by a car, and died.

Some two weeks later Rosa appears at Manuela's door, and shows her the lab report; she is HIV positive. Manuela agrees to take her in and take care of her. Huma appears to give Manuela her salary. Agrado comes bringing ice cream and champagne to celebrate Manuela's performance as Stella. The four women laugh and enjoy each other. As Huma leaves, she gives Manuela a large check and a note that says that this is the autograph she did not give to Esteban.

Some months later Manuela invites Rosa's mother to visit her. The mother says she never understood her daughter. She always felt her to be an alien. When she leaves Manuela sobs; we see her shaking back and shoulders.

In a parallel scene Agrado substitutes for Huma and Nina when they are unable to perform because they tried to kill each other. Agrado fascinates the audience by telling them what each of her surgeries to become a woman cost her. She says this is the high cost of becoming authentically who she feels herself to be. Everyone laughs. The contrast between the inauthentic mother of Rosa and the brutal reality of Agrado startles; young people cheer, while other people walk out of her talk. She finishes with the idea that being authentic is being what you dream yourself to be.

Rosa's mother comes to the hospital but cannot stay for the birth. Rosa makes Manuela promise that she will not conceal anything from her son. The next scene is Rosa's funeral in the rain. Manuela sees Lola, the heavily made up woman who is both her husband and the father of both her and Rosa's sons. She tells Lola that her son was Esteban, named after him as was Rosa's baby. Lola, now a woman albeit with a penis, now knows that he is the father of two sons, both named Esteban after him. She shows him a picture of her son, reads to him from Esteban's notebook, and allows him to meet his and Rosa's child.

The new baby Esteban will know everything about his birth. Rosa takes him away from the home of Rosa's parents and brings him back when he is two years old and free of the HIV he was born with. She sees Huma play a mother whose son was killed in an automobile accident. Huma keeps the picture of Esteban on her dressing table mirror. Lola gave it to her when he died. Manuela smiles at the miracle of her son's rebirth.

Discussion

The title of the movie is enigmatic. Is it that the movie is everything about the woman who is my mother, or is it that the movie is totally about her and no one else? Is it a reference to *All About Eve*? A clip from that movie electrifies the conversation between Esteban and Manuela when they are eating dinner together. Because the clip shows Bette Davis as Margo Channing furiously denigrating her fans, it sets her up as a fraud when she accepts the adulation of a young woman who presents herself as a fan. The fan who calls herself Eve Harrington, becomes her assistant, but manipulates Margo and her friends and colleagues into making Eve a star while Margo chooses retirement.

This reference to *All About Eve* is the basis for a plot theme about lesbian love. Just as Margo was seduced by Eve's adoration, but betrayed by her, Huma in *All About My Mother* is betrayed by Nina. Huma is the star, in love with her co-star Nina and helpless without her. The lesbian relationship in *All About My Mother* ends when Nina goes home, marries and has a baby. She thus joins the patriarchy.

What happens in the *All About My Mother* movie is first a death. Esteban, the teen aged prospective writer and presumably Almodóvar's representative or avatar, is accidentally killed as a consequence of his passion for the actress Huma, whose name means smoke. Then Esteban's mother goes in search of his father Esteban, her lover, husband and betrayer. Finally a new Esteban is born and reborn. In this way, the film reverses time. Life goes birth, love, death; the movie reverses the order death, love, birth. The reversal creates a melodrama. In tragic drama as in life, death is the ending. In melodrama the nearness of death is averted in the end by a birth. This echoes the religious myths of Christianity. Christ's story ends with resurrection, as does Esteban's.

The heroine Manuela is an avatar of Mary. She is pale, long suffering, and at the beginning of the film when we meet her, she is the angel of death. She announces death to a shocked wife, she arranges a resurrection for parts of the body that are donated to save lives, she endures. [The name Manuela is derived from Emanuel, which means God is with us.] She is also the woman of love, the woman the first Esteban has married and with whom he has a child. And she is the mother of the third Esteban, Rosa's baby. In this way she reverses the order of natural life. She is the mother, lover, bringer of death Freud posited in his essay "The theme of the three caskets" (S.E. 12: 291–301). In that work Freud showed that stories in Shakespeare, fairy tales, and ancient chronicles all feature a scene in which a character must make a choice between gold, silver, or lead caskets. In each case the lead casket contains the great prize. Similarly many stories feature the choice between three women as in Paris's choice of who was most beautiful among the goddesses, Hera, Aphrodite and Athena. Similarly, King Lear chooses which of his three daughters truly loves him. Freud concludes, "We might argue that what is represented here are the three inevitable relations that a man has with a woman— the woman who bears him, the woman who is his mate and the woman who destroys him; or that they are the three forms taken by the figure of the mother in a man's life— the mother herself, the beloved one who is chosen after her pattern, and lastly, the Mother Earth who receives him once more. But it is in vain that an old man yearns for the love of woman as he had it first from his mother; the third of the fates alone, the silent Goddess of Death, will take him in her arms." (S.E. 12: P.301)

In drawing this conclusion Freud introduces the element of time. An old man cannot find his mother's love again, she, presumably will have died before him. He cannot have the kind of sexual love he had in his youth, time has deprived him of that. The only woman he can have to love is death.

The idea of time as a natural phenomenon prevailed in human society in many forms, such as the form of the recognition of seasons, the time from dawn to dusk and the time of life both for animals and humans. Each town or village would have its own town clock set to local time measured by the rising and setting of the sun.

So it might be fifteen minutes later in the town one left. With the coming of railroads in the early nineteenth century came a need for a standard time so that boarding or leaving a train would occur at a predictable time and so that trains coming from different directions would not crash. Charting latitude and longitude had made long sea voyages easier, creating the possibility that time zones could be set along those lines. This made time a man-made thing, as opposed to natural time.

Henri Bergson responded to the change in the status of time with a thesis that asserted that intuition at the moment was the basis of freedom of thought. This idea parallels Freud's idea of free association as a way of allowing what was unconscious to play on the mind and be communicated and thereby understood. In the same era and social milieu Marcel Proust made time the centerpiece of his epic novel *In Search of Lost Time.* He said, "Love is space and time measured by the heart." Marcel Proust used the image of the train and watching the landscape speeding by as contrasted with the idea of the landscape seen on a walk. Space was thus defined by time just as time was defined by convention. The revolution in thought and social mores caused by the technology is similar to what is at the heart of Almodóvar's work: the change in thought about sexual identity caused by technology that allows physical sex change.

Einstein disagreed with Bergson. For a physicist the arbitrary nature of time as defined by cultural agreement did not work. He defined it in terms of movement through space, thus regarding the interaction of time and space as universal and the arbitrary time zones as a convenience, not a truth. China's policy of putting the whole country on the same time further emphasized the cultural and political implications of time. For China time was a way of unifying a country with many languages and diverse cultures. Thus definition shifted from the physical to the emotional and from the reality of consciousness to the power of the unconscious.

Proust was a forerunner of the idea of the return of events in the past from the unconscious to consciousness and the return of power to the writer or speaker of those events. By communicating the events to an audience, the speaker or writer gains power over what events inflicted long before the writer seized control of them. By writing about the long gone past, especially the events of childhood, he was able to trace the effects of these events on his development. Both his sexuality and his work came out of the events. Neither would have been possible to accept without the work of telling. In this way, the artist is a spinner of enchantment as well as a teller of truth.

How does this play out in the movie *All About My Mother?* As we have seen, the movie reverses time in the life cycle. It runs over several years yet the viewer is only watching for an hour and a half. The time sequence does not depend on natural time. In fact, movies shown entirely in "real time" like those of Andy Warhol and even partially in "real time" like the brilliant Chantal Akerman's 1975 *Jeanne Dielman, 23, quai du Commerce, 1080 Bruxelles*, one of cinema's most hypnotic and complete depictions of space and time, quickly become unbearably boring. Why should this happen? Why do we bear real time in our lives, but need tremendously speeded up, cut and flashback sequences in movies in order to focus attention? Almodóvar's reversal of time poses the question. I do not know the answer, but I believe that playing with time is an important part of the movie's power. Perhaps it is an important part of all movies. Perhaps it is no coincidence that the movies came soon after the railroads and just before the fluidity of gender. By showing still images quickly flickering, the viewer's eye and brain are tricked into seeing movement, time is socially constructed. The step by step movement away from the natural and into social construction shocks as it fascinates.

What powers the story in *All About My Mother* is the older Esteban's breast implants. These allow him to live as Lola, a prostitute, to compete with his wife and to eventually drive her and their about to be baby to take a train to another city. Manuela leaves him because she cannot bear his insistence that she cover her body while he exposes his female-looking breasts. Pregnant, she is the embodiment of traditional, church sanctioned reproductive sexuality. By contrast, equipped with both breasts and a penis, he is the pleasure-seeking sybarite, the exponent of sexual identity of choice. Manuela's taking a train makes plain the parallel between the revolution in understanding time as man-made and the revolution in understanding gender as human-made. Just as time is set by cultural agreement, gender is also. In this way, the twentieth century was the moment when gender became arbitrary, just as the nineteenth century had seen time become arbitrary.

What has all this to do with psychoanalysis? Proust makes recalling the past, bringing it in to face the present, and confronting the reality of the juxtaposition, into what is arguably the most original and influential novel of the twentieth century. Almodóvar gives Agrado the most important scene in *All About My Mother*. Agrado recounts her alterations of her body as a sequence of becoming in reality what she was in her mind. Whether we call this "self actualization" (Horney, 1950) or becoming one's authentic self (Winnicott, 1960), or consolidating the ego (Freud, A., 1965), it is a process, expensive as psychoanalysis is expensive, personal, as psychoanalysis is personal, and transformative in a way that is apparent to the outer world as well as the self.

Agrado's way is not the way for most people. For most it is not the body but the mind where transformation takes place. But the goal is the same: an authentic self. And Agrado's performance is what heals. At the beginning of the movie he was prostituting himself and getting beaten up. After the performance he keeps his new job as Huma's assistant. Given the success of his performance, it is not impossible that he will establish an acting career just as Eve in *All About Eve* first got a job as assistant to the star Margo Channing and then replaced her as an actress.

Another suggestion the movie *All About My Mother* makes is that Manuela's role is parallel to that of Stella in *A Streetcar Named Desire*. Like Stella, she walks out on a man who bullies her. Like Stella, she takes her baby with her. Having a baby empowers a woman. As long as she is a mother, she is not alone. Blanche in Streetcar is the childless woman; she is helpless, unable to have a real life, lost in fantasy, trying to become what she can never be. What gives women power in *All About My Mother*, is the capacity to bear, nurture, heal and soothe a baby. Blanche has none of these.

Psychoanalysts believe that the blueprint for the woman a man loves is the one who gave birth to him. Of all Freud's ideas about women, this is the most enduring. Object relations theorists, self psychologists, interpersonalists, contemporary conflict theorists and therapists of every sort believe this. The mother is a shorthand name for the first nurturer, be it wet-nurse, nanny, father, grandparent or another person. Freud's idea of the "three caskets" continues with the woman who sees a man to his death. Manuela does this when she allows the dying—first Esteban to see the baby he has fathered. She grants his last wish in an act of charity. Despite his heavily made up face and long beautiful hair, he still wants to see his son. He still wants to know that he is a father. He somehow recovers his manhood in seeing the child. And despite what he has done to her by denying her sexual attractiveness, and done to himself by using drugs and getting HIV, and to Rosa who is the biological mother of this baby, and to the baby by getting and transmitting HIV to them, Manuela still has enough pity on him to give him this last comfort. In this she is the ultimate mother. We learn all about her and the film is all about her. Both meanings of the title are delivered in the film.

References

Almodóvar, P. (Director). (1999). *All About My Mother. [Motion Picture]*. Spain. El Deseo.

Bergson, H.(1910). *Time and Free Will: An Essay on the Immediate Data of Consciousness (Essai sur les données immédiates de la conscience, 1889)*. Mineola: Dover Publications, 2001.

Freud, A. (1965). *Normality and Pathology in Childhood: Assessments of Development*. New York: International Universities Press.

Freud, S. (1935). The theme of the three caskets. *Standard Edition* 12:291–301.

Horney, K. (1950). *Neurosis and Human Growth*. New York: Norton.

Kazan, E. (1951). (Director). Saul, O. & Kazan, E. (Screenplay with Tennessee Williams). *A Streetcar Named Desire* [Motion Picture]. (Adapted from the play by Tennessee Williams). USA: Warner Brothers.

Mankiewicz, J. (1950). *All About Eve.* [Motion Picture]. USA: Twentieth Century Fox.

Proust, M.(1913–1927). *In Search of Lost Time.* New York: Modern Library, 2012.

Winnicott, D.W. (1963). Ego Distortion in Terms of True and False Self. In: *The Collected Works of D. W. Winnicott:* Volume 6, 1960–1963.

CHAPTER 14

Death and Dialogue in
Pedro Almodóvar's *Talk To Her*

Danielle Knafo

Hable con Ella (Talk to Her), a psychologically complex and emotionally resonant film, was written and directed by Pedro Almodóvar,
Spain's most famous director since Luis Buñuel. Released in 2002, the
film garnered numerous awards, including an Academy Award for
best screenplay. Of all his films, Almodóvar claims that *Talk to Her* has
the least amount of scenes he dislikes (Max, 2016).

Simply put, the film is about two lonely men who love two comatose women, but it is about much more. It is also about male
friendship and achieving a level of authenticity in relationships. One
of the titles Almodóvar considered for this film was *Solitude, I Suppose* (Almodóvar & Almodóvar, 2002), because all of the characters
in the film struggle with their solitude. Most of Almodóvar's films
have centered around women; therefore, his focus in this film on
men's inner lives and fears, and their peculiar relationships with
women and each other, is unusual. The film is an unlikely story, yet it
is one that affects us deeply because it succeeds in raising important
ideas about our notions of masculinity, femininity, morality, and the
complexity of gender politics. It moves at a slow and deliberate pace
and it is accompanied by a beautiful, melancholic score by Alberto
Iglesias, all of which accentuate an emotional atmosphere of social
isolation and alienation.

Since *Talk to Her* centers on male love of comatose women, it invites a psychoanalytic interpretation of necrophilic perversion. Attraction to the sleeping, comatose, or dead is at the heart of the film. Because it is presented with romantic tenderness, however, the usual repulsion to such behavior may be largely attenuated. Despite this, we are aware that something is happening that makes us uncomfortable and this is due to the power of the concept of necrophilia, which links the physical and the metaphysical and attempts to bridge the gap between sexual desire and the object that lies beyond that desire (Downing, 2003), whether that object is someone one has no chance of being with, the forbidden Mother of one's childhood, or immortality itself.

The film opens with a theater curtain—the same curtain that appeared at the end of Almodóvar's previous film, *All About My Mother* (1999), thus linking the two films. Although the major characters in *Talk to Her* are two men and the women they love, we shall see that the mother, albeit mostly invisible, remains an important figure throughout. The bookends of *Talk to Her* are dance scenes created by German choreographer Pina Bausch to symbolize the bizarrely beautiful and poignant dance of life, love, and death. The opening dance, *Café Müller*, shows two women (one of whom is Bausch herself) with their eyes closed who look and move as if they are sleepwalking, bumping into walls and objects, even falling. A sad-faced man frantically rushes about, moving chairs out of the women's way, to avoid danger. Bausch's dance directs our awareness, from the start, to human blindness, perpetual impending danger, and our dependency upon others to survive—all central themes that will be elaborated in the film. We encounter two men, strangers to one another, seated next to each other in the audience. One notices the other who is weeping as he watches the dance. Both men are unaware that their lives will soon be intricately intertwined.

The two men are Benigno and Marco, each superficially very different, yet both alike in that they continue to struggle with traumatic loss and have difficulty connecting to women who are alive and well. Marco Zuloaga is a good-looking journalist from Argentina who writes about travel. He is the more macho of the two, yet the first time we see him, it is he who weeps while watching the performance of *Café Müller*. We will see him weep again on many occasions. We later learn that he has lost a former love to drug addiction, and that it took him ten years to "get over it". Benigno Martin is the more ostensibly effeminate and sensitive man: he is a nurse, skilled at styling hair, putting on makeup, and embroidery. He honed these skills by caring for his bedridden mother for fifteen years until she died.

The two women are Alicia and Lydia, each of whom engaged in a performance art. Alicia was a ballet dancer and Lydia a matador. Both women lived physically active lives before they were rendered comatose by their respective accidents, the first in a car crash and the second gored by a bull in the ring. Throughout much of the film, the women lay silent and immobile in their hospital beds, becoming fetish objects for the men who love them.

Benigno transfers the care-giving skills he acquired from tending his invalid mother onto Alicia. "You have to pay attention to women," he says.

Coincidence plays a large role in the film. The apartment Benigno shares with his mother happens to face the ballet studio in which Alicia trains. One day, he notices her wallet fall to the ground as she walks home from dance class. He runs to catch up with her. She is apprehensive until he hands her the wallet, after which she speaks openly with him, telling him about her interest in silent films, dance, and travel. He watches her jaywalk carelessly into traffic, a premonition of what is to come. He also notes her address, taking stock of her psychiatrist father's office, which is attached to their home. This is the only scene in which Benigno and Alicia are both upright.

Benigno begins to stalk Alicia by seeing her psychiatrist father. Despite the fact that he falsifies the true reason for his visit, when asked why he came, he honestly responds: "I miss my mother". He tells the psychotherapist that he specializes in "beauty therapy", juxtaposing his surface therapy with the depth psychology he is being offered. Following his appointment, he invades the family home, even entering Alicia's bedroom and secretly watching her shower. Before leaving, he startles her as she emerges from the shower, reassuring her that he is "not dangerous". Benigno steals her hair clip, foreshadowing later actions as well as his sense that he cannot get what he wants directly, and so he takes it without the other's knowledge or consent.

Benigno spends many hours voyeuristically spying on Alicia and watching her every move. Now he watches from his window while aggressively snapping the hair clip he stole in biting motions. We never witness the accident that results in her coma. But coincidence once again ensues when the improbable chance event lands her in Benigno's grateful and loving care at the hospital where he works, El Bosque, "the forest", where she becomes a sort of Sleeping Beauty. As Alicia's private nurse for the past four years, Benigno shows himself to be devoted beyond professional duty, putting in many extra hours on the job. He tends to Alicia's physical needs with an almost religious devotion, by carefully washing her and arranging her hair. The film's most sensual scenes show Benigno methodically and expertly massaging Alicia's body and face, and the abundant close-ups of her skin bring it to life as a vital, flesh and blood field of Eros.

He talks to her about dance performances and silent films because he knows she'd enjoy hearing about them. After attending the performance of *Café Müller*, he brings Alicia an autographed photograph of the choreographer, with the inscription, "I hope you overcome all of your obstacles." Engaging in a perverse reversal of the talking cure, here Benigno speaks incessantly to the woman who lies on the bed but cannot respond in any way. Interestingly, talking to the dead was something Almodóvar was introduced to early in life. One of his fondest memories is of the women of Calzada de Calatrava, his birthplace, talking in the cemetery while tending family graves (Max, 2016).

Marco is the boyfriend of Lydia, a name that means "bullfight" in Spanish. She is a famous matador who engaged in the Spanish sport known for its glorification of ritualized death. He is intrigued after seeing her interviewed on television and asks to write a piece on her. They develop a relationship, especially after he kills a snake for her (she is phobic). When she asks him why he chose to interview her, he says he knows nothing about bullfighting, but he knows about desperate women. We later find out that he had a girlfriend whom he loved and lost, and for whom he also killed a snake.

As we watch Benigno dress and undress Alicia's body, we also watch as Lydia is dressed by her male assistant. The camera moves up and down her slim, androgynous body and her magnificent strong face, with her hair tightly pulled back in a braid. The torero costume is revealed to us in all its splendor, with its bright pink socks, burgundy velvet, gold and jeweled embroidery, cropped pants and jacket, literally sewn onto her body. Before she goes to meet the bull, her sister tells Marco about nuns who were raped by priests in Africa, adding the words, "If you can't trust missionaries, what's to become of us?" The message is clear: Men are not what they seem.

Unlike Alicia's accident, we do witness the blood and gore of Lydia's. In the second bullfighting scene, we watch as she kneels with her pink cape before her as she courageously waits for the bull to emerge from the gate. Within moments, he charges at her, gores her, and drags her bloody, limp body until another matador succeeds in distracting him. This is followed by an interesting moment in which the bull turns his gaze back toward Lydia, as if expressing contempt for her arrogance and underestimation of his strength (Wilson, 2009). After Lydia is gored by the bull, she coincidentally lands in the same hospital as Alicia.

Marco is a novice at having a comatose girlfriend and, unlike Benigno, cannot bring himself to touch her. When he enters Alicia's room, he is awed by Benigno's relationship to the comatose Alicia and intrigued by certain objects that attract his attention: a clock (as if she can tell time), and a book with a page marked where she left off reading. The book is *La Noche del Cazador* (The Night of the Hunter), a compelling novel (and film) about a man who pretends to be a priest and is a serial killer. Almodóvar throws out clues like this one, priest rapists, and Benigno's name—which ironically means benign—to let the audience know that surface good can mask deep evil.

Benigno advises Marco that "the first night is the worst, but then you get used to it". Benigno takes it upon himself to mentor Marco, gently instructing him to "talk to her," advice Almodóvar believes all men should follow (DVD commentary). However, Marco cannot take Benigno's advice. In fact, he had trouble communicating even before Lydia's accident. In one flashback scene, Marco and Lydia drive through the hills of Cordoba. She says, "We have to talk." He replies, "We are talking". She retorts, "No, you are talking". She wanted to tell Marco that she was breaking up with him in order to go back to her previous boyfriend and fellow matador, El Niño de Valencia. The theme of talking to a woman is very important, but so is the theme of listening to the woman. The two men are clearly in love with their comatose "girlfriends"; however, there is a strong homoerotic tie between them as well.

Coma is an interesting state of being, in which one is alive but completely unconscious, a state between life and death. Almodóvar presents us with successful and attractive women who are rendered comatose—unconscious and immobile. Yet, in parallel, we are introduced to two men who, though not comatose, are unconscious in a different way, for they are unaware of their inner lives, unable to transcend their traumas, and lacking the ability to deal with a conscious woman. Necrophilia is usually understood in terms of pathological mourning and identification with the dead. Furlong (2013), compared the "helpless openness" and vulnerability communicated by the prostrate human form, which elicits "powerful urges that unconsciously direct our behavior toward them" (p. 476).

Having studied necrophilia (Knafo, 2015), a condition that is primarily male, as well as iDollators, men who love sex dolls (Knafo, 2015), I am well aware of the fear of women felt by many heterosexual men. I have often posed the question: why would a man prefer an inanimate, sleeping, comatose, or dead object to an alive flesh-and-blood woman?

I have found that many men are afraid of the power they feel women may wield over them. Some of these men, like Benigno, have had strong, symbiotic, and dependent relationships with their mothers. Although we never see Benigno's mother, we hear her voice once, and we know she is an absent presence throughout. These men seek to control women so they don't feel controlled by them. And they seek reunion with the lost/dead object. They seek a woman who cannot reject, shame, or retaliate. With an inanimate woman or doll, the man denies his own helplessness, dependency, castration, and even death. Sexualizing the dead or comatose is a way of protecting oneself from deadness, creating an illusion of excitement and vitality to ward off dread and fill an emptiness inside one. Ultimately, it is a strategy for managing one's fear of death.

Cultural tropes reinforce the fear of a woman who is alive and self-possessed, sometimes presented as the bitch, the witch, the maenad, or the castrating harpy. It is not unusual to see images that idealize female surrender and passivity, which, taken to an extreme, symbolize the feminization and erotization of death. May (2009) coined the term "necro-gaze" to denote "a masculinized gaze directed at a dead subject or directed as fantasy at a subject whom the gazer wishes dead for his benefit" (p. 169). Bronfen (1992) considers the trope of women's dead bodies as a social symptom, claiming that death, sexuality, and otherness have almost always been located in the female signifying body. The philosopher and psychoanalyst Slavoj Žižek, in the film *The Pervert's Guide to Cinema* (Fiennes, 2006), claims that Hitchcock's *Vertigo*, like many other films, represents the realization of a male fantasy in which women must be "mortified" before they are acceptable sexual partners. He paraphrases the old saying, "The only good woman is a dead woman." Women, like death, have been feared and desired.

Both May (2009) and Bronfen (1992) conceive of the necro-gaze as encouraging gender stereotypes to the extreme, with masculinity as possessing, consuming, conquering, invasive, and powerful, and femininity as receptive, submissive, powerless, lacking agency, and dead. The doer/done-to, penetrator/recipient dialectic clearly represents socially encoded models of desire that are present in the necrophile and somnophile.

It is not surprising, then, to find that *Talk to Her*'s centerpiece is a seven-minute black-and-white silent movie, *The Shrinking Lover*, a film Almodóvar claims to be the proudest of from his entire filmography (Almodóvar & Almodóvar, 2002). On the surface, the movie is rather comical, yet it possesses some serious deeper meanings that mirror and amplify the film's themes and that can be understood as a dream sequence or a projected fantasy of Benigno's. Indeed, the camera cuts back and forth between the film and scenes of Benigno sensuously massaging Alicia's naked body. In the fantasy sequence, Amparo, a scientist, accuses her husband, Alfredo, of being egotistical and he, in turn, volunteers to drink an experimental weight loss liquid she concocted in order to prove that he is not selfish. He shrinks (becomes a child) to the size of her hand and leaves her to go to his mother's. While there, he discovers that his mother is evil and has killed his father. The wife later rescues him and carries him in her purse, taking him to a hotel. After she reads to him, she falls asleep, leaving her giant body for him to explore. He climbs her breasts like mountains, tumbling down the hill of her abdomen to discover her vagina, which he enters as he would a cave. His body, now the size of a penis, pleasures his wife in her sleep; but he is swallowed up by the vagina, in the ultimate castration/reunion, never to emerge again. Once more, referring to the mother, Almodóvar comments on this scene: "His destiny is to fulfill a cycle that starts and ends in the same place. That place has to do with pleasure, birth and death" (Almodóvar & Almodóvar, 2002). Benigno, who narrates the film's plot to Alicia, says that Alfredo "stays inside her forever." As he recounts the film's storyline, it is clear that he is sharing his own fantasy. The two stories—the film and Benigno's fantasy—are one and the same.

With this short film, Almodóvar shows us the boy's/man's fears that his organ is too small to satisfy his mother/woman and that her sexual power can diminish him to the point of consuming him. It symbolically mirrors the two male characters' struggles by alluding to their smallness and their sense of being overwhelmed by women they experience as "larger than life"(Freud, 1905). Indeed, both men are social misfits who have been deeply affected by their respective losses, Benigno's dead mother and absent father and Marco's ex-girlfriend. Their solution is to reverse the power balance and to sexualize their relationships with inert women, thus overcoming their sense of impotence and ineptitude. One of the movie's interesting twists is how these men, infatuated with their comatose women, are ultimately revealed as the true (emotional) cripples. At one point, Marco says, "There is nothing sadder than losing the one you love. Love is the saddest thing when it goes away." Rather than grieve their losses, Benigno and Marco act them out through desperate attempts to master them by keeping the comatose women alive. At one point, Benigno tells Marco that his favorite travel book is the one Marco wrote on Cuba because it describes people "who've got nothing and invent everything".

Soon after the short film, the camera zooms into a close-up of a lava lamp in which a red bubble bursts, symbolically reflecting the approaching rupture in the film's tragicomic ambiance.

One day, Lydia's former boyfriend, Niño, shows up and a new triangle is formed. Marco enters her room and catches him talking to her—something he still is unable to do. Marco defers to Niño and leaves, but, before he does, he wants to say goodbye to Benigno and Alicia. Benigno confesses that he wishes to marry Alicia. He argues against Marco's rational objection that he is engaging in a monologue and delusionally insists that he and the comatose Alicia have a better relationship than most married couples. Marco cannot hear the desperation in Benigno's communication (Wilson, 2009). When he insists, "Alicia can't say with any part of her body 'I do'", he unconsciously forewarns him about the rape.

We soon learn that a real transgression has been committed, for which the short film and lava lamp closeup were symbolic. It is discovered that Alicia is pregnant, and the finger is naturally pointed at Benigno, who is arrested and imprisoned. Although Benigno's offense does not come entirely as a shock, the outrage of his rape seems mitigated by several factors: the rape occurs off screen, the loving attention we've seen Benigno show Alicia, and the miraculous result of the rape—the birth of Alicia's still-born child is also a re-birth for Alicia—she emerges from her coma. In addition, *The Shrinking Lover* is a symbolic film that deals with potentially explosive material in a carefree manner. Almodóvar himself has said, "I came up…with *The Shrinking Lover* in order to cover up what Benigno has done" (Strauss, 2006; p. 97). Despite the fact that the rape is somewhat masked by a comical film and a beneficial outcome, it is nonetheless a classical male violation that aggresses against the woman's body and soul. Having Alicia emerge from her comatose state as she gives birth is Almodóvar's way of presenting the definitive necrophilic fantasy: through sexual intercourse, the man can bring the woman back to life (Knafo, 2015). Such reversals are meant to reassure him of his power and virility and bolster his self-esteem.

Fluidity of gender and sexuality is a frequent interest in Almodóvar's films. He himself claims to have lived a bisexual life until the age of 35 (Max, 2016). We are told that Lydia's father considered her a male because of her passion for bullfighting. Benigno's interests are more typically associated with female pursuits. Benigno tells Alicia's father that he likes men, but feels he needs to lie in order to assuage the father's suspicions regarding how intimate he has become with Alicia. As the film progresses and Benigno and Marco become more friendly, one questions whether this is a lie at all.

Indeed, Marco leaves Jordan, where he has fled to write another travel book, when he learns that Lydia has died and Benigno is in prison. He visits Benigno and attempts to speak to a female clerk behind a glass window. Echoing the film's theme, neither man nor woman can hear the other, despite the large sign—COMMUNICATION—above their heads. Benigno tells Marco that some of the inmates think Marco is his boyfriend. Marco cries once again and reassures Benigno that it's OK for them to say this. Benigno wants to hug Marco, and the two men press the palms of their hands onto the glass partition, illustrating the mutual love that now exists between them. The camera moves back and forth alternately focusing on the face of one and then the other. Interestingly, the glass partition indicates that they are mirror images of one another, two sides of the same coin. In one shot, Benigno's face is reflected on the glass and superimposed onto Marco's. They literally become one.

The film, like the dances that frame it, comes full circle in the end. Marco completes his merging with Benigno by taking over Benigno's apartment. Marco now begins to watch the dancers across the street, as Benigno had done before him. He is taken aback when he notices Alicia sitting on the sideline.

Benigno cannot bear having no further contact with Alicia. He wishes to be in a coma since he falsely believes Alicia remains in a coma. He decides to take an overdose, but not before writing to Marco asking him to promise he'll continue to "talk to" him and tell him everything. Marco weeps at the discovery of Benigno's death. He goes to Benigno's gravesite and talks to him. He has evolved over the course of the film. He has adopted the positive qualities that Benigno embodied. He has learned not only to talk to the dead; he has learned to communicate more openly and more emotionally. Marco, travel writer and perpetual visitor, is perhaps ready to settle down. He tells Benigno that Alicia is alive and that he, Benigno, woke her up.

The film's final scene brings us back to the beginning. Coincidentally, Marco and Alicia happen to be at the same performance to watch the final dance, Pina Bausch's *Masurca Fogo*. Although the bookend dances are similar at first—now a woman's limp body is passed around the arms of men to a song's lyrics that include the words "Intimate strangers"—the second part of the final dance is more lyrical and romantic. Alicia is accompanied by her dance teacher, Katarina, who leaves her momentarily during the intermission. Alicia and Marco speak. She asks, "How are you? Are you OK?" He replies, "I am better because I am talking to you". Katarina notices the two have spoken and anxiously approaches Marco. Marco reassures her and informs her that Benigno is dead. Returning to the film's theme, she says, "One day you and I should talk". They go back to their seats to watch the dance. Now, several heterosexual couples dance the Bachata, a romantic and sensual Latin dance. Is there hope for love after all? Watching this dance, as well as the gaze exchanged between Marco and Alicia, leaves us with the possibility that they will come together as two alive, albeit flawed, human beings. Importantly, the seat between them indicates that Benigno remains as an absent presence.

The polarities of life-death, big-little, activity-passivity, speech-silence, selfishness-selflessness, innocence-guilt are beautifully rendered in Almodóvar's film, which has been read both as a sensitive love story (Edelstein, 2002) and a misogynous, morally bankrupt veneration of rape (Bechler, 2004; Suarez, 2009; Eaton 2009). At the very least, one can say that the movie contains a powerful statement about how communication between the genders has gone awry and how so many of us are trapped in a prison—whether physical or spiritual. The male denies his vulnerability, and the female denies her vitality and pleasure. Such gender stereotyping, enacted in "subtle collaborations," wrote Louise Kaplan (1999), are the "crucibles of perversion". Perhaps best summarizing this touching yet disturbing film are its final words spoken by Katarina: "Nothing is simple". Indeed, the film began with a theater curtain, but there is no curtain in the end. The conclusion is neither simple nor clear.

References

Almodóvar, A. (Producer), & Almodóvar, P. (Director). (2002). *Talk to Her.* [Motion Picture]. Spain: El Deseo.

Bechler, R. (2004). Rape and redemption in the West: Pedro Almodóvar's *Talk to Her. Open Democracy*, September 2.

Bronfen, E. (1992). *Over Her Dead Body: Death, Femininity and the Aesthetic.* Manchester: Manchester University Press.

Downing, L. (2003). *Desiring the Dead: Necrophilia in Nineteenth-Century French Literature.* Oxford: Legenda.

Eaton, A.W., 2009. Almodóvar's immoralism. In *Talk to Her*, Ed. A.W. Eaton, pp. 45–68. London: Routledge.

Edelstein, D. (2002). Arrivederci, coma: Almodóvar's *Talk to Her* is stupendous. *Slate*, November 22.

Fiennes, S. (Producer), & Žižek, S. (Director). (2006*). The Pervert's Guide to Cinema* [Motion Picture]. The Netherlands: Kasander Film Company.

Freud, S. (1905). Three essays on the theory of sexuality. *Standard Edition* 7:130–243.

Furlong, A. (2013). An example of dehumanization as a shield against our helpless openness to the other. *Journal of the American Psychoanalytic Association* 61:471–490.

Kaplan, L. (1991). *Female Perversion: The Temptations of Emma Bovary.* New York: Doubleday.

Knafo, D. 2015. For the love of death: Somnophilic and Necrophilic acts and fantasies. *Journal of the American Psychoanalytic Association.* 63: 857–86.

Max, D.T. (2016). The evolution of Pedro Almodóvar. *The New Yorker,* December 5.

May, R. (2009). Morbid parts: Gender, seduction and the necro–gaze. In *Sexual Perversions, 1670–1890,* ed. J. Peakman. New York: Palgrave.

Strauss, F., Ed. 2006. *Almodóvar on Almodóvar.* Revised edition. London: Faber.

Suarez, J.M. (2009). Woman or object: Selected female roles in the films of Pedro Almodóvar. *Pop Matters,* November 17.

Wilson, G. 2009. Rapport, rupture, and rape: Reflections on Talk to Her. In *Talk to Her,* Ed. A.W. Eaton, pp. 45–68. London: Routledge.

CHAPTER 15

The Lost Father and Regressive Desire in Almodóvar's *Talk to Her*

Albert J. Brok

Introduction

The "Father" as an important factor has been ignored in much of the writing about Pedro Almodóvar's film *Talk to Her (2002)*. To elaborate and illustrate the impact of a "lost father", I will focus on the character Almodóvar gives the name of Benigno. Benigno is a nurse who lives with and takes sole care of his mother, as his father left the family during his youth.

Benigno is an adult man who does not go out, but becomes fascinated by a young woman he sees from his window who is practicing ballet at a school across the street. What unfolds and how their paths cross, and what eventually happens, will be described below as part of my discussion of the impact of a lost father and the search to refind him.

Psychodynamic explanations of Benigno, the principal protagonist, have been ascribed to an over-involvement with his mother due to regressive wishes and needs. Correctly so, but not sufficient in my opinion to fully understand his dynamics and behavior. Therefore, it is my intention to fill what I consider to be a gap in our understanding of Benigno, by placing in sharper focus the internal location of "Men" and "Fathers" in his psychological life, as illustrated by the film narrative.

Fathers are very important both realistically, and symbolically. In a child's experience, fathers are often in the role of an additional, though different "Other", to the mother, and as a "Third" in the triadic relationship of Mother, Father, Child. Though not the main thrust of this chapter; the existence of a "third" in a young child's relationship is important, even when parenting figures are the same gender.

My overall thesis is that the life narrative of the protagonist Benigno, as constructed by Almodóvar, was reflective of the absence of a significant "third" in his development. A "third" that he ambivalently searches for, but only to limited avail. As the script indicates, when Benigno was young, his father abandoned the family, formed a new relationship, and was not heard of again. As a result, whatever positive involvement Benigno did experience with his father might have been just barely sufficient to somewhat prevent his total immersion with his individuation–inhibiting narcissistic mother.

Benigno's mother appears in the film only once and briefly as a disembodied voice from another room calling her son away from looking out through their apartment window into a ballet school across the street. What is across the street is hope embodied in the form of a young ballet student. Benigno is fascinated and silently involved at a distance with the young woman he sees during her ballet lessons. The young woman, whom we come to know as Alicia, has no sense of being observed. Benigno's fascination is that of a longing hunter, more than of an appreciator and observer of her aesthetic. In this key scene, his mother's voice in effect takes Benigno away from his voyeuristically organized process of seeking an "Other."

Clearly, for Benigno, an interest in and towards an "Other" is percolating during the window scene.[1] His mother is still alive at this

---

[1] The absent father has a space—he is remembered as unavailable. M. Target and P. Fonagy, p. 58. We also know from early infant observation that as early as four or five months infants engage in triadic as well as dyadic interchanges with their parents (Stern, 1995).

time, and he is looking outwards and away from her, shielded, however, by two window panes and a thoroughfare in between. To my mind, Benigno is a voyeuristically interested intruder, rather than solely involved in a regressive search to find and cling to a mother substitute embodied by the "girl next door". After all, his mother is quite alive as she calls him away from his distant involvement with Alicia. Our protagonist's mother narcissistically uses her gravitational pull to keep him close. Benigno of course surrenders to it, in effect dampening his attempts to go beyond her gravitational pull. There is no well internalized "Third" to reinforce his nascent yet underdeveloped need to individuate. As we shall see, he eventually partially succeeds in a distorted and regressed way. For Benigno, maturity is a tough effort which never reaches full fruition.

My reading of the above mentioned window scene, where he looks outward towards an object of desire, illustrates that the damage created by the loss of a supportive father did not totally squash Benigno's latent though evident individuation desires; but as we shall subsequently see, made it harder to act on his desires in a mature way.

As noted by Freud (1921) as well as others such as Chasseguet-Smirgel (1975), the early pre-conflict father is idealized and looked up to and can serve as a guide to leaving mother before he is experienced as a rival. I am suggesting that Benigno indeed partially experienced this stage, a stage that was ambivalently internalized, with insufficient potency in the face of the regressive needs which indeed inhibited full mourning of his mother as lost love object. His object desires were thus marked by a distortion of reality under the influence of unconscious fantasy wishes.

I shall also suggest that for Benigno, a possible substitute "Third" is played by his friend Marco, who befriends Benigno while visiting his own comatose girlfriend at the hospital where Benigno works. Marco almost salvages Benigno's regressed developmental state from further devolving. As a voice of reality, Marco even attempts to help him evolve in a progressive manner—but unfortunately fails. Too little too late?

In sum, I suggest that Benigno, as depicted in the film, not only is organized solely in a regressive manner, as most writers have emphasized (Fried, 2017, Sabbadini, 2012, Lichtenstein, 2005), but is also struggling for a hope, albeit in a damaged way, to escape the gravitational pull reinforcing his adhesive connection to his mother. A hope characterized by being interested in a live attractive woman (via his initial glimpses of Alicia) but organized by the limited developmental supplies available in his psyche. His deep regressive fantasy, and his need to relate to an object rather than a subjective person, is fully revealed once Alicia enters into a coma as a result of a accident.[2]

Aspects of the Plot

The plot weaves back and forth in time, brilliantly intertwining background information with current experiences of the characters. Significantly, it opens with a sense of desperation and ends with images of harmony. Ultimately it is a film about hope for one person, Marco, but unrequited and unrealistic hope for another as portrayed in the character of Benigno. In Marco we see shades of the "posibilista" quality that Almodóvar talks about[3] (2016, *New Yorker* interview), while in Benigno we see poignant hope as a fantasy, devoid of reality.

The film opens with a dance scene, from Pina Bausch's "Café Muller". On stage, two women in nightgowns blindly stumble about a large room in a disjointed manner. They crash into walls, and don't

---

[2] I am not implying that Benigno has not reached Oedipal stage conflictual issues; indeed he is organized both pre-Oedipally and as an Oedipal winner as depicted.

[3] The Posibilista movement in its political and emotional meanings in particular, is as it sounds. It involves believing that things are possible, i.e. there is hope, which is a motivator and an emotion that combats a sense of depression. Almodóvar's desire to create is one aspect of this. And, most likely, this helps him maintain a life affirming equilibrium that might not be otherwise present in his way of being. I am a posibilista, Almodóvar told me repeatedly, a word that can mean both a practical person and an optimist (Interview, New Yorker, Dec 5, 2016).

see obstacles such as chairs in their way. A man barely keeping in front of them hurriedly clears furniture out of the way of their unpredictable wanderings. He looks tense and is manically focused on preventing the women from crashing into objects. There is no speech. In the audience, we see two men sitting near each other. They are Benigno and Marco. At this point in the film narrative they are strangers, but are fated to meet later on. Marco is teary and crying as he watches the scene: Benigno notices Marco's emotion, but his own face registers no feeling other than an obvious interest and awareness of Marco's state. Similarly to his voyeuristic gaze out the window towards Alicia, Benigno is looking outside towards an "Other" who doesn't experience being observed. Benigno is a male nurse, who has lived with his mother his whole life and taken full care of her the past twenty years. We have no idea about his social life, though the implication is that he has none.

As noted above, before and after his mother died, Benigno, from the safety of his window, has been watching Alicia, a ballet student, go through her exercises in the school across the street. One day, some months after his mother died; as he voyeuristically looks out his window towards the ballet school, he notices Alicia accidentally drop her wallet as she walks home. Benigno takes this as a call to action. He rushes downstairs, picks up the wallet, and hurriedly catches up to her. As they walk, she initially ignores him; notably he doesn't say anything to get her attention as they walk rapidly in parallel. Finally, Alicia stops and "talks to him". Perturbed, she aggressively asks, "Why are you following me? What do you want?" Benigno shows her the wallet she'd dropped and as if to reassure her asks, "Nothing is missing?". Alicia gratefully smiles, calms down, as and they walk together we see his interest, apparently not hers, as she says, "I'm just going home." Alicia makes no comment about how strange it was that he initially didn't say anything to her as they walked in parallel. They discuss interests. She shares that she enjoys travel and silent movies. Benigno answers that he doesn't go anywhere, and that he took care of his mother until she died. Alicia shares that her mother died when she way very young. And then she excuses herself, needing to cross a busy street in order to go home. Notably she crosses recklessly, to the sound of honking cars. Clearly she is endangering her life. Benigno observes where she enters, and resolves to find a way to meet her again. He crosses the street and notes the name at the buzzer. It's that of a psychiatrist, Dr. Roncero, her father, who has an office attached to their living quarters. Benigno resolves to see him for a session. Interestingly, his thoughts are shared with us as film viewers; as he says to himself, "I might as well take advantage of the session in order to share that I miss my mother". Could this be a very veiled sign of his interest in seeking a man to connect with about loss, and to serve as a Third?[4] Someone to help him mourn the loss of his mother? After all, he could have simply decided to call up and see if Alicia would receive him for a date. Instead, he goes to her father and through him to get to her.

Alicia's father, the psychiatrist, is an austere man, who sits behind a desk and shows a detached interest but no warmth. The interview is short. There is some discussion about Benigno's sexuality as he reveals he hasn't had sex with a man or a woman. He also reveals his father is absent, having left many years ago and that he now has a new family in Sweden. Benigno advises that he hasn't seen his father since he left. He also shares that he takes sole care of his mother, does her hair, paints her nails, etc. when not at work as a nurse. Dr. Roncero takes no empathic stance. Rather, he says that Benigno has had "special experience" that needs to be "analyzed". Benigno, in a dissimulating manner, replies with feigned agreement "Of course we must analyze". Here is a clear veiled hostility to the "father", a trait that carries through all his relationships with men, with one exception, that of Marco, who I will argue plays the role of a "father" who shows affect over loss, and is well organized within reality rather than fantasy; two basic needs Benigno seems to appreciate from a

---

[4] This dynamic is multidetermined, as it is both a way of getting closer to Alicia as well as a veiled attempt per my thesis, to find a man to be known by, to clear up his confusions, as well as to foil in a competitive manner, in order to get to his daughter, who is both a fantasied object of desire, as well as substitute replacement for a lost mother.

distance, perhaps experienced early on, and still has a latent though ambivalent desire to recapture.

Especially relevant is what happens right after the session with Dr. Roncero. Benigno, an obvious boundary violator and invader, who ignores all "interdicts", notices that Dr. Roncero's secretary is not at her desk, so instead of leaving, he begins to explore other parts of the apartment to which the office is connected. Here we see his aggressive unbridled intrusiveness. There is no internal mechanism stopping him, no developed superego.

Interestingly this appears to be the very opposite as to what one writer on the film reported as, "He certainly does not mean any harm" (Lichtenstein, 2005). Indeed, Benigno, in a certain sense, "means no harm" (Almodóvar himself construed this character as naïve), but his intentions are embedded in aggressive fantasy and anger marked by respect for no authority. He enters Alicia's personal space, in effect metaphorically raping her: a harbinger of things to come when he actually enters her body. He gives her no choice. He waits for no invitation.

As portrayed in the film, to Benigno, Alicia is clearly an object rather than a subject, an object that he can enter into and do things to at will. William Fried capably describes in detail Almodóvar's depiction of Benigno's obsession with Alicia, manifesting in Benigno's fetishistic search of Alicia's private room. He focuses on Benigno discovering a series of collectible toys on a shelf. Almodóvar's eyes mirror Benigno's eyes, showing Benigno first visually surveying everything in the room, then soaking everything in by touching her things as if touching her personally. He picks up a toy truck from the shelf and puts it down, then picks up a toy acrobat with which he momentarily plays. I see that this finding of a plastic hair clip a very personal intimate item, as not something that is to be played with or put on display, but something that was in contact with Alicia herself, something when worn, is attached to her hair and goes with her no matter where she goes.

On one level the hair clip is the most intimate item in the room, outside of her clothes, but unlike her clothes it is a powerful symbolically primitive object, which seems to me resembles a set of sharp interlocking teeth, like the jaws of an aggressive shark. Fried interprets Benigno's choice of the hair clip as "symbolizing the primitive oral greed provoked in him by Alicia and her belongings. This impulse to devour the envied object is the sadistic counterpart of the passive wish to be enclosed and disappear into her" (Fried, 2017, pp. 73–74).

I agree with Fried about this dynamic but it is too narrow a diagnosis. I wish to amplify it to include feelings about Benigno's abandoning father; a father who may have been initially loved as well as organized with intertwined pre-Oedipal dynamics and nascent Oedipal rivalry. Specifically, I would suggest that the aggression symbolized by the hair clip represents not only his "biting oral aggression" (Fried, 2017), but also a counter-castration, aimed at Alicia's father Dr. Roncero, as well as Benigno's wounded and controlling mother and abandoning father and towards Alicia herself.

While Benigno is roaming around Alicia's private quarters she discovers him as she emerges from bathing. She is vulnerable, wrapped in her bathrobe, but does not scream. She looks startled, and he reassures her that he is "harmless" and then simply leaves. Alicia remains silent, perhaps in shock. She does not call out for her father, ostensibly down the hall in his office, or the secretary. This is unusual, and prophetic, as she allows danger to happen to her; Benigno leaves rapidly with his fetishistic symbolic object, the hair clip composed of a clamp with two sides of aggressive looking teeth.

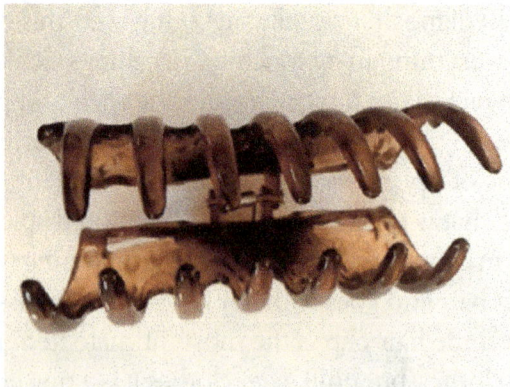

Submitted by A. Brok: A teeth-like clasp clip.

The film does not fill us in about what happened afterward between Alicia and her father. Didn't she tell him?

As time goes on, Benigno returns to Dr. Roncero, the psychiatrist, for a second session, but there is no answer when he rings the bell. Benigno does not interact with Alicia again until a fateful experience occurs. Alicia, given her recklessness, is hit by a car while crossing the street. She winds up in a coma and is interned in the hospital where Benigno works. On the basis of Benigno's excellent reputation as a nurse, Alicia's father allows him to take charge of her nursing needs, with some assistance from other nurses. Benigno bathes, feeds and takes care of all her physical needs, and importantly, talks to her, as if they were in a real relationship and they are having a conversation. He enters into a fantasy relationship with Alicia, proposing questions and answering them in his mind, as if he heard them from her. He is convinced that she hears and listens to him.

At one point Alicia's father visits the hospital and sees Benigno ministering to his daughter in an intimate way as he washes her inner thigh. Dr. Roncero is concerned, reminds Benigno of their one session, and again asks Benigno if he likes men or women. Benigno quite astutely again dissimulates by lying, saying he prefers men, thereby indicating he is gay and will pose no danger of sexual interest in Alicia. Here is another subterfuge, against a Father. Benigno not so benignly goes behind the Psychiatrist/Father's back to maintain an Oedipal victory with his silent fantasy prize woman, a woman, whose last conscious experience of him was the shock of his violation of her private space. That same man now takes care of her private parts, organizing her role in a play in which she does not know she is participating. Is this evidence of a relationship based on projective identification? As I've noted (Brok, 1998, 2009), when you relate to another via projective identification you push him/her into a role you need to be played out, but this also serves as a defense against "discovering" who the other actually is. You find what you are looking for rather than discovering the "Other". You discover who the other is only when you are interested in who they are objectively and subjectively, as opposed to who you want them to be.

To my mind this, second, encounter with Dr. Roncero represents a fantasied oedipal victory for Benigno. I am suggesting that Benigno's motives are not one dimensional, but rather multi-developmental, with differing dimensions of strength. In implying he is gay, does he Oedipally defeat and thwart a hated father whom he also wanted to love? It is helpful to recall that Benigno wanted a session to discuss that he missed his mother, and did show up for a second session, but no one answered the bell. He refuses to admit his heterosexuality, albeit mixed with regressed motives, to a father he fears, yet misses and yearns for, a father who did not help him maintain boundaries.

Benigno has individuated somewhat, but not to the developmental point where he is interested in the other as a subject as well as an object, at least when it comes to love. However, when Marco arrives on the scene, we see a type of involvement by Benigno that combines the hope of finding a man who can befriend him, as well as a man, potentially a father, he can re-educate, by advising that women are to be talked to (and with), as well as listened to. I am hypothesizing he is trying to re-unite mother and father, while at another level he is in conflict with his father and wants his mother. On an additional level, instead of going forward, as we shall see subsequently, he regresses to being literally in the womb, fully in fantasy, and only partly in reality via his sperm, which impregnates Alicia.

In sum, I am suggesting that Marco becomes a refinding of aspects of a father Benigno only somewhat had and then lost via abandonment.

Marco: the impact of a relatively healthy though damaged man in Benigno's life

Marco, by happenstance, enters into Benigno's life a second time, via his involvement with Lydia, a female bullfighter of some notoriety, who, like Alicia, is a risk taker. Benigno previously was interested in his presence, through his involvement with Marco's teary eyes, in the theater. Lydia takes on more bulls at one time than a man. This need is apparently a way of proving her worth and surpassing her father, who was a bullfighter assistant, but not a full fledged "toreador". Lydia is involved in an on and off relationship with El Niño, a famous bullfighter who has spurned her and to whom, in the film plot, she eventually returns, much to Marco's mournful acceptance.

Lydia was gored by a bull, and she too is in a coma, with considerable brain damage, and winds up in the same hospital as Alicia. Marco's engagement with Benigno occurs as he passes by the room in which Benigno is tending to Alicia; he momentarily hovers and looks inside. Alicia's breasts are exposed, in a stimulating way that Benigno observes, and Marco denies. Benigno notices Marco's curiosity, and beckons him in. Marco, with hesitation, complies. This is a plot design to reunite them, but interestingly, and in keeping with my thesis, also reflects a need of Benigno to want a man in his life. Fried (2017), on the relationship between Marco and Benigno, speculates: "Benigno's attraction to Marco, is driven initially by hope of recruiting a man in circumstances similar to his own, as a secret sharer or a proselyte to his own delusion" (Fried, 2017, p.79). I would instead suggest that the affiliated need of Benigno towards Marco was motivated by the fantasy fulfillment of re-finding a good Father, a father who has feelings and sentiment. This failed with Dr. Roncero (Alicia's father) because of his demeanor and the conflict over Alicia. It was indeed easier to befriend Marco, who was needy and vulnerable, as well as not an overt competitor. He also fulfilled an important capacity for reality testing, which Benigno was missing, and probably wanted, but also successfully managed to avoid.

Marco is a journalist who wanders the world, writing about travel. He is represented in the film as a combination of a strong man lodged in reality and a poor soul in a state of mourning. He is in mourning for a second time, having already lost a significant girlfriend to addiction, and then to her recovery and a happy marriage to someone else. He indeed is stuck in a repetitive circle of finding, losing, and mourning. Now he has lost Lydia to her former boyfriend "El Niño", who has returned to love her again even though she is in a coma.

In a poignant scene, prior to her being gored, Lydia had tried to "talk to Marco" about her reuniting with "El Niño", but Marco had been so involved in his own narrative that Lydia had no chance to be listened to.

Marco's hopes for remaining with Lydia, hoping for her recovery and a relationship, are dashed by his discovery of "El Niño" at her bedside one day. He has returned to be with her, even in a coma. A severe blow, as Marco is once more isolated, and this too moves him closer to Benigno.

Benigno shares with Marco the importance of talking to Alicia and eventually confides that he intends to marry Alicia and that they will live together in his apartment. Marco, the voice of reality, confronts Benigno in an angry way, attempting to have him realize the unreality of his delusion. Benigno is not moved by this, and simply brushes it off. When Marco reacts with horror and concern, Benigno, unfazed, indignantly argues that he and Alicia "get on better than most married couples." Her lack of a voice in the matter goes completely unmentioned by him, a voice that Marco provides, with no apparent impact!

Marco, sad and depressed, leaves the country to continue his international journalistic work, while Benigno, stimulated by a silent movie, breaks an important nurse–patient, man–woman, human–human boundary.

Silence and isolation

An important part of the film is the significance of silence, juxtaposed with the importance of talking. Alicia likes silent movies. Benigno, in an attempt to get close to her, also goes to silent movies. Silent movies are the opposite of talking with someone. Charlie Chaplin, for example, refused to make talking pictures for many years, believing he could better communicate with international audiences via pantomime, which he felt was universally understood.

Chaplin maintained this approach until he began to make more serious films about political and social events (*Modern Times, The Great Dictator, Monsieur Verdoux, Limelight,* etc.), (Brok, 1998, 2006; Villegas López, 1998). I have suggested that one of the unconscious reasons Chaplin held on to the use of silent film, even though the technology for talkies was available, was that it symbolically kept him close to his mother. He too, like Benigno, had an estranged and distant father. Language and talking are a way of communicating when one is separate from an Other. In this light, I have elsewhere suggested that the transition from silence to talking represented for Chaplin his leaving the world of the mother and entering the world of the father[5] (Brok, 1991, 2006; Lynn, 1997.pp.428–431; Robinson, 1985, p.519; Brok, 1998). Serious themes are best recognized through speech. Talking involves the bridging of a space via language, a space not totally necessary in very early development, due to a good-enough mother's non-verbal empathic reading of her baby. In this sense, Benigno's emphasis on talking with her (to her) involves his attempt to be a separate person with a female but sadly without needing her to be a responsive subject who can talk to and with him. With a responsive male like Marco, it's a little easier for Benigno, as it meets a developmental need, albeit ambivalently desired.

Deep in his psyche, though, is Benigno's biting aggression, as demonstrated by his stealing the hair clasp that looks like a pair of teeth. In addition to oral aggression, as I hypothesized earlier, it represents a castration tool, which is identified with, rather than feared. In this he is identifying with the aggressor as a defense: "I am the castrator, I am in power, not my father or castrating mother."

The narrative of this film takes a breathtaking and surprising turn when Benigno impregnates Alicia. We learn of this through a clever

---

[5] I have suggested that Chaplin entered fully the world of the father when he married Oona O'Neill, who represented his young mother. She was 17 and he was 57. This coincided with his making films in which he, Chaplin, talked. In addition, Chaplin's marriage to Oona was a clear oedipal victory. Her father, the playwright Eugene O'Neill, hated Chaplin. Oona worshiped Charlie, and was his total self-object, and after his death gave no interviews, i.e. talked to no one (Brok, 1998).

technical device used by Almodóvar to hide from his audience "what should not be seen" (interview, Guardian, 2012). What should not be seen is seen, a primal scene that should not be experienced, a meta-phoric incest that ought not to be committed, a rape that should not be expressly demonstrated. Almodóvar inserts a film within a film, a short silent film with explicit sexual content to represent the motiva-tion for Benigno's future transgressive sexual act.

Benigno, as a way of "being with" Alicia via identification, attends a silent movie, *The Shrinking Lover*. The content of this film-within-a-film gives us a deeply nuanced look into Benigno's mental life of erotic ambitions and desires.[6]

The silent movie is about Alfredo and Amparo. The opening sce-ne is in a laboratory where Amparo, a scientist, is working on a new formula for nutrition. Alfredo, her boyfriend, who is slightly over-weight, has been accused of being selfish. So, he attempts to prove his lack of selfishness by impulsively drinking Amparo's experimental new weight loss potion, serving as a subject in her experiment, so she can test it out. His taking in her product proves to be tragic; instead of making him lose weight, the potion makes him shrink. He gets smaller and smaller.[7] At some point, he leaves in order to avoid making Amparo feel bad, and goes to his mother, a woman he does not like, but who will hide him. Ten years go by, and Amparo even-tually finds Alfredo, and rescues him from his mother. He is still a shrunken man, who could fit in the palm of her hand. But, they are together again. One night, as the go to sleep, tiny Alfredo, no bigger than a bug, explores her naked body as she sleeps, and eventually quite willingly and out of desire, completely enters her vagina. Amparo seems to feel pleasure without waking up as tiny Alfredo disappears into her vagina. One infers that Alfredo will not come out. The implication is he cannot be with a woman as an adult man,

---

[6] Almodóvar has been quoted as saying, there are some things one should not see among friends, in alluding to the insertion of the silent movie to the script.

[7] To my mind the shrinking symbolized that mother's nutrition was not nurturing and empowering but rather diminishing. Bad milk from a bad breast?

but only as a child, going back into the womb. Sexuality is organized around losing oneself in another.

After Benigno sees the silent movie, the next scene in *Talk to Her* has Benigno back in his role as nurse to Alicia in the hospital and talking to her about his experience. He tells her he saw a "disturbing film", and narrates the plot. Soon after, during normal routine nursing tasks, a co-worker nurse notices that Alicia has missed her period, which Benigno explains away as a happenstance, i.e. that she is often late. Eventually there is an investigation and its discovered that Alicia is pregnant.

There is a staff meeting about this. The administrative head of the hospital is hostile and in a rage, exclaiming, "Who is the son of a bitch who would do such an egregious act in my hospital?". Benigno's immediate medical director takes a more kindly tack, saying, "Let's not accuse anyone until we know they are not innocent". But he too eventually is shocked by the fact of Benigno's non-benign actions.

Talk to Her: and perhaps to Him

Activated by the silent film, Benigno could no longer hold it together, and crossed a final boundary. He gave in to a combination of sexual desires, the need to prove his manhood, and, at the same time disappear into someone. A final, naïvely constructed Oedipal victory.[8]

Ultimately he is jailed for his act. Alicia delivers a still born baby. To have fathered a healthy baby, would have been proof of his phallic potency, of an Oedipal victory, the possibility of his being a father or taking the place of his father through his being the one who impregnates his Mother/Alicia. In the process of giving birth, Alicia wakes up from her coma. So we have a rape, and yet an act of bringing full life to a "sleeping beauty".

While in jail, one of the sentimental nurses, (Rosa) receives a call

---

[8] His identification with the diminished Alfredo in the silent film also demonstrates this, but with a twist. Unlike Alfredo, he doesn't go "all in" but rather part in, via impregnating her as a separate person.

from Marco, who is in Jordan writing a travel book. Marco, while discussing his shock at reading about the death of Lydia in a newspaper, is also informed of Benigno's incarceration. Rosa, I suggest, plays the role of retrieving the missing lost father that Benigno probably wished for. Notably, Marco asks if Rosa visits Benigno, and she replies that she emotionally can't after what he has done, but does encourage Marco to see him. Marco rushes back to see if he can help his friend. They speak in jail, Benigno is told the baby died, and falsely, that Alicia is still in a coma.

Benigno suggests that Marco stay in his apartment, and Marco agrees, thereby taking Benigno's place. Why Benigno suggests this is relevant to Benigno's dynamics. I am suggesting that, Benigno is putting Marco, representing his father, back in his rightful place; as well as identifying himself with Marco.

Benigno, feeling all is lost, believing that he will never get out of jail, unconsciously gives father back to mother, giving Marco to Alicia, and takes an overdose of pills, from which he dies. Benigno's act has a quality of Liebestod, a mutual death in order to be together. She is in a coma, he is in a coma of death. However, as Almodóvar has constructed the narrative, we also see a return of a father surrogate to a mother surrogate.

In the case of Benigno, we see that his drive to have a baby, i.e. to be a "Father", was deeply intertwined with a regressive need to be "in another woman" as well as to "give a woman his semen", a part of himself to join with her egg to create baby. We might note that what activates his impregnation of Alicia is the scene in the silent film where Alfredo disappears totally into Amparo. Benigno cannot do that; he is an adult. He just won't fit. His rape of Alicia is an act of an adult man who treats a woman as an object of his creation and has coitus in the service of wanting too to be a father, yet needing to do this by breaking through an incest barrier and getting himself well punished and truly confused about it. Indeed, I am hypothesizing. As Almodóvar's script indicates, Benigno is an adult, but in shrunken form, as symbolized by his identification with Alfredo in the silent film. Part child, part adult, Benigno is a mixture of both. His rape of Alicia puts him back into a locked womb as represented by his incarceration. Yet he evinces a faint hope of wanting a relationship with a realistic and compassionate "third", as evidenced by his involvement with Marco, a third who represents his father, and who he re-installs in the correct place with his mother/Alicia. For Benigno, component feelings towards Alicia are a mixture of a regressive wish to fuse with mother, an Oedipal wish to win mother from father and have her baby, and a wish to return mother to father (Marco), and take his appropriate role as a child.

We might note that Benigno gives Marco his apartment and in effect returns his father to his mother. The denouement comes with his death, ending his dream of individuation and futile attempt to be a father/husband to his mother, symbolized by having sex and impregnating Alicia. Benigno is in a mixed up world of being his father, being like a father and surrendering to his father as represented by placing Marco in his apartment that was to be for him and Alicia.

The film, unlike its beginning, ends on a hopeful note. It is again a theatre scene.[9] Marco is in attendance and so is the now awake Alicia. They both notice each other. The performance they watch involves men dancing with enticing women in a sexually evocative manner. In the final scene, a man and woman have a lovely private dance. Things are returned to normal. A couple is formed, a couple who can talk with each other. At intermission, Alicia notices Marco without knowing who he is, and Marco notices Alicia; they have some conversation and there is a resonance between them, a resonance that has a quality of normality rather than pathology. The implication is that they will be together.

---

[9] Almodóvar notes about his structure for the film: "I was clear what I wanted to do with this movie. It's very simple to explain. I started with the performance of "Café Muller" by Pina Bausch. She actually gave me the autograph that Benigno gives to Alicia in the movie six years ago. That autograph was mine. The atmosphere is darker in this film. We end the film with another Pina Bausch piece, which brings closure"(Guardian interview, 2012). And to this author's mind, a double experience, of a life not being fulfilled (Benigno) and a possibility of two lives (Marco's and Alicia's) evolving positively.

References

Almodóvar, P. (Director). (2002). Spain. *Talk to Her.* [Motion Picture]. Spain: El Deseo.

Arroyo, J. (2002). Interview with Almodóvar, Wednesday, July 31, 2002. *The Guardian,* UK.

Brok, A.J. (1991). The playing alliance in film and on the couch. Paper presented, Spring meeting, Div. 39, APA, Chicago.

———(1998). Attachment and involvement as modes of romantic coupling. Paper presented, Division 39, Spring Meeting, American Psychological Association, Boston.

———(2006a). What can we learn from Charlie Chaplin? Invited presentation, Annual Conference, American Psychological Association, New Orleans, La. August 4.

———(2006b). The obtainable moment of desire, the elusive construction of love. Invited Presentation: Sponsored by the Pacific Northwest Psychoanalytic Society, Section I, Division 39 APA, The Northwest Alliance for Psychoanalytic Study, and the Seattle Psychoanalytic Society and Institute, Oct 14, Seattle, Washington.

———(2008). Section 1 Invited Presentation on "Discovering vs. Finding in Analytic Work for both analyst and Patient." Annual Spring Meeting, Division 39 (Psychoanalysis,) APA, New York. April 4.

Chasseguet-Smirgel, J. (1985). The Ego ideal. London: Free Association Books, p. 15.

Freud,S (1921). Group Psychology and analysis of the Ego. *Standard Edition* 18:65–144.

Fried, W. (2017) Critical Flicker Fusion: Psychoanalysis at the Movies. pp. 71–83, London: Karnac.

Lichtenstein, D. (2005) Talk to her. *International Journal of Psychoanalysis* 86(3):905–914.

Lynn, K. S. (1997). *Charlie Chaplin and His Times.* New York: Simon and Schuster, pp. 430–431.

Mackenzie, S. (2002). All About my Father: *The Guardian,* UK.

Max, D.T. (2016). The evolution of Pedro Almodóvar. *The New Yorker,* December 5, 2016.

Robinson, D. (1985). *Chaplin, his life and Art.* New York: McGraw Hill, pp. 519–528.

Sabbadini, A. (2007). The Talking Cure: from Freud to Almodóvar, Hable con Ella, in *Projected Shadow*, ed. A. Sabbadini. London: Routledge, pp 65–72.

Target M. and Fonagy, P (2002). Fathers in Modern Psychoanalysis and Society, The role of the Father in child Development. In *The Importance of Fathers: A Psychoanalytic Re-Evaluation, ed.* Trowel, J, & Etchegoyen, A. New York: Taylor and Francis.

Villegas López, M. (2003). *Charles Chaplin, El genio del Cine,* Ediciones. Argentina, SA: Ediciones Folio.

CHAPTER 16

Crocodiles, Lambs and Soul Murder:
Reflections on Pedro Almodóvar's *Bad Education*

Lucille Spira

What happens to a lamb when cornered by a crocodile? In Pedro Almodóvar's *Bad Education* (2004), murder is the subject and a young boy—the object. In the throes of a sexual encounter with a man he doesn't trust, Enrique Goded, a film director and auteur, recalls a tale of a woman who embraces a crocodile as it is devouring her. She had deliberately thrown herself into its pit. Was she suicidal? Or, was she trying to escape from something even more frightening? The manifest content of Almodóvar's film centers on murder and death; here I consider an underlying theme—the abuse of a child. To me the film stimulates us to consider the perspective of both victim and predator.

No synopsis or commentary can substitute for the pleasure of watching Pedro Almodóvar's *Bad Education*. The provocative themes and the perfectly cast actors, with their expressive faces and nuanced body language, pull the audience in. It is a complex movie with fluid boundaries between past and present and between movie-as-frame to movie-within. As with a Chinese box, when one question is answered, another emerges.

The stunning opening credits accompanied by music consisting of a full orchestra relying heavily on percussion and strings, portend a movie with serious themes.

A Director at Work

Enrique, the auteur director, is searching a newspaper for inspiration. A story about a dead man sitting on a motorcycle, alone, in the desert catches his attention. Aloud, he fills in the missing pieces, drawing upon his imagination. A knock on the door interrupts his creative process; he becomes irritated and tells his assistant to say that he's out. The visitor overhears this, and sees Enrique at his desk. Undeterred by the director's obvious lack of interest in seeing him, the visitor inches forward and announces himself as Ignacio Rodriguez. Enrique recognizes that as the name of an old friend, a man he has not seen in sixteen years. But very soon he becomes uneasy. The man before him does not resemble the Ignacio that he remembers.

He tells Enrique that he is a stage actor in amateur theatre, and that he would like to transition from theatre into films. He hopes that Enrique will have a part for him in one of his movies. He calls himself by his stage name these days: Ángel Andrade. He has a story that he says that he wrote and gives it to Enrique, saying that he hopes he will be able to adapt it into a script for a film.

During the encounter, Enrique twice refers to Ángel as Ignacio, but Ángel stiffly corrects him, saying that he wants to be called Ángel so that Enrique will think of him as an actor. The roles are reversed temporarily; he acts more like a director than an actor looking for a part. And Enrique tenses up when Ángel corrects him.

Ángel is surprised when Enrique ends the meeting, saying that he will contact him after he reads the script. After Ángel leaves, Enrique's assistant asks the director if he will see him again. Enrique responds that he will not, adding that an actor wanting a part is not erotic.

Ángel is portrayed as hungry, clumsy, and naive--no match for Enrique, who appears analytical and tough, not easily seduced, except by a story.

A Director and a Story

The story that Ángel gives Enrique is titled The Visit. It is a film noir page-turner with a back-story, and the audience sees the story transform into a movie. Almodóvar structures his movie in a way that the outer movie gets defined as real life and The Visit as the movie. The audience suspends disbelief.

Almodóvar, in an interview, said that his hope is to meld reality with fantasy (Hirschberg, 2004).

The Movie Within: Zahara[1]

The Visit initially centers on Zahara, who, when performing in drag at gay clubs, lip-synchs to the songs of a famous Spanish film star, Sara Montiel. After a club performance, Zahara, a transvestite, picks up a guy with whom she had been flirting. They go to a hotel to have sex. While busy with her pickup, her friend, Paquito, is arranging to steal the man's motorbike. The hotel scene has comic bits, though its seriousness becomes clear later on as the underlying theme develops.

When Zahara realizes that her pick-up is actually her first love, also named Enrique, she ditches the scheme to steal his motorbike. Searching his wallet she learns that he is broke, so she leaves him money and a note inviting him to catch up. As she has also learned that he is married and has a child she writes in the note that she will not make trouble. Is the money she leaves to repair him? Or, is it a way to empower herself?

Her pickup is drunk and barely awake, and he has difficulty getting an erection frustrating Zahara's efforts at fellating him. Yet he prods her to keep going without any consideration to what this might mean for her. Later, as she is about to leave, and he is soundly sleeping, she notices that he has an erection. She mounts him to

---

[1] Pronouns used for Zahara, and the adult Ignacio, are intended to respect the gender-fluid characters as portrayed in the scene discussed.

pleasure herself, saying aloud that she has been longing for years to have sex with Enrique.

In the real world, having sex with a person who is asleep or otherwise unconscious is generally considered rape. Here, for Zahara, it is a romantic encounter—a wish or a fantasy fulfilled. Zahara has her own moral code; she can steal money from unknown Johns, but not from a first love.

Zahara Goes to Church

The scene shifts to a nearby church. The priest there, Zahara's former principal and teacher, Father Manolo, sexually abused her when she was Ignacio, a boy at his school. Zahara and Paquito come in as Father Manolo is saying Mass. Zahara stands out wearing a bright green dress, a hot pink sweater, and platform shoes. Zahara intends to confront the priest while her friend steals the church vessels. Father Manolo is leading the parishioners in the mea culpa (through my fault), but instead we hear her say, "through your fault." The priest looks alarmed, and eyes her with suspicion.

At the end of the Mass, she follows the priest into the sacristy. He asks why she is there. As if she were a messenger, she responds that she is Ignacio Rodriguez's sister, and that she wants him to know that Ignacio is dead. He pretends that he cannot recall Ignacio, but says that he is sorry. He tells her that she should not be there. She leaves.

As fast as she slips out, she slips back in. But now they are no longer in the sacristy but rather they are in his nearby office. Father Manolo had just been looking tenderly at an old photo of Ignacio; the way he looks at him seems as if he still has feelings for the boy in the photo. He is angry when he notices that Zahara has returned, and tells her that he does not believe that Ignacio is dead, or that she is his sister, or even that she is a woman. In a condescending manner, he orders her again to leave.

But here Zahara is not the easy-going character of the hotel scene. She does not allow him to intimidate her, and she angrily pursues her desire for revenge. As she tells him that she was/is Ignacio, Father

Manolo seems distraught. He must reconcile the person whom he sees before him, with the boy in the photo whom, acting upon his own desire he violated. Though he reacts angrily, his facial expression is one of suffering. And Zahara does not let up on her intent to punish him for sexually abusing her; as she puts it, for giving her a "bad education." If he does not give her a large sum of money, she says, she will expose him to the newspapers.

The theme of exchanging sex for money connects the two scenes; when Zahara picked up the man in the club, she wanted both sex and money. But when she realized that he was her first love, she was willing to forgo money. Unlike the way Father Manolo behaved with Ignacio, implied here is that Zahara does not purposefully abuse the one she loves/d.

In this scene, Zahara is not a scammer, but a former victim demanding her rights. Once she was powerless with the priest, but now their positions are reversed. She is an avenging angel.

As Zahara argues with Father Manolo, Father José knocks on the door and reports that the church vessels are missing. After he leaves, Zahara tells Father Manolo that when she was at school she hated Father José. How this encounter between Father Manolo and Zahara turns out, the audience learns at the end when The Visit, and the movie that frames it, moves toward conclusion.

School Days: Ignacio and Father Manolo

Now the scene flashes back into the distant past. We hear the voice of young Ignacio, and see him as a schoolboy on an outing. Boys are swimming and enjoying themselves in a beautiful country setting. Ignacio, separated from the other boys, is singing a version of Moon River; Father Manolo accompanies him on the guitar. One line of the song might be a prequel to the danger that lies ahead: "I am longing to know what is hidden in the dark."

But the idyllic setting belies any lurking danger. Father Manolo looks both rapturous and tortured by the boy's beautiful voice and presence. Orality is expressed through the hungry eye. He seems to be struggling not to act on his sexual feelings for the boy, but if this is so, his better angels lose. Hidden from the audience's sight by a tree, Father Manolo moves in and attempts an assault. We hear Ignacio say no and we see him running away. Falling, he injures his forehead. Blood flows from the wound toward the center of his body, as if splitting him in half. I understand this as a graphic representation of a psychic split.

The story teller has put words in Ignacio's mouth that suggest how an adult might retrospectively understand the impact of such an act—"it was then that my life was split in two, never to come together again." Almodóvar draws attention to the fact that even an attempt at assault on a child becomes a negatively transforming event, and a death blow to innocence. Junot Díaz (2018), the prize-winning author and victim of child rape describes the aftermath following the abuse he suffered. He says, "That shit cracked the planet of me in half, threw me completely out of orbit, into the lightless regions of space where life is not possible" (p. 24).

The Priests Enjoy a Meal

The next scene may explain why Zahara says that s/he hated Father José. Father José has arranged for Ignacio to sing in honor of Father Manolo's promotion. A large towering, overweight man, Father José escorts Ignacio from the school lunchroom to the priest's dining room. Ignacio looks unhappy and anxious. Coached by Father José, he sings in a clear voice, and with his graceful gestures—spreading out his hands—he seems to be offering himself. Given the toxic atmosphere, it's ironic that the song is about a gardener lovingly cultivating his flowers; this is both a metaphor and propaganda.

The camera focuses in on Father Manolo's face; he is barely able to look at Ignacio. The viewer is under the illusion that he/she is privy to Father Manolo's inner struggle. He looks tortured—as if the boy's beautiful voice and evocative gestures arouse him. It appears that Father José's "gift" of the boy was an act of hostility both toward Ignacio and Father Manolo.

In trying to avoid gazing at Ignacio, it's as if Father Manolo is attempting to ward off his feelings—sexual feelings, or, perhaps ones of shame. While they dine, the priests watch the boy's performance, and also Father Manolo's reaction to him. They act as though they are oblivious to the suffering depicted. This suggests that they in *Bad Education* (2004) are complicit—hypocrites. It seems that Almodóvar here wants us to see the group, not one individual, as guilty.

Almodóvar has said that predators blend into society and are known only to their victims (Strauss, 1994/2006). To me the dining room scene is similar to a crocodile pit; getting too near is dangerous. If one is pushed into the pit, as it appears here, the verdict likely is murder, not suicide.

In contrast to the heaviness of the dining room scene, the next one is lulling in its beauty. Shot partly in slow motion, it shows the boys and the priests playing a game of soccer. Ignacio and his teammates are running, scoring goals. During the game, the action freezes. Ignacio's eyes fix on the boy on the other team, who, in turn, fixes his gaze on him. They both appear struck—pierced by Cupid's arrow. This is the beginning of the love between Enrique and Ignacio. Later, the boys are at Mass, and we see Enrique smiling at Ignacio who is singing in the choir.

The two boys manage to find some pleasure at a local movie house. As they watch a film, Enrique and Ignacio fondle each other; for Ignacio, evidently, this type of intimacy is new.

Pleasure and Pain

That evening, restless in bed, Ignacio goes to the bathroom. Enrique soon follows. They talk about their feelings about what happened at the movie. Ignacio says that although he enjoyed what they did together he believes that in the eyes of God he committed a sin. He has incorporated the teachings of the church; sex is for procreating; sex for pleasure is prohibited. Enrique sees it differently, and explains that he does not believe in God, but in pleasure. While they are conversing, they hear heavy footsteps and realize that it's Father

Manolo. Fearing that they will be punished, they lock the bathroom door and huddle together hoping to evade him. After what looks like a frenzied pursuit, he finds them and threatens to knock down the door unless they open it.

As the door opens, Father Manolo pulls Enrique out, causing him to fall. Then he orders him to leave. Fearing for Ignacio's safety, Enrique says he will not leave him alone with the priest. Does Ignacio intuit that Father Manolo is a sexual predator? Ignacio, also wanting to protect Enrique, tells him to leave, which he does.

While searching for the boys, Father Manolo's expression and movements are ominous, reminiscent of a character in a horror movie. This scene captures the horribleness of an adult's overreaction toward a young person who is first becoming aware of his sexual self and relational needs.

A Sacrifice

Father Manolo escorts Ignacio to the chapel to assist him at Mass, as if God's holiness might wash over Ignacio. De Masi (2007) says that pedophiles may have either a cynical view of the child or an idealizing one. Here it appears that in Father Manolo's eyes Ignacio has lost the idealization he once attributed to him, but that he looks to the religious service to restore that state. By pushing him toward religion in this way, it suggests that if he cannot have Ignacio's body he can control his mind through religion. Such behavior is a compromise; a way to appease both id and superego. The fantasy is that uniting with God will allow purity to overtake carnality. After the Mass, Father Manolo demands to know what occurred between the boys. He seems not to be able to temper his obsession with sex and Ignacio, and obviously suspects something sexual.

His questioning of Ignacio suggests that it is a way to gratify voyeuristic impulses, to look into a private moment. To be curious, to want to learn about what we do not know or understand is not perverse. The wish to see beyond our self and immediate environment is human nature, and thought by Freud to be rooted in our wish to know how babies are born. Here Almodóvar shows us an unwelcome intrusiveness into the secrets of an other.

Though the questioning takes place in church rather than in an actual confessional, a child raised in the Catholic faith, being asked by a priest to report on his behavior, likely would associate the questioning with confession. Coercing a confession—inside or outside the confessional—is to debase the intent of confession and as such is perverse.

Ignacio denies that anything occurred between him and Enrique. Not reassured, Father Manolo tells Ignacio that he must promise never to do whatever he did again. The suspiciousness that Father Manolo shows verges on paranoia. Does Almodóvar want us to see that Father Manolo perceives Enrique as his rival for Ignacio?

Father Manolo makes a comment that he ought to expel Enrique. By doing so he could imagine that he was saving Ignacio from the badness Father Manolo attributes to him rather than clearing a path for himself. Father Manolo temporarily appears kinder and calmer. We see him gently wiping away Ignacio's tears. In a real situation, the unconscious splitting off of aggression, or projecting it allows the projector the illusion of goodness. Here, however, the audience understands what Father Manolo caused is not goodness but pain.

In a desperate attempt to keep Enrique from being sent away, Ignacio says that if Father Manolo does not expel him, he will do what Father Manolo wants. I presume that Father Manolo allows himself to be gratified; if so, by sacrificing himself in this way he has violated his own beliefs. What was once forbidden is now sanctioned, at least when it is under my auspices, with me. Benvenuto believes that the perverse person draws pleasure from breaking a rule and as such welcomes rules (Richards, A.K., 2018).

As Blackman and Dring (2016), along with De Masi (2007), correctly remind us, that not all pedophiles abuse children. When an adult does use a child as a sex object, they are more accurately termed child abusers rather than pedophiles (Blackman and Dring, 2016).

The Aftermath

The next morning Ignacio and the other boys are in the yard exercising. Ignacio is searching for Enrique. A boy is outside by the gate standing with a woman with a car. Father Manolo expelled him after all, and he is crying. He is crying because he realizes that he has been separated from Ignacio. Hypocrisy and sadism have won out, fueling Father Manolo's jealousy and lust, not love. The rival had to be eliminated. A boy was sacrificed. Fathers' readiness to sacrifice or kill off their sons is the stuff of myths and biblical stories, the story of Abraham and Isaac famously among them. Molofsky (2004) discusses *The Return*, a film that raises the question of whether a father's cruelty toward his sons is necessarily sadism, or his way of preparing them for what he might perceive as the harsh life ahead. She considers the possibility of an "Abraham complex" in which a father needs to sacrifice his son to maintain his own sense of his virility and youth. Here, the priest is a stand-in for the father, and although he is in conflict, his behavior appears motivated by his inability to control his lustful and abusive impulses.

Back to Business: Producing The Visit

After reading Ángel's story, Enrique decides that he will make the movie after all, but as the movie develops producing The Visit is fraught with conflict and melodrama for Enrique and Ángel. The two celebrate at a club, and later Ángel drives Enrique home. In the car, a song from their past plays on the radio; Enrique looks to Ángel for a sign that he recognizes it. When he realizes that Ángel does not, he becomes defensive and suspicious.

At Enrique's the action is erotic and tense. They argue when Ángel tells Enrique that he wants to play Zahara, a role that Enrique cannot imagine for him. Before this interchange there is a sexy scene with Enrique swimming naked while he watches Ángel undress again, again another instance of the hungry eye. As Ángel notices Enrique watching him, he decides not to step out of his jockey shorts. He is behaving as if he is fearful of a sexual encounter, or wants to avoid sexual intimacy. Enrique calls him a cockteaser. This leaves open the possibility that Enrique cannot empathize with what Ángel suffered when he was Ignacio.

Later, it seems that if Ángel agrees to have sex with Enrique he will get to play Zahara. But Enrique wants the story without conditions. Ángel wants the part, or he will take back the story. Enrique angrily tells him to leave. He already had told Ángel that he does not trust him and that he is not the Ignacio that he once knew. Ángel says that if he had remained that boy, he would not have survived. This recalls to the viewers the abuse that Ignacio suffered, and Almodóvar gains sympathy for Ángel by presenting Enrique as somewhat callous.

The scene ends with both men frustrated in their desire. But the story is not over. Much like an analyst, Almodóvar intends to uncover what is being defended against,—"that which is hidden in the dark." Unable to quell his lingering doubt about Ángel, Enrique goes in search for answers—Is Ángel lethal? Is he even Ignacio?—the audience wonders: Is Enrique paranoid?

Another Visit

Enrique visits Ignacio's hometown. He talks with Ángel's mother, who tells him that Ignacio has been dead for several years. Ángel is not Ignacio but Ignacio's younger brother, Juan.

Ignacio's mother gives Enrique a letter that he wrote to him not long before he died. In that letter he writes that he knows that Enrique is a director and tells him that he wrote a story that he would like him to read. That story is The Visit, the same story that Ángel brought to Enrique's office. He also mentions there that Father Manolo is not any longer a priest but a publisher who calls himself Señor Berenguer.

As Enrique understands that Ignacio is dead, his concerns are: How did he die? How far will Juan/Ángel go to achieve his desire? Many truth-seekers find that what they uncover is painful. But for others the truth can be freeing. Enrique seems shocked, and perhaps sad. But now he, again like an analyst and patient, cannot resist a more complete understanding. To direct this film and to answer his questions he cannot rely solely on his imagination. He must jump into the pit with Juan/Ángel.

Enrique and Juan/Ángel

When he reconnects with Juan/Ángel, Enrique is surprised to see that he is thinner. Less masculine-looking, he now appears as if he could play Zahara. He apologizes for having tried to coerce Enrique into giving him the part; he only wants a chance to audition for it. Almodóvar has shown us that in Enrique's absence, Juan/Ángel studied with an impersonator who is a drag queen to learn how to play Zahara. Enrique agrees to give him the role. He had experienced, first hand, Ángel's acting skill. Enrique now knows that Juan/Ángel acted the victim when he is, actually, a perpetrator. Enrique does not reveal that he knows that Ángel is Juan, that Ignacio is dead, and also that Ángel stole Ignacio's story.

Their relationship becomes a sexual one. As Enrique embraces Ángel/Juan it is then that he recalls the story of the lady and the crocodile pit. This suggests that Enrique considers Juan/Ángel to be a crocodile. Is Enrique on a path of suicide? In an interview with Almodóvar, Strauss (1994/2006) pointed out the carnivorous aspect of the sex depicted here. When Enrique takes the initiative, the sex scene between them is not tender; Juan/Ángel appears to be suffering. Almodóvar shows, through Enrique's aggressive approach with Juan/Ángel, that you cannot let a crocodile get the upper hand. A director must take charge.

Another Visitor

Enrique and the audience are still to learn what really happened to Ignacio. In the movie that developed from Ignacio's story, Enrique changed the ending. In Enrique's version, Zahara is strangled by

Father José while Father Manolo stands by; he is complicit in the murder. Whereas in Ignacio's version of the story, Zahara is not killed. When Juan/Ángel questions why Enrique changed the ending, Enrique explains that it is necessary to ensure that Zahara could not ever expose them. Here it is clear that Enrique sees the priests as crocodiles. Juan/Ángel had to act the scene. I consider that Enrique changed the script partly to get revenge on Juan/Ángel—make him feel emotional pain. The shooting of The Visit ends. The ending has had an effect on Juan; he appears shaken and tearful.

As Enrique is about to leave the set, a visitor approaches him— Señor Berenguer, formerly Father Manolo. Through his eyes we see what caused Ignacio's death and what his life had been. He/she displays his/her perfectly formed female breasts and hoped, through surgery, to get what he/she believes is a more perfect body. He/she is also a junkie who was blackmailing Señor Berenguer for what he did to him when he was a boy. We see that Ignacio humiliates him and Señor Berenguer tolerates this. When Berenguer tells Ignacio that then he had loved him, Ignacio sets him straight—you do not love a ten year old like that. Though Ignacio seems on edge, angry, and sadistic toward Señor Berenguer, Almodóvar shows us, Ignacio did not incorporate or identify with Father Manolo's sexual perverseness.

Berenguer tells Enrique that Juan seduced him in Ignacio's apartment. They had an affair and he fell madly in love with Juan. The audience sees Juan teasing Señor Berenguer and extracting gifts from him. Señor Berenguer imagines that with Ignacio out of the way, he and Juan will be together. Juan encourages Señor Berenguer's fantasy.

The audience can imagine why Juan might want Ignacio dead. We see his anger at Ignacio for stealing money from the family. There is the suggestion that Ignacio is the mother's favorite child. Is Juan jealous? Juan has a grudge against Ignacio for his cross dressing; making a spectacle of himself in their small town. Does Almodóvar want the audience to see that Juan's ambition is what propels his role in Ignacio's murder? With Ignacio dead Juan would have his brother's manuscript to leverage his way into the movie business.

Juan and Señor Berenguer supply Ignacio with a lethal dose of heroin that he/she self-administers. After the murder, Juan abandons him. With the loss of Juan, Señor Berenguer seems desperate. In the scene with Enrique, he appears disheveled. Obsessed by Juan, as he was with the young Ignacio, he says that he will not give up trying to get him back. Without access to the object of his desire, aware that the other is separate and that he cannot control him, Berenguer's defenses break down; he appears as if he is on the verge of hysteria.

Enrique now knows what happened to Ignacio, and with this knowledge, he can no longer continue his relationship with Juan/Ángel, whom he understands to be not simply an ambitious con artist, but a murderer, and lethal. Enrique tells Juan that he must leave. With seeming reluctance Juan does, but not before casting himself as a victim of his brother's cross dressing and stealing from the family. Pontalis(2013), in a beautiful monograph about brothers, suggests that envy or jealousy between brothers is about winning the mother's love; the wish to be the favorite, or sometimes the only one; Juan wants to be a star.

At the end of the movie, news blips show how the characters fared. Juan we learn marries a woman, and achieves his stardom, but later is relegated to TV. Señor Berenguer, until his death, continued his fruitless pursuit of Juan—who may have been responsible for his death. Enrique continues to create stories for the movies; his passion is to create. In portraying Ignacio's story, Enrique has honored Ignacio. As D'Lugo(2006) points out, Almodóvar has shown how sexual desire transforms into the desire for a story. This is not unlike Freud's idea about the importance of sublimation. The ego has gained dominance over the id.

Discussion

D'Lugo (2006), brings an historical perspective to his rich analysis of *Bad Education*. He says that by inserting nostalgia in the form of old songs, scenes from old movies, and other cultural memorabilia into each of the three time periods depicted in the film, Almodóvar connects his Spanish audience with their history. This gives the film personal meaning to those viewers. To me creating nostalgia generally sharpens the difference between past and present—what is old and what is new. This emphasizes the dynamic aspect of change.

Gutiérrez-Albilla (2017/2018), in his scholarly work analyzes the themes, symbols, and the circumstances depicted in particular Almodóvar films, including *Bad Education*, for what they tell us about the cultural trauma suffered by the Spanish people during the Franco reign and how it might impact the survivors.

My focus is on how a particular type of soul murder—sexual abuse of a child that has a devastating effect on the child. In *Bad Education* Almodóvar has Ignacio murdered twice. The first murder is the soul murder committed by Father Manolo when he sexually abuses him as depicted in The Visit. My understanding of soul murder mostly derives from Shengold's (1978; 1989) work and from my experience as a psychotherapist. Shengold (1978) sensitively uses this nineteenth century concept—soul murder—to elaborate on the dynamics and impact of child abuse.

As I understand Shengold (1978;1989), soul murder is the persistent attempt by an adult, often a parent, or another person acting in loco parentis, to take the joy or spirit out of a child's life. The soul murderer cannot tolerate the child as a separate being. Control is maintained by use of physical force, verbal bullying, withholding of love, or other acts of mental torture and threats.

The case in California where parents are accused of imprisoning and seriously maltreating their thirteen children may be considered an extreme example of soul murder (Medina, 2018). What is interesting here is that while two children escaped together to get help, only one continued in her purpose, while the other returned to the scene of the abuse (Shilliday, 2018). Perhaps the one who was able to persevere with her intent to get help was less internally in the grasp of these seriously abusive parents, and thus, more differentiated.

Where soul murder takes hold, the victim's identity is compromised. The abuser manipulates the child and makes him/her believe that he/she deserves the abuse. The child incorporates an image of himself as bad with the abuser as good; a split in his object world.

This allows him/her some control in a situation of relative helplessness. He deludes himself: If I do what is wanted, life will be okay. This does not often work, as Almodóvar showed when Ignacio made his bargain. Often the abuser cannot change without an outside intervention—external control (Blackman & Dring, 2016). The abuser often does not believe that he needs to stop his behavior as he does not see that he did anything wrong: "The child lured me in." Warner (1995) says that those who adopt a view of a child's sinfulness, "fail to see that it is we who have lost innocent eyes." (p. 59)

When Ignacio submits to Father Manolo he is not mature enough to understand the emotional cost of giving himself in this way. When Father Manolo does not keep his part of the "bargain" and sends Enrique away, Ignacio loses his self-object or soul mate. A real child in such a situation might also lose his sense of himself as powerful. It is as if Ignacio is symbolically castrated. This recalls the sadistic scene in the dining room where Ignacio sings the priest's song about the gardener cultivating his flowers; flowers, typically, are associated with femininity.

Benvenuto's work on perversion focuses on the perverse person's wish to create pain (Richards, A.K., 2018). Richards in her discussion of Benvenuto's work says that we cannot know why a person inflicts pain on another without knowing his/her deeper feelings. She questions whether the abuser's wish is to cause pain as an end in itself, or is it to satisfy a wish to feel powerful. Both Father Manolo and the adult Ignacio cause pain. How Ignacio reacts toward the ex-priest when he is Señor Berenguer can be considered an example of a wish to inflict pain; s/he humiliates him and also taunts him by flashing her/his perfect female breasts. Berenguer tries to excuse his behavior toward Ignacio when he says that it was motivated by love. This is not the way we typically understand love.

Yanof (2005), in her excellent paper discusses the movie from the point of view of impaired object relations and defense. She points out that in *Bad Education* relationships are about gaining power rather than mutuality. She makes the case that the perversity depicted between the adults exists in the quality of the relationships rather than in any particular behavior. But in the movie-within, when Father Manolo abuses Ignacio and deceives him, he commits a dual assault—on soul and body—I see this as both an example of perverse object relations and child abuse.

Shengold (1978; 1989), points out that the anger at being abused is superimposed on a child's innate aggression. We eventually see the adult Ignacio as angry, cynical, vengeful, and self-destructive. The abused child must absorb, and later find an outlet for, not only his own anger but also the hostility projected into him. Stoller (1975/1986), believes that hostility is an intrinsic part of perversion. Child sexual abuse, as I alluded to above, is perverse in its object choice and though the perpetrator's hostility might be unconscious it negatively impacts the child. Such behavior on the part of the abuser might also encompass the desire for the thrill of feeling powerful.

In a recent account of widespread sexual misconduct at a tony private school, a man who was abused by a teacher during his teenage years linked his inability to trust and his difficulty of sustaining relationships to the abuse (Kamil, 2015).

While likely there were multiple factors that contributed to the situation of the man mentioned above, what he reports dovetails with the experience of other abuse victims. Junot Díaz (2018), says following the abuse he suffered as a child, he was plagued by frightening thoughts, persistent nightmares, and depression. He describes his experience as a teenager including heavy use of illicit drugs, suicide attempts, and, later, infidelity to escape painful feelings. After hitting bottom, he turned to intensive long-term psychotherapy and credits it with helping him to cope with the residue of the trauma. What is striking is Díaz' report that the abuse continued because the abuser told him he would kill him if he did not return. The fear engendered by the abuser overtakes the child and it is how a child abuser becomes a soul murderer and controls his victim. Sadly, recently, Díaz is accused of behaving abusively toward women. One woman was a graduate student (Alter, & Bromwich,2018). Without knowing what was on Díaz' mind, it is not possible to know what motivated his alleged behavior. With a patient one might wonder if such reported abusive behavior was an identification with the aggressor. Or, was it a way to exert power? Or, even was it a result of impaired consciousness due to drug or alcohol use? It could also be understood as a call for help—a wish for limits—gone awry.

Almodóvar shows the child abuser to share qualities with a thief: abusers damage or steal the child's ability to trust in the world. When Ignacio lost his friend, he lost the one whom he loved and had wanted to protect him, as he, in turn, had wanted to protect Enrique. For children boarding at school, child friends may be their only comfort; particularly where they believe that they cannot trust the adults.

Victims of child abuse often fear that they will become abusers. Of interest is that the mother of the thirteen abused children I mentioned above is reported to have been repeatedly sexually abused, as a child, by a family member (Eltagouri, 2018). Though she is not accused of sexual abuse, her husband, the children's father, is accused of a lewd act with their 14 year old.

Feit (2013) reports work with a male patient who was sexually abused as a pre-teen by a prominent member of his Orthodox Jewish community. Apparently he found equilibrium in his adulthood until his own son reached the age when he himself had become a victim, at which time, he experienced severe anxiety and panic, what may be understood as caused by a return of the repressed breaking into consciousness. He then began psychoanalytic treatment. That he did so speaks to the power of love for his son. At the time that he sought treatment, such matters were not openly discussed or considered in that particular segment of his community but, in the last five years, or so, therapy in his community has become commonplace (A. Feit, personal communication, April, 2018).

Identifying with the aggressor is one way a victim can defend against fear or passive wishes. Use of certain potentially harmful drugs may be understood as attempts to self-soothe, to withdraw from overstimulation, and/or as an identification with the aggressor. To the extent that heroin use alters one's consciousness and perception, Ignacio's use of heroin repeats within him/her the dissociative experience that Father Manolo's behavior had caused.

Ignacio wants money to complete his/her transition—to make himself/herself more perfect. Almodóvar left the answer to the question of what might have motivated his/her character's wish open. With a patient in analysis, patient and analyst can tease out more about what drives one's wishes. If a patient wants to transform his/her sexual identity, is it to embrace an authentic self? Does it have to do with a fantasy of attracting a particular object? For a real victim of sexual abuse, transforming one's self in this way might support the fantasy of undoing the body that was desired by the perverse abuser. It might also encompass a fantasy of being reborn as a better, cleaner self. Where the abuser is a male, the victim's desire to identify with a maternal object rather than a paternal one might fuel the wish. There is power in being able to choose one's sexual identity and/or, to assume one's authentic self. A person's resolutions are multiple and various, and are best understood when there is a window into what lies below the surface. How a person perceives his/her overall identity is complex with both with internal aspects, both conscious and unconscious, not only external manifestations. Understanding our internal world more fully, allows us to better connect with our deeper wishes, our self, our soul. We can hope that such understanding leads to more attuned resolutions to our conflicts.

When cornered by a crocodile one needs a suit of armor—a strong ego, and a belief in the self. Almodóvar's film suggests that power lies in the ability to create, and not, while hiding behind a veil of virtue, abusing those less powerful. A child is an unequal match for a crocodile. Children flourish where the environment is safe. For those who are, or were, victims, support groups, personal therapy, and, as Rogers (2007) suggests, the opportunity to give voice to one's trauma, can help. Even the awareness that one has survived can empower a person (Shengold, 1978). Almodóvar (Hirschberg, 2004), said that art has its own world. While as he shows, that in movies unrestrained passion can make a good story, in life as we know, to act without considering the needs and feelings of others, risks harming not only the other, but also the self. The perpetrator, often, becomes a victim of himself, as Almodóvar portrays here.

References

Almodóvar, P. (Director).(2004). *Bad Education* [La mala educación]. [Motion picture]. Spain: El Deseo.

Alter, A. & Bromwich, J. E. (2018, 5/5). A Fellow Writer Accuses A Celebrated Novelist of Forcibly Kissing Her, The New York Times, p. A 7.

Blackman, J. & Dring, K. (2016). *Sexual Aggression Against Children.* New York: Routledge.

De Masi, F. (2017). The Pedophile and his Inner World: Theoretical Considerations on the Analysis of a Patient. *International Journal of Psychoanalysis* 88:147-165.

D'Lugo, M. (2006). *Pedro Almodóvar: Urbana & Chicago.* University of Illinois Press.

Díaz, J. (2018). *The Silence: Confronting the Legacy of Childhood Trauma.* The New Yorker: April 16, pp. 24-28.

Eltagouri, M. 2018. Before Police Rescued their 13 Children, California Couple had a History of Strange Behavior, Family and Neighbors Say. Washington Post online. Jan. 22.

Feit, A. (2013). Modesty from Cats, Sexual Morality from Doves: Jewry's Silence in the Face of Sexual Misconduct. *International Journal of Psychoanalytic Self Psychology* 8(2):154-172.

Gutiérrez-Albilla, J. D. (2017/2018). *Aesthetics, Ethics and Trauma in the Cinema of Pedro Almodóvar.* Edinburgh: Edinburgh University Press.

Hirschberg, L. (2004). The Redeemer. New York Times Magazine online, September, 5.

Kamil, A. (2015). *Great is the Truth: Secrecy, Scandal, and The Quest for Justice at the Horace Mann School.* New York: Farrar, Straus and Giroux.

Medina, J. (2018) California Girl's Escape from 'Human Depravity' Led to 12 Children's Rescue. January, 18. New York Times online.

Molofsky, M. (2004). The Return. The Psychoanalytic Review. 91: (6) 853-859.

Pontalis, J.-B.(2006). *Brother of the Above.* New York: The Unconscious in Translation.

Richards, A.K. (2018). Review of: What Are Perversions by Sergio Benvenuto. 2016). London: Karnac. *American Psychoanalyst:* Awaiting publication.

Rogers, A. (2007). *The Unsayable: The Hidden Language of Trauma.* New York: Ballantine Books.

Shengold, L. (1978). *Kaspar Hauser and Soul Murder: A study of Deprivation.* International Review of Psychoanalysis. 5(4):457-476.

_____(1989). *Soul Murder: The Effects of Child Abuse and Deprivation.* New York: Fawcett Columbine.

Shilliday, B.(2018). California Couple Brainwashed Family to Think Escaping Wasn't an Option. wwww.hollywoodlife.com. January, 18.

Stoller, R. (1975/1986). *Perversion: The Erotic Form of Hatred.* London: Maresfield Library.

Strauss, F. (1994/2006). *Almodóvar on Almodóvar* (Revised Edition). New York: Faber & Faber.

Warner, M. (1995). *Six Myths of Our Time.* London: Vintage.

Yanof, J. (2005). Perversion in *La mala educación [Bad Education]. International Journal of Psychoanalysis* 86(6):715-1724.

CHAPTER 17

Almodóvar's *Broken Embraces* (2009)
Voyeurs, Vampires and Going Blind:
Trying To Survive Oedipal Exclusion and Loss

Sandra Cohen

Almodóvar's oeuvre is desire.
"It is rare that two desires meet," he tells us.
What prevents them meeting is the question.
In *Broken Embraces*, the answer centers on Ernesto Martel.

The image of an Eye emerges on the screen. We're invited to see through Almodóvar's unique eye. Are we Voyeurs? Maybe. Yet, what is the intention of our looking? Is it to intrude; to possess; to control; or is it to understand? If our intention is the latter, we are in harmony with Almodóvar's (2017, p. 357-361) view that: "Film is a 'representation' of reality and at times its most faithful reflection." I agree. Come with me and look through my eye. I will take you into the infantile psychic realities living in the adult minds of *Broken Embraces'* troubled, traumatized and terrified souls. Cinema, for Almodóvar (2004, p. xii), is "the psychologist's couch and the priest's confessional". And, because he likes "to discover new explanations in [his] films" (ibid, p. xiv), my focus is on the problems of being the excluded one in an Oedipal triangle, with all the dark urges and unmanageable feelings exclusion brings. That is the story I will tell.

"Ernesto Martel is dead." This pronouncement begins Almodóvar's *Broken Embraces* (Almodóvar, 2009). Who Ernesto

Martel is and what he has to do with the collage of torn up photos of a happy couple is at the heart of a story we don't begin to understand until almost halfway through the film. We are left in the dark, as blind as our writer-filmmaker-protagonist Harry Caine (once, Mateo Blanco). Why Mateo Blanco has changed his name to his pseudonym and why he is blind are also mysteries.

We're slowly introduced to the other characters: Judit Garcia, Harry's agent and caregiver; her teenage son, Diego; and a man named "Ray X," who suddenly knocks at Harry's door and asks to make a film with him. We soon discover that "Ray X", a clearly disturbing figure from the past, is Ernesto Martel Jr. His entry begins the remembering of 1994 and Magdalena Rivera, the tragic and beautiful woman at the center of more than one love triangle. As Almodóvar (2017, p. 361) tells us: "Mateo, Lena, and Ernesto Sr. make up a typical noir trio. The three love fiercely, and one is very powerful, violent, and unscrupulous. Combustion is served. The trio becomes a quartet with Judit Garcia, who brings treachery, a secret son, and a guilt complex to the group - ingredients that will make the relationship between the four even thicker and more oppressive".

The story unfolds in broken bits, weaving back and forth between 2008 and 1994. We have clues. We know Ernesto Martel is dead. We don't yet know the nature of his central importance in Almodóvar's devastating but poignant story of jealousy, lust, obsession, love, revenge and very likely murder. Our first clue to the hot emotions brewing beneath the surface is in the images of guns and words in the paintings in Martel's mansion: "Lust-Love, Crime, Gun, Hot, Love-Lust, Murder, Shot, Blackmail, Weapon" (Almodóvar, 2009). These passions live in every human psyche; first stirred in the earliest Oedipal drama, quieted only with good enough infantile experience (the infant's desire reasonably met).

Ernesto Martel, Sr. and our other lonely characters seem not to have had this early meeting of their baby needs. Old anxieties and grievances hide in secret, ready to take possession since, as Boris (1994 b, pp. 256-257) poetically reminds us: "the infant [is] ... heir to ... dark urges ... that push its mind as teeth will its gums, creating a

Kafkaesque nightmare of being controlled by unclear choices and unnamable agencies". We see what happens when the baby still living inside our characters acts in ways that ignite the desires or troubled feelings in the others. It is in Ernesto Martel, Sr. that we find the most destructive and dark urges unleashed. Given both our innate vulnerabilities and particular early histories, there are different babies living inside us. Martel's is more envious and vengeful than others, especially when faced with being the one excluded; the one left hungry and desperate; the 'wronged party' in a love triangle: his desire unmet and obstructed by another man. We see what happens in an Oedipal story gone terribly, terribly wrong.

One, Two ... Or Three

"One is the loneliest number that you'll ever do" (Nilsson, One, 1968). Two (and only two), between mother and baby, is what a baby desires most. Three is the most difficult number. Almost invariably, one in that threesome is excluded and one is not.

Desire begins at birth. The original desire is "a universe without obstacles, without roughness or differences ... the fantasy of the empty and completely accessible mother's belly" (Chassaguet-Smirgel, 1978, p. 77). After all, to the baby there exists the fantasy of "an ideal breast, which never frustrates, a mother and child in a purely loving relation to each other" (Klein, 1945, p. 23). Awareness of "the other twosome", the parental couple, produces the biggest obstacle of all.

Facing that fact of life, the father, the other, is hard enough. A baby must be met with openness and understanding, by a willing object to take in and contain communications of hunger, desire, distress and hate. A baby must be able to evacuate "its unmanageable, indigestible, conglomeration of good and bad experiences into a care-taking part object ... [in order to realize its] inborn expectation that there is somewhere in which the unmanageable can be made manageable, the unbearable bearable, the unthinkable thinkable" (Isaacs Elmhirst, 1983, p.87). When this doesn't happen, as we see in differing ways in our characters, the anxieties involved in exclusion, separateness and unmet need are, indeed, intolerable. Lena shows symptoms of such early trauma hidden beneath her beautiful but false self (Winnicott, 1965, pp. 140-146). What this trauma drives her to do ignites the Oedipal drama in *Broken Embraces*.

One: Lena

Lena is the lonely one. Her mom - beleaguered, helpless, needy, is unmindful of her daughter's needs. Her dad is dying, and they can't afford medical care. To make ends meet, Lena sells sex as a high-end call girl, her pseudonym Severine. She uses her beauty to disown her real emotional hungers. As many vulnerable children, she must take care of her mother; the first to capitalize on what Lena can give. A tough façade: that's the only answer.

By definition, Severine means stern and reserved, severe. We see that on the surface. But, doesn't Severine also suggest to sever, to cut, to break off, to divide? Lena's defense is splitting a locking out of awareness her feelings and needs, typical of early trauma. Her exterior might be coolly unreachable. But buried inside lives a vulnerable little girl, longing for love and never expecting it. When she meets Mateo Blanco, she'll do anything to have him.

Lena has complicated things, though, by her desperate willingness to sell herself to Ernesto Martel. Her talent for acting, fake smiles, portrayal of desire, has made her Martel's obsessive love. Yet, existing on the outskirts of emotional reality proves dangerous when Martel's reaction to being left for Mateo is humiliation and betrayal.

Two: Lena and Ernesto Martel

Ernesto Martel is manipulative from the start. Putting his wealth and influence to use, he digs up as much information as he can to gain power over his beautiful secretary, Magdalena Rivera. When he sees to private medical care for Lena's father, she becomes Martel's hostage. Later, his voyeuristic inclinations intensify, intruding more insistently into Lena's private world to control loss, to possess her, to indebt her to him, making it impossible to refuse what he wants. Martel's consuming desire for Lena knows no bounds. She must be a steadfast mirror of this desire, her gaze entirely focused on him. He'll have it no other way.

Desire, of course, doesn't come from manipulation and control. What can we understand about Martel, then? That his infancy was complicated by a lack of containment for the primitive anxieties and Oedipal exclusions that are an inevitable part of the beginnings of life? We see, in Martel's extreme reactions, that he is taken over by an overabundance of envy that renders any previous good experience bad. He cannot bear "the implication of a mother who is separate ... and not under the infant's control, having a life of her own, which includes principally a relationship with father, with all that it implies, including feelings of exclusion, envy and jealousy" (Segal, 1989, p.3). It's true: "the initial recognition of the parental sexual relationship involves relinquishing the idea of sole and permanent possession of mother and leads to a profound sense of loss which, if not tolerated, may become a sense of persecution" (Britton, 1989, p. 84).

We see it. We watch what happens to Martel when Lena decides to assert her independence and follow her dream of acting. We see his demands, desperation, anxiety and greed as she appeals to him for what would be, in a healthy relationship, a reasonable need to live her own life. Martel is none too happy when Lena tells him she's auditioned for a film. Even her saccharine sweet reassurance that they'll come home at night and tell each other about their days is not enough. He tries to remind her that she was going to redecorate their house. But, Mr. Mateo Blanco, the new director, is on the phone. He wants to meet with her again. Martel asks, challengingly, as if he expects her to say no, "What are you going to do?" (Almodóvar, 2009). When she says she'll take the second audition, Martel's response is telling and dangerous: "And, what about *me*?"

Three: Lena, Ernesto Martel & Mateo Blanco

The triangle is now created. Re-created, on a more primitive level, from Martel's early life. His hold on Lena threatened, he pleads with her to marry him. When she says, "No", this cements the danger of his being left lonely, pining, starving, while she turns to someone else. Just as the baby tries to fight the fact that he doesn't own his mother, Martel can't accept that Lena is not his possession. "Greed ... is inherently insatiable ... it wants everything; nothing less will do." (Boris, 1994 b, p.255).

Vampires and Starving Babies

Greed and vampires are inveterate partners. Diego's vampire story, seemingly out of place in *Broken Embraces'* overall arc, is an apt metaphor for the unrequited desire of the characters in the film. Plus, Diego's own origins are kept as secret as the existence of the vampires in his fantasy, who live behind the scenes in legitimate blood donation centers in the city of Madrid. Blood is as essential to life as love. Blood is what vampires hunger for; blood is the only thing that keeps them alive. They need it from others, just as a baby needs milk (and wants exclusive love). Blood is a given. Love is not. Sometimes love protects. The vampire girl in Diego's story is not greedy for blood, and she won't bite the 'normal' boy she loves. Sometimes, though, when satisfying a need for love is difficult to come by, hunger turns to greed.

Greed is desire gone mad. A baby's greed is provoked by the threat of starvation. Lena, our vampire girl, because of poverty, desperation to save her father, and hidden cravings for real love and care, draws Mateo Blanco into a deadly triangle. Out of necessity and fear, she's lived a shutdown emotional life. Her hunger awakened, she's starving. She needs Mateo. Mateo, the seemingly 'normal' boy, is hungry, too. He takes what he wants, exacts his own triumph over the other man, and turns Ernesto Martel's greed into an envy that will destroy. Unlike Diego's story, there is no sane love to protect any of them; and because love has failed each and every one, they cannot protect themselves.

These are the problems of unfulfilled desire. Desire is Almodóvar's oeuvre and the color red features prominently in his films. Red is Lena's suit and the shoes she wears walking away. Red is the color in the background of the painting with guns and words: "Lust-Love, Crime, Gun, Hot, Love-Lust, Murder, Shot, Blackmail, Weapon". Red is passion. Red is rage. Red is betrayal. Red is Mateo Blanco's car, the color of Ernesto Martel's hurt. Red is the flowers in the window box after "Ray X" shows up at Harry Caine's door, a reminder of love now gone.

Red is the color of greed: vampire greed. The vampires in Diego's saga steal much of the blood donated "…but without attracting attention" (Almodóvar, 2009). They exist as hidden forces of disappointed hunger that live in all of us, with "sun cream … thick, like armor, to protect them all day" (ibid). As rigorously as we armor ourselves against hurt, greed and anger rear their heads when love is denied. Biting (Klein, 1945, p. 21) expresses hatred towards the breast that starves (O'Shaughnessy, 1964). As Diego's story goes: "These vampires don't proselytize; they don't bite people – unless it is really necessary …" (Almodóvar, 2009).

Ernesto Martel's sadism is set into motion when he becomes the one excluded from the love triangle. Lena is the breast. And, Martel can bite. Hard. "The child's natural greed for his object will make him further resent its absence and so will his jealous wish to prevent his object having a relationship with anyone but himself" (O'Shaughnessy, 1964, p. 30).

Martel tries. He will be the Producer of *Girls and Suitcases*, the film Lena stars in, also about triangles, jealousy and revenge. He won't take "no" for an answer. He won't be left out. Yet, Martel is just as afraid of what eludes his eyes. He must know everything. Using voyeurism by way of Ernesto Jr.'s camera, Martel proves that what is not given willingly can and will be taken.

Voyeurs and Terrified Infants

Ernesto Martel's voyeurism is driven by the torture of watching what he cannot have. "Voyeuristic phantasies … appear at times of separation" (Meltzer, p. 70). Hatred of Lena's separateness is a powerful determinant, taking residence inside him as a jealous monster, in place of a tolerable degree of loss. Loss cannot and will not be felt.

Watching Lena is meant to eliminate the pain of exclusion: "an instant cure, a magic bullet" (Stoller, 1985, p. 20). She is not out of reach. He can get inside her with his eyes, severing barriers and reducing "the anxiety of waiting; of separateness" (O'Shaughnessy, 2008, pp. 234–235). At a deeper level, he fights off infantile psychotic anxieties, survival terror: "… the breast is instinctively felt to be the source of nourishment and therefore, in a deeper sense, of life itself" (Klein, 1975, p. 178). To the baby, being cut off means he's dying. Martel saves himself by intruding whenever he pleases. He will see everything. The couple will not be alone.

Each night, he watches his son's daily documentary takes on the making of *Girls and Suitcases*. A lip reader sits by his side. He can't read the often-agonizing language of feeling. He wants the interpreter to confirm all the ways he deludes himself about Lena and "their love". He isn't cured. In fact, he's tortured. He watches Lena and Mateo work together on the screen. Not wanting to see what's right before his eyes, he grills the translator about whether they like each other. In his unconscious infantile world, relived as he watches, Lena is the mother who exposes him to her sexual goings-on. His terrified, hungry, small and envious self cannot bear that she is not his. His brooding face, captured full screen, is the picture of a cuckolded man, a hurt little boy, pushed aside, forgotten, left out. This is the part of him he's tried to disown – forced, as it is, inside the other Ernesto: his son.

Martel is waiting for Lena when she comes home after making love with Mateo. She's confident and happy. He's gloomy. He insists they go to Ibiza for the weekend. No, she must rehearse, she says. He reminds her that he sets the rules. He's the producer. This time, she cannot refuse.

In Ibiza, Martel forces himself on her repeatedly: taking her own-ing her. After being with Mateo in the thrall of new love, being used makes her sick. Returning to the set of *Girls and Suitcases*, Lena cries to Mateo: "I had that son of a bitch on top of me for 48 hours ... I'm living on 'tranq's'" (Almodóvar, 2009). This too is recorded. We see Martel's face watching the whole ugly truth. She doesn't love him. She's tricked him with her acting, just as he's tricked himself. The last frame in the scene is a picture of Ernesto Martel as he witnesses Lena and Mateo kiss. Their kiss, an ordinary kiss of two people in love, is also the last image in the film ... a tragic image because, in the end, it's followed by death, loss and broken embraces.

Envy, Revenge, and Broken Embraces

The fantasy of splitting the couple apart is one of the dark urges in an Oedipal baby who cannot bear the existence of a combined parental couple "always getting sexual gratification from one another" (Klein, 1975, p. 198): a couple that leaves it out. That couple is now Lena and Mateo, arousing, in the baby still living inside Martel's mind, "vengeful thoughts because it shatters the assumption of the exclusive relationship between mother and child" (Steiner, 2011, p. 134).

After viewing Lena's fraught confession to Mateo, Martel watches footage of a physical fight between Lena and Ernesto, Jr. As much a voyeur as the elder Martel, "Ray X" uses his X-Ray vision, his camera, to get inside the couple, too. He wants Mateo, the idealized father; the father he couldn't have. His is another untold Oedipal story. Ernesto, Jr. films Lena as she leaves Mateo's apartment. Furiously, she tries to stop him. He refuses: "My father wants to see everything". And so his father does. We see, in company with a tormented Martel, the photographed images of Mateo and Lena, their naked bodies only barely hidden by sheer curtains. As Martel watches, Lena walks into the room behind him. Standing coolly, in her red suit, she demands: "Focus on me. Yes, I'm talking to you". In double time, on screen and in person, we hear her confess: "I've just been with the man I love and I'm happier than I've ever been ... don't worry. I'll leave you in peace very soon. You needn't spy on us … there is nothing more to hide" (Almodóvar, 2009).

Leave him in peace? That's a naïve, wishful fantasy. There will be no peace for any member of this triangle. Lena doesn't grasp Martel's sense of betrayal, how she's castrated and humiliated him; his need for victory to overcome these feelings; the rage and murderous jealousy that have now been inflamed. She has no idea what he's capable of. Frustration breeds hate. Hate and revenge trade places with love. Envy, more vicious than jealousy, will kill what it cannot have.

Lena turns, as if leaving him is as simple as that. She walks up the curved staircase and, for a moment, sits in the dark under a painting inscribed with the words: "Je T'aime". She's made a mockery of his love. The camera pans to Martel's black shoes walking up the stairs behind her, then to her red high heels walking away. He wants to talk. She's erected a cold wall against her fear, anger, years of obligation: a debt hard-paid for her father's medical care. She's reduced Martel to pleading; an unacceptable weakness to a man who prides himself on power and control. With her back to him, Lena heads down the stairs to go. He reaches out his hand, gives her a push.

Martel's face is now a mask of superior disdain. He stands at the top of the stairs eyeing her as she lies at the bottom, crumpled and broken, needing him now. An example of projective identification in blatant Technicolor, this is Martel's bitter triumph over his own broken, crumpled, helpless self. Almodóvar (2017) says, "I am very proud of the staircase scene. It shows his enormous cruelty", a cruelty born out of self-hatred for needing her. Yet, he does need her. For a moment, his brutality scares him. Frightened he's destroyed her love forever, Martel gathers Lena in his arms and carries her to his big, black, phallic Rolls Royce. He rushes to the hospital, calling for help.

Lena is again his prisoner. Now scared, she stays. But with conditions. Mateo will finish his film however he wishes. She'll live under the same roof until then, but in separate bedrooms. Martel has no rights. He can't win her over. His only option is to get back at her in any (and every) way he can. Before long, Martel beats her and throws her onto the street with only her underwear. She won't leave him with nothing; he'll do it to her. Arriving at the studio in a taxi, bloodied and terrified, she begs Mateo to take her away. She blindly wants to believe she can escape from Martel's destructiveness with the love she is frantic to have.

Going Blind

Love is complicated. Sane love, healthy adult love, is hard to find, colored as it is by infantile anxieties and frustrations that lurk, hidden deep inside, from earlier situations of unrequited love. In *Broken Embraces* these anxieties lead our struggling characters to obsessive love, possessive love, idealized love, masochistic willingness to take the little that is given. The origins of these anxieties, as my re-telling of the film goes, frequently date back to Oedipal hungers and exclusions.

Mateo, our main Oedipus, commits the unconscious "crime" of transgression into the (parental) sexual couple. He takes the object of the father's love. He steals Lena. He thinks he has a right to her. In his fantasy, he's the victorious one. But, Mateo's bloodthirsty Oedipal desire blinds him to the dangers inherent in his rivalry. He takes an uncalculated risk with the object of Ernesto Martel's obsessive love. In turn, Martel's wrath at Lena's betrayal serves the unconscious purpose of blinding him to humiliation and loss. His love and longing are obliterated as completely as she's gotten rid of him. The Oedipal baby on the outside of a couple, Martel is filled with all the jealousy, envy, and hostility exclusion brings.

Lena and Mateo flee to Famara Beach on the island of Lanzarote leaving no trace, or so they think. Living in a blind refuge, the peril of Ernesto Martel and their precariously won love is as out of mind as he is now out of sight. They play at being a carefree couple, hiding from the external and internal forces that hunt them down. She cooks. They cuddle. He writes *The Secret of Golfo Beach*. But, there will be no secrets from a desolate and vengeful lover. To find her, Martel tricks the couple by making a travesty of Mateo's film. Reading about the film's premiere in the newspaper, a distraught Mateo, urgent to save his film and his ego, carelessly discloses their whereabouts in a message to Judit. Self-absorbed, he has no room to see how much he's hurt her by flaunting his love for Lena. Accustomed to her readiness to satisfy his every need, he does not suspect Judit's complicity in Martel's plan.

The couple's location revealed, Ernesto, Jr., voyeur to the end, follows Mateo's small red car as he drives Lena home before leaving Famara for Madrid. Filming them, Ernesto's camera captures a black SUV (all too reminiscent of Martel's black Rolls Royce) as it smashes into them. Is this an accident? I think it's safe to say that if Martel can't have Lena, no one will. "With violent and disruptive projection into the couple in order to separate them or make them sterile" (Feldman, 1989, p. 126), we have one of the most "pathological versions of the Oedipal situation" (ibid). And, when Judit enters their bungalow in Famara to help Mateo home, she finds a bag of photos (the ones Diego helps piece together in 2004), ripped in the center, splitting Lena and Mateo apart. A vindictive 'someone' has been there first, making certain the couple's embraces are broken.

Mateo loses his eyesight in the crash. Lena is dead. Mateo refuses to answer to Mateo any longer. Taking his pseudonym, Harry Caine, he blinds himself to his guilt and his grief. Not unlike Oedipus who stabs his own eyes out, he cannot feel the pain of his loss. Is emotional truth served in *Broken Embraces*? I don't think we can say it is. "Since we are dealing with human characters we are also concerned with lies, deceptions, evasions, fictions, phantasies, visions, hallucinations — indeed, the list can be lengthened almost indefinitely" (Bion, 1977, pp. 41–42).

All our characters have turned away from something for unique but not dissimilar reasons. Seeing can be painful and the desire not to know overrides a capacity to face emotional reality. In each of our characters, we have "… a total personality who has at some time, consciously or unconsciously, chosen a particular view or a particular vertex from which to see the view. This always involves inhibition of the capacity to see the views that one does not want to see" (Bion,

1977, p. 52). A movement onward, in development or in life, can't be taken because it means something too agonizing to feel.

Only Diego tries to reconstruct the truth of all that's hidden from sight. Diego: Judit's (and Mateo's secret) son, born of a love affair that makes Judit another rejected 'third.' He, the vehicle that unearths the real story is, perhaps, the psychoanalyst in this Almodóvar film. He is also the healthiest child among all our characters, intent on piecing together what has been broken. To some degree, Diego does help Mateo begin to face his past and finish *Girls and Suitcases*. Yet, in the end neither Mateo's film nor *Broken Embraces* is complete. For, although Mateo says in the voice of filmmaker Almodóvar (2009): "Films have to be finished even if you do it blindly," there are consequences to turning a blind eye to very real sadness.

When There Are No Tears

"What the eye don't see, the heart don't grieve" (Boris, 1994 a, p. 100) – but we know that isn't true. Unexpressed sadness hides in symptoms and perverse defenses. Almodóvar has a unique capacity to understand and portray the most raw, primitive, dark emotional situations lurking in the human psyche, heirs of the original conflicts between love and hate. Our characters in Almodóvar's *Broken Embraces* offer a window into what happens deep inside when Oedipal rivalries are not resolved. We see anxiety about separateness and loss, obsession, jealous possessiveness, voyeuristic intrusion, vengeful acts. We see blindness to the grief.

Harry tells his story to Diego. Judit admits the hurt that led her to join Ernesto Martel's plot to make a mockery of *Girls and Suitcases*— while downing drink after drink. Her purpose is more to expunge her guilt than grieve. Our characters, humanly limited as we all are, do the best they can to put things right. Judit, after all, didn't destroy Mateo's best takes, making it possible for him to redo his film. The three become a family of sorts, although a damaged one. Yet, it's not quite enough. Mateo, Judit (and certainly Ernesto Martel, Sr., now dead) cannot bear the pain or the guilt that must be felt. They try, too quickly, to remodel what happened and move on, not really settling with the past.

True reparation means feeling the regrets; mending the spoils of hostilities and hate; of jealousies, missteps, and mistakes. This we don't see. We see instead Judit's fantasy that her "catharsis" is an end point. We see Mateo taking back his real name, a start – but carrying on in blind determination to re-make *Girls and Suitcases* as originally intended: a comedy about betrayal and revenge. But betrayal and revenge are far from funny. For those in *Broken Embraces*, there is more sorrow than any can handle and no one sheds a tear.

Ernesto Martel's death does not free them. Our characters are bound by childhood defenses. They cannot do "the work of mourning and often with it the painful work of thinking and worrying … fundamental to any concept of separation and separateness … not to be confused with physical separation, rejection, or abandonment" (Conran, 1999, p. 42). For those in the film, separation and separateness are translated into cruel exclusion; being unwanted, rejected, abandoned and betrayed. These beliefs lead to grievances, guilt, feelings of deep-seated unfairness, a sense of persecution, but not to an acceptance of the reality of differences or loss. Helplessness is terrifying if there is no one there. A baby must find ways to manage its fears, its feelings of unacceptable smallness, its unmet needs. All babies need someone to hold unmanageable feelings, losses and sorrows, and, even later, to hear the infant living inside the adult mind. With no one to hear the hurt of exclusion, hatred sometimes gets out of hand. Vampire-like greed is stimulated. Voyeurism reverses helpless watching to a fantasy of power over the pain of loss. When these methods don't succeed, we have the tragedy of *Broken Embraces*.

The combustion, as Almodóvar (2017) calls it, is embodied in the brutal car crash, filmed by Ernesto, Jr., in Famara. At the end of *Broken Embraces*, as Diego and Mateo watch Ernesto's documentary, the sighted Diego confirms that Ernesto, Jr. was the first at the scene of the accident to help them. We see him on the screen, running towards the crash in horror. His documentary pans to the image he captured just before the black SUV hit Mateo's small red car and took off. Ernesto's last image is Mateo and Lena's last kiss: "a normal kiss; the kind of kiss a couple give each other out of habit" (Almodóvar, 2009).

As *Broken Embraces* comes to a close, we watch Mateo caressing the screen, frame by frame. With remembering and longing, he tries to capture mere remnants of the happiness of an ill-fated couple that could not be, their attempt at love tainted by unsettled Oedipal cravings and impossible triumphs. In the end, their embraces are broken by the biting revenge of an envious (and hurt) baby still living inside Ernesto Martel. The one excluded, the one who's hungry desire and unmanageable feelings were, from the start, never openly met and tragically never heard.

References

Almodóvar, P. (2017). Broken Embraces. In P. Duncan with B. Peiro (Eds.). *The Pedro Almodóvar Archives* (pp. 346–367). Taschen America LLC.

———(Writer and Director). (2009). *Broken Embraces*, Spain: Sony Pictures Classic Release and El Deseo.

———(2004). P. Willoquet-Marcondi, Ed., *Pedro Almodóvar Interviews*. Jackson: University Press of Mississippi.

Bion, W.R. (1962). The Psycho-Analytic Study of Thinking. *International Journal Psycho-Analysis* 43:306–310.

———(1977). *Two Papers: 'The Grid' and 'Caesura'*. Taylor and Francis. Kindle Edition.

Boris, H. (1994 a). *Envy*. New Jersey: Jason Aronson Inc.

———(1994 b). *Sleights of Mind: One and Multiples of One*. New Jersey: Jason Aronson Inc.

Britton, R. (1989). The missing link: parental sexuality in the Oedipus complex. In J. Steiner, Ed. *The Oedipus Complex Today: Clinical Implications* (pp. 83–101). London: Karnac Books.

Chasseguet-Smirgel, J. (1989). *Sexuality and Mind: The Role of the Father and the Mother in the Psyche*. London: Karnac Books.

Conran, M. (1999). Sorrow, vulnerability and madness. In P. Williams, Ed. *Psychosis (madness)* (pp. 27–43). London: The Institute of Psychoanalysis.

Feldman, M. (1989). The Oedipus complex: manifestations in the inner world and the therapeutic situation. In J. :.Isaacs Elmhirst, S. (1983). Bion and Babies. In J. Grotstein, Ed. *Do I Dare Disturb The Universe: A Memorial To Wilfred R. Bion* (pp. 84–91). London: Marsfield Reprints.

Klein, M. (1945). The Oedipus Complex in the Light of Early Anxieties. *Love, Guilt, and Reparation.* The Hogarth Press, 1983. [Reprinted in J. Steiner, Ed. (1989). *The Oedipus Complex Today: Clinical Implications,* pp. 11–82,1989. London: Karnac Books.

Klein, M. (1975). *Envy and Gratitude & Other Works 1946–1963.* London: The Hogarth Press and The Institute of Psycho-Analysis.

Little, M. (1990). *Psychotic Anxieties And Containment: A Personal Record of an Analysis with Winnicott.* New Jersey: Jason Aronson Inc.

Meltzer, D. (1973). *Sexual States of Mind.* Scotland: Clunie Press.

Nilsson, H. (1968). *One.* Produced by Rick Jarrard. Label: RCA.

O'Shaughnessy, E. (1964). The Absent Object. *Journal of Child Psychotherapy,* 1: 39–43. Reprinted in R. Rusbridger, Ed. *Inquiries in Psychoanalysis: Collected papers of Edna O'Shaughnessy,* pp. 19–31, 2015. London: Routledge.

——(1989). The invisible Oedipus complex. Reprinted in J. Steiner, Ed. *The Oedipus Complex Today: Clinical Implications,* London: Karnac Books, pp. 129–150.

——(2008). Intrusions. In J. Steiner, Ed., *Rosenfeld in Retrospect.* London: Karnac Books. Reprinted in R. Rusbridger, Ed. *Inquiries in Psychoanalysis: Collected papers of Edna O'Shaughnessy,* pp. 232–245. London: Routledge, 2015.

Segal, H. (1989). Introduction. In J. Steiner, Ed. *The Oedipus Complex Today: Clinical Implications* (pp. 1–10). London: Karnac Books.

——(1964). *Introduction To The Work Of Melanie Klein.* New York: Basic Books, Inc.

Steiner, J. (2011). *Seeing and Being Seen: Emerging from a Psychic Retreat.* London: Routledge.

——Ed. *The Oedipus Complex Today: Clinical Implications* (pp. 103–128). London: Karnac Books.

Stoller, R. (1985). *Observing Erotic Imagination.* New Haven: Yale University Press.

Winnicott, D.W. (1965). *The Maturational Processes and the acilitating Environment: Studies in the Theory of Emotional Development.* London: The Hogarth Press and the Institute of Psycho-Analysis.

CHAPTER 18

The Skin I Live In[1]

Arlene Kramer Richards

This horror film by Almodóvar shows us the making of a woman. It uses loneliness and social isolation as metaphor and as bedrock for the process of becoming a person. Where Freud posited penis envy as the bedrock of femininity, Almodóvar posits a very different beginning and a very different process for the formation of a woman and by extension for the formation of a human being.

What makes a woman? The Hebrew bible tells of the creation of woman: Eve is created because Adam is lonely. She is made for his companionship, to accompany him and give him pleasure. This idea has persisted in Western civilization as the foundational myth of femininity. Female sexuality is made for man's pleasure. Their roles are not equal; their purposes are different. Modern women have been insisting that our sexuality and our own selves are just as important as those of men. But it is an uphill battle. I will discuss a movie that opened up for me the question of female sexuality once again and that seems to me to illustrate the dilemma of female development in a new social context.

The horror film *The Skin I Live In* by Almodóvar shows us the making of a woman. It uses loneliness and social isolation as metaphor and as bedrock for the process of becoming a person.

---

[1] Reprinted from: *Encounters with Loneliness: Only the Lonely.*(2013). Edited by: Arlene Kramer Richards, Lucille Spira and Arthur A. Lynch. New York: IP Books.

Almodóvar calls her "Vera"; Vera means truth. Where Freud posited penis envy as the bedrock of femininity, Almodóvar posits a different beginning but a very familiar process for the formation of a woman and, by extension, for the formation of a human being. Both Freud and Almodóvar posit the woman as having been a castrated boy. Where Freud went for the internal and the "dark continent," Almodóvar goes for the external as window into the soul. The story he presents is one of sorrow and mourning. A scientist loses his beloved wife in a car accident that burns her skin off. He develops artificial skin that would have saved her if he had it to use while she was dying. The skin is flawless and impervious: It will not burn. It does not feel.

How does he use this wonderful invention? We see him drive his expensive car to his palatial house. In it he has a lab where he performs surgery, and a rehabilitation clinic where a beautiful and mysterious patient lives. Her skin is flawless and is kept perfect by her second skin: a flesh-colored leotard. But she lives in near total isolation. She has contact only with a motherly woman who feeds her via dumbwaiter and provides her with books to read, also delivered by dumbwaiter. She exercises and she reads, but she does not get out of her room.

As the film unfolds we learn that she is actually a person who was once a man but has had a sex change. Yet she is not a usual transsexual. This change was not done in the usual trans-sexual way, with hormone treatments and gradual reversible steps leading up to the permanent change of surgery. Instead, the young man had penile ablation and an artificially created vagina first. In this, Almodóvar is mimicking the creation of a woman rather than a trans-sexual. The woman is created on the basis of a female genital, not by changing the secondary sexual characteristics that would present her to the outside world as a woman. She starts out as a genital female, then gets the smooth hairless face, soft skin, breasts, hips and female suppleness that actual women develop at puberty.

But how is she to become a psychological woman, how can the feminine image become her way of seeing herself? The book we first see her reading is written by Alice Munro, a Canadian feminist author. She lives with art made by Louise Bourgeois, a French feminist sculptor. She is taught by women artists what it means to be a woman. She is isolated from actual women except by the intercom connection to the woman who feeds her from a distance and supplies her with art materials from a distance. Her social isolation is carefully dosed with female ideas. This is the adult equivalent of giving little girls baby dolls to play with so as to prepare them to think about themselves as nurturers and caretakers, and giving them fashion dolls so that they can think of themselves as becoming ladies of fashion. Her skin is the interface between self and environment, protecting her self against the impingements of the outside world and at the same time keeping her self together, protecting her self from leaking into the outside world. In developing this impervious skin, she is confined to a solitary room. The price of protection is high: her skin isolates her from the world.

We find out that when the surgeon's wife recovered from her terrible burn, she saw a reflection of herself with horribly scarred skin, jumped out a window and killed herself. We now know both how and why the impervious skin was so important to the surgeon who invented it. But the story is even more complex. The isolated woman is in solitary confinement. She lives in a prison, in the most punitive of all prison situations. She is all alone, almost all the time. Who can she identify with? Who is the witness to her life? Only the surgeon sees her. Only the surgeon has the power to keep her in her prison or release her from it. Only the surgeon represents the outside world to her. His will determines her fate. His choice of how she is to live determines her only possibilities. Isolated and alone, she can only long for his visits. She lives an exaggerated version of the life of 1950's housewives described by Betty Freidan (1963); alone in a beautiful suburban house with nothing to do all day long but take care of her body and wait for her lord and master to come home. He puts her in a situation which maximizes her loneliness and minimizes her possibilities, yet it is also a situation that seems luxurious and is similar to what upper-middle class housewives choose for themselves in the twenty-first century. She has the smooth skin that so many women achieve through injections of poison and through plastic surgery. Her yoga practice is her only consolation. She believes the televised yoga teacher who promises that it will give her a way to reach her inner core. Yoga gives her some semblance of choice. She can do it without having it imposed by the surgeon. What she does not have is another person who wants to know what she feels or wants to listen to her thoughts. This makes her lonely and also makes her a non-person.

Psychologically, the skin is the border of the self. It is the first boundary. Being stroked, held, caressed, slapped, cut, burned, beaten is experienced through the skin. It is the organ of feeling. It is the edge of me/-not-me and is implicated in perversions as pleasure inches over into pain and pain becomes pleasurable. When the surgeon gives his patient impermeable skin, he is depriving her of both her vulnerability and her capacity to blemish her humanity.

The surgeon has been coaxing her to use dilators to enlarge her vagina so that she will be capable of sexual intercourse without pain. The movie shows the surgeon's brother as his cruder alter ego. The brother rapes her, hurting her but shocking her into life. She complains. The surgeon promises her pleasurable intercourse. But this is not to be. She has feelings. She is shown brutally raped, then tenderly cared for and consoled. She shows herself frightened and weakened by the pain of first intercourse experienced as rape. She has taken on what the environment showed her as her place.

Yet, in the end, the surgeon is not successful. Vera is physically a woman, but psychologically still a man. In the end she will go back to her mother's second-hand ladies clothing shop and reveal herself as the mutilated version of his mother's son. Psychologically this person is still a man. The irony of her situation is underscored by her mother's occupation. She runs a store in which she sells women's second-hand clothes. She is her mother's second-hand woman.

Almodóvar tells a modern version of the Tiresias myth. Tiresias lived as a man, was punished by the goddess Hera by being turned into a woman for seven years, and rewarded for a good deed by being returned to his life as a man. Asked about the sexual pleasure he experienced as a man as compared to that of a woman, Tiresias replied that a woman has ten times as much pleasure as a man. The hero-victim of Almodóvar's story had no such satisfaction in being a woman. For her, it is pain and ultimate calamity. At the end she has returned to being a man just as Tiresias did.

The loneliness of living in an artificial skin is unbearable. Anzieu (1989) proposes a parallel between the psychological function of the mental image of the skin and the physical function of the bodily skin: the psychological skin ego skin serves to keep in everything needed for mental health and functioning, while at the same time keeping out everything that could harm the self, just as the bodily skin keeps in the other body organs and keeps out what could harm them. This implies that the skin ego is necessary for sexual functioning. It seems to me that the act of sexual intercourse becomes frightening when it is seen as intrusion on the body in the same way that psychological intimacy threatens to intrude on the self. To ward off this danger one needs to keep away from others who might intrude. Self-imposed social isolation that leads to unbearable loneliness protects both against being intruded upon and intruding on others. The theme of intrusion is taken up by Lemma (2010) in her study of body modification. She describes several cases in which people sought plastic surgery even though the their surgeons thought that the their body parts would not be substantially improved by the procedures. The patients insisted that the changes they wanted made were important to them because they chose them. The body they were rejecting was that provided by the mother who was experienced as either too intrusive or too neglectful, or as alternating between these two noxious extremes. The modifications of the body were felt to be assertions of a separate self that had nothing to do with the mother and therefore would free the patients from the anxiety of intrusion as well as the depressive affect associated with abandonment.

Among the artists who modify their bodies as a form of art Lemma cites Orlan, a woman who has had multiple plastic surgeries recorded on video and broadcast to show the extreme procedures which induce horror and revulsion in the viewers; and a man named Stelarc, whose art consists of mutilating his body by adding extra functional parts like a third arm. Orlan's form of change is a change in being, and Stelarc's is a change in function. Orlan's is passive in that she provides the face and the image of the face, while the surgeon and the viewer provide the action. For Stelarc, the body is modified to produce new action on his part. Stelarc himself, as quoted by Lemma, says:

> I've moved beyond the skin as a barrier . . . Skin no longer signifies closure. . . The hollow body becomes a host. . . . It is time to recolonize the body. (p.127)

Lemma sees this as a fantasy of using the body as a womb, thus undoing the experience of having been enclosed in the mother's womb so that the artist can undo the loss of the mother by becoming a mother. In all, Lemma sees bodily mutilation as a way to either: deny separation, attempt separation, cover shame, defend against fear of fragmentation, or to retaliate against the parent. She thus offers many avenues to explore with patients who mutilate themselves or who, like the surgeon in the movie *The Skin I Live In*, are motivated to mutilate others.

In the movie, the surgeon lost his wife some years earlier when her skin was burned beyond repair in an automobile crash. He very recently lost his daughter to a rape-murder. Having lost his entire family, he lives alone. He is doubly castrated in having lost both of the women he loved, his wife and his daughter. He is utterly lonely. By first castrating and then isolating the young man who raped and killed his daughter, he is leaving the person who isolated him as helpless and alone as he has become. The story equates castration and social isolation with femininity. The young man becomes a woman by being rendered helpless and alone. After completing the transformation from male to female, the surgeon tries to teach the young woman he has created how to become a sexually functioning woman. His attempt fails because the young woman longs for her mother, longs to return to her life as her mother's son. Yet his mother's work as the purveyor of second-hand womanhood seems to have doomed him from the start to his fate of becoming a second-hand woman.

The theme of the second-hand woman appears in Gilbert's (Sander 2010) version of the myth of Pygmalion and Galatea. In the original myth, Pygmalion is a sculptor who falls in love with a statue he makes of a woman and his love causes her the statue to come to life. In Gilbert's version, he makes the statue using his own wife as the model; and he falls in love with the statue only after he experiences loneliness and longing when his wife leaves him for a day with the promise that his sculpture of her will keep him company as he waits for her to come back. Unfortunately, the newly alive statue falls in love with him and he, in response, falls in love with her as well. Only when she is frozen back into marble will he achieve peace. The surgeon in *The Skin I Live In* has also created a woman to substitute for the wife who left him. But his creation does not fall in love with him. He must suffer his loneliness without a substitute.

Another variation on the theme of creating a woman to love is shown in Shaw's Pygmalion, and again in Lerner and Loewe's My Fair Lady (both the stage and movie versions), a musical based on Shaw's play. In all of these, the creator of the woman, like the surgeon in *The Skin I Live In*, ends up alone and lonely as does the surgeon in *The Skin I Live In*. The creator is the father who must see his daughter go off with another man to a life of her own with a love of her own choosing. But the surgeon's creation, the woman he has made for himself, goes off leaving both the surgeon and himself devastated. In the end, he experiences the ultimate loneliness: he longs for himself as a man. By longing for his former self s/he experiences what is impossible to fulfill, he must be lonely for the rest of his life. In this movie, Almodóvar has shown us a form of loneliness that no one has ever seen before. To the ideas of longing for a specific object (Brenner, 1959), longing for an empathic object (Kohut, 1977), longing for acceptance in an elite group (Proust, 1997), and longing for a national or racial group's acceptance, Almodóvar has added longing for oneself. This idea is implicit in Freud's assertion that narcissistic love can be longing for one's former self, longing for one's ideal self, or longing for one's mirror image. But Almodóvar gives us a picture of someone longing for his former sexual and gender identity in a way that was not possible in Freud's time; because the possibility of sex reassignment surgery was not available. The closest thing to it that could be achieved was adopting the gender role of the opposite sex in life and the sexual role of the opposite sex in love making. So a psychological change was possible. Castration was possible, but trans-sexuality like that of Tiresias only became possible with modern surgery.

What has all of this to do with clinical practice? When a Chinese person gets a divorce, he or she may say: "I have lost my skin." When he or she is disillusioned or disappointed, he or she may say something similar. Skin has the meaning of a layer of protection from the world. The skin provided by a spouse is a reassurance that one is a wife and therefore a female or that one is a husband and therefore a male. Our sexual roles reinforce our gender identity. And our gender identity reinforces our sense of self. To have a gender is be a person. If a man speaks as a husband, it reinforces his sense of self; if a woman speaks as a wife, that reinforces her sense of self. To lose that status is to lose a part of oneself.

When angry at another person one says in English that the other person is "getting under my skin." The expression conveys the feeling of being intruded upon that causes psychic pain to the person who has been aroused to anger. The other person who has "gotten under" her skin is an alien presence that does not fit with the image of herself that she values and wants to protect. And nothing is as important to protect as one's sexuality. But, by contrast, a popular song of the last century by Cole Porter called "I've Got You Under My Skin" describes being in love as having the other person inside oneself but again against his own will and better judgment.

Concealing sexuality and concealing one's sexual organs are part of most societies. In both China and the west, modesty is based on covering the sexual organs. That part of the skin that covers the sexual organs is both the most delicate, the most abundantly supplied with nerve endings, and most to be protected from intrusion. In this sense sexuality is the basis and foundation of the innermost self. And the skin is the organ of touch, and touch is the sensation of sexual arousal. The senses of smell, sight and hearing are involved in the earlier stages of sexual arousal, but the skin on skin contact of sexuality is the essential part of both arousal and fulfillment. So the skin stimulates, and the nerves it shields and stimulates are the road in to sexual experience and to the sense of oneself as a sexual being.

The sense of being a sexual person is crucial to adulthood for most people. Whether one sees oneself as heterosexual male, homosexual male, heterosexual female or homosexual female, having a firm sense of being one of these helps makes most people feel grounded in their own bodies. Some people believe that they are free to choose and to change their sexual choices as they meet new possible lovers. They still feel themselves to be male and potent with male partners, for example, even though they also have female partners. Blechner (2009) argues for the consideration of any sexual desires as non-pathological as long as they give pleasure to the persons who practice them. He thinks that psychoanalysts harm their patients when they categorize any forms of sexuality as abnormal.

But this attitude, while sounding modern and cool to New York City therapists, limits psychoanalysis to a way of thinking that fits a particular society at a particular time. What about sex with children? With patients? With students? All of these can cause harm. One way of dealing with this problem is by limiting what we consider normal to what happens between two consenting adults. But this standard does not fit into everyone's way of defining limits, and it is not recognized by societies with different moral standards. Psychoanalysis faces a crisis whenever we try to fit our concepts to a new social reality. Blechner (2009), among others (e.g., Dimen, 2005), is trying to widen our horizons to accommodate a widening social acceptance in the United States of the rights of homosexual people. Marriage between two men or two women is already socially acceptable and legal in several states in the United States including New York and

Massachusetts, where many analysts practice. The shame that used to attach to homosexuality is gone. The blame for feelings of sexual desire has stopped. Men and women are publishing their same-sex marriages in The New York Times, our most prestigious newspaper.

At the same time, young people who are starting their adult sexual lives worry about their sexual orientation. They tease homosexuals and even push some of them to suicide (Parker, 2012). Young people are anxious about their new sexuality. Are they going to be good lovers? Will someone want them? Will they be attracted to the right sort of person? Will the right sort of person be attracted to them? Are their bodies disgusting? Do they smell bad? Are they too hairy? Not hairy enough? Are they too fat? Too skinny? Too short? Too tall? Is their nose too big? Too small? Are their eyes the right shape? Do they look too pimply? Will they do well in the preliminaries? Will they be too fast? Or too slow? Will they be able to sustain sexual contact long enough? These worries, and many others, make them vulnerable to disappointment in their own sexuality.

When people feel vulnerable in these ways, one way to protect themselves is to find others who are less attractive or less popular, or who have sexual preferences that are different from those of most people. If most people are heterosexual, then homosexuals make good targets for teasing and put downs. People who do not fit the model of sexual attractiveness of their society may also easily become targets.

If "blonds have more fun," then darker hair or darker skin makes a good target. The idea that different is worse makes the alienation of the other, especially the other of a different skin color, a permissible target of for rejection, ridicule and persecution. People who do not fit the model of sexual attractiveness for their society may also easily become targets. Adolescent sexuality pushes young people into cruelty because they project their uncertainty and anxiety about their own attractiveness onto anyone with less socially valued attributes and features.

The social value of sexual attractiveness is a combination of innate and socially differentiated elements. For example, all known social groups value symmetrical features, almost all value the look of health. These traits seem to belong to an innate system of values. By contrast, only very special circumstances make obesity or extreme thinness sexually attractive; although there are some social groups in which obesity in women is seen as a sign of fertility and therefore of sexual attractiveness, and there are groups in the western world that value the extreme skinniness of fashion models. Young people are extremely sensitive to these values and go to extreme lengths to alter their bodies and their faces to achieve what they see as the ideal of sexual attractiveness in their society. And many older people are willing to go to great expense and take great risks in order to try to look young and sexually attractive (Sinkman, 2012). Like the surgeon's wife, they are disgusted and repelled by the signs that age and experience have left on their skins. Like her they would rather die than look scarred. They prefer to risk their lives and tolerate pain and discomfort rather than risk the social isolation and loneliness that they see as inevitable concomitants of wrinkled skin, droopy muscles and white hair. They are willing to risk looking ridiculous, in clothing worn by much younger people, shoes that torture older feet, hairstyles that require hours at the colorist and more at the stylist's. They work at looking younger as if their very lives depended on it.

Ironically, Eco (2011) shows that ugliness in women is represented in art as old age masquerading as beauty by hiding behind cosmetics, seductive clothing or seductive poses. This idea has particular relevance to our current aging society. More and more, women past menopause are unwilling to see themselves as ugly. Yet it is not age, but the attempt to imitate youth that is seen as ugly. But Eco reminds the reader that what is beautiful in art may not be the same as what is beautiful in life. A beautiful woman may be painted by Picasso with green cheeks or a single eye, yet a woman in life who had such features would be ugly. So we cannot take what is represented in art as a depiction of what would be beautiful in life. The girl who starves herself to look like a model in a fashion magazine does not get elected homecoming queen. The old woman who uses cosmetic surgery and/or chemical cosmetics may or may not look beautiful to her aging husband or her children or her grandchildren. They may want her to look the age that fits the role she plays in their lives. Yet to her friends and even to her age mates she may look wonderful when she looks young enough to make them feel young also. The role of cosmetics and plastic surgery may be to enhance a woman's attractiveness or these may make her look fake and even frightening.

Often, by rejecting one's body and face as they have been, one manages to alienate the body from the self, leaving a person lonely in the most radical way imaginable, lonely for oneself. Aging forces this alienation on the person, especially in adolescence when the secondary sexual characteristics change one's body and face, and again in the process of aging when menopause or male climacteric change the body and face. Longing for who one used to be is a kind of loneliness that is even more radical than longing for another person. Plastic surgery offers the possibility of rejecting the newly acquired changes but at the cost of still further alienation from the self, and still further loneliness and longing for the self she once had, but can never really recover. Almodóvar has shown us in this film a wonderful instance of the complexity of changing one's body and the loneliness for the former self that transcends the social aspects of this exquisitely painful feeling.

References

Anzieu, D. (1989). *The Skin Ego*. New Haven: Yale University Press. Blechner, M. (2009). Sex Changes. New York: Routledge.

Brenner, C. (1974). On the Nature and Development of Affects: A Unified Theory. *Psychoanalytic Quarterly* 43:532–556.

Dimen, M. (2005) Sexuality and suffering or the Eew! factor. *Studies in Gender and Sexuality* 6:1–8.

Eco, U. ed., (2010). *On Beauty*. New York: Rizzoli.

———(2011). *On Ugliness*. New York: Rizzoli.

Friedan, B. (1963). *The Feminine Mystique*. New York: Norton.

Kohut, H. (1959). Introspection, Empathy, and Psychoanalysis—An Examination of the Relationship Between Mode of Observation and Theory. *Journal of the American Psychoanalytic Association* 7:459–483.

———(1977). *The Restoration of the Self.* New York: International Universities Press.

Lemma, A. (2010). *Under the Skin.* London: Routledge.

Parker, I. (2012) *The story of a suicide.* The New Yorker, Feb 6, 2012.

Proust, Marcel. (1896–1919). A race accursed. In: *On Art and Literature,* transl. Sylvia Townsend Warner, introduction Terence Kilmartin. New York: Carroll & Graf Publishers, Inc. pp. 210–229, 1997.

———(1913–1927). *In Search of Lost Time.* (6 volumes), transl. C.K. Scott Moncrieff & T. Kilmartin, rev. D.J. Enright, introduction Richard Howard. New York: Modern Library Edition, 2003.

———(1956). *Letters to His Mother,* transl. & ed G.D. Painter with an essay by Pamela Hansford Johnson. New York: The Citadel Press.

Richards, A.K. & Spira, L. (2003). On being lonely: Fear of one's own aggression as an impediment to intimacy. *Psychoanalytic Quarterly* 72:357–375.

Spira, L. & Richards, A.K. (2003). The "Sweet and Sour" of being lonely and alone. *Psychoanalytic Study of the Child* 58:214–227.

Sander, F. (2010). *Created in Our Own Images.* New York: IPBooks.

Sinkman, E. (2012). *The Psychology of Beauty.* New York: Rowan, Littlefield.

CHAPTER 19

Conclusion

Arlene Kramer Richards and Lucille Spira

Almodóvar's genius for creating films that grab us emotionally is the thread that runs through our authors' contributions. This narrative builds on Herbert H. Stein's *The Importance of Film for Psychoanalysis* (Chapter 1). He tells us that film brings concepts used in psychoanalysis into living color. The vivid colors of Almodóvar's movies embody the intensity of desire, passion and compulsion. They arouse these states in the audience as we watch them, they expose them in the characters' actions. In what follows we will look at desire, passion, and compulsion as they are expressed in our authors' discussions of Almodóvar's movies.

Desire

Almodóvar named his film studio "El Deseo". He sees his movies as all about desire. French Freudians focus on desire, German Freudians on wish. Freud said that a wish is characterized by the aim. Desire implies that the object or person is the most impelling aspect of the longing. For example, a wish is to be fed, the desire would be to be fed by mother or to be fed a delicious meal. The Lacanian idea is that one wishes to be desired as other. Almodóvar shows the wish to be desired as an exciting sexual object. A wish is a wish in the moment; desire implies longing over time. Sexilla and Riza in *Labyrinth of Passion* look hungrily at men's crotches as Bennett Roth mentions in Chapter 3. They do not wish for any single one, their eyes are on the penis — any penis.

Here William Fried's discussion of *The Law of Desire* (Chapter 7) provides an explication. Desire implies a lack; to desire something is to acknowledge that one does not have it. In that film the sister was once the director's brother. She later changed her gender to satisfy her desire to be loved by her father. She was willing to sacrifice her gender in order to be sexually desired. This is about the desire to be desired.

Desire is a theme that runs through all of Almodóvar's work. The conflict between desire and being desired motivates men who change their bodies to resemble those of women. In *All About My Mother* (Chapter 13) the father of both sons has had breast implants, dresses and uses make-up like a woman even when he fathers his second child. He presents himself as a woman; she impregnates a woman. The character has aspects of both genders. He is Esteban and Lola.

In *Women on the Verge of a Nervous Breakdown* (Chapter 8), Jeffrey Stern shows how Pepa desires Ivan as the father of her child, but fails to see that he is incapable of being a father to their baby. Her desire is strong enough to overcome her reason. To Stern this comes from a system where women are taught to see themselves as deficient. In such a situation some will turn to men for their esteem and emotional balance. He sees a risk to men as well as women. The men are also victims of a destructive patriarchy, and consequently are inadequate when relating to women, leading women to be on the verge of a nervous breakdown. Then Pepa, as she moves toward motherhood, desires Ivan to bolster her self-esteem.

In *Live Flesh* (Chapter 12), Adriana Prengler analyzes the way the character Victor rushes through life. He has sex with a girl at a club and the sexual contact kindles his desire for her; a desire to possess her. Victor is blamed for shooting a detective who comes to investigate the noise in her apartment. She allows Victor to enter her apartment while under the false impression that he is her drug dealer. After a series of complications he achieves his desire. He marries her and has a child with her. Desire begets life.

A similar plot structures *Tie me Up, Tie Me Down* as described by Herbert Stein in Chapter 9. The hero Ricky wants to marry and father children with the drug addicted porn star Marina. Paradoxically, he is a sociopath, she is also. When she refuses him he beats her up. Yet she also cares for a sick horse and for him when he is beaten by drug dealers while out getting drugs for her. She falls in love with a victim; he falls in love with a caring motherly person. As in screwball comedies one is to think that they marry, have children and live happily ever after.

Danielle Knafo in *Talk to Her* (Chapter 14), discusses the desire of some men for sex with dolls rather than a live woman as rooted in necrophilia. From Knafo we learn that sexualizing a dead or comatose woman is a way to protect the self from deadness as it creates an illusory excitement. The aim is to ward off fear of loss, castration anxiety and the fear of one's death.

In *Matador* Diego, the matador, when he has sex with Eva, his model girlfriend, demands that she pretend to be dead. Then it is the woman who is rendered impotent, not the man; he can be the powerful enlivened one.

In Chapter 11, another romantic comedy, *The Flower of My Secret* tells a story that Selma Duckler relates to the theory of "toxic nourishment" created by Michael Eigen. She highlights the playing with reality through an opening scene in which a mother is apparently being convinced or coerced into donating her dead son's organs to people in need of transplants. The scene is shown to be a training session with the mother played by an actress. While the movie shows the heroine, Leo, struggling to reject the bitter side of herself and make her life more like the romantic comedies she writes, it also ends with her accepting the love of a man who knows her romantic, soft, sweet side. We think it interesting that the heroine has a name that is both masculine and animal. It is the masculine and animal side of herself that gives her trouble; this is a Jungian idea.

Passion

Luhmann (1987) described the original concept of passion as longing, a state for which the person could not be held accountable. To this day crimes of passion are judged differently than other crimes. Murdering an adulterous wife when she is found in the embrace of her lover is still seen as something different from murdering a stranger on the street. Passion comes to you; being struck by Cupid's arrow is not volitional. He reports that in pre-modern times passion was seen as a disease while sexual desire was normal. Passion was passive longing; sexual desire was active. Luhmann contrasted this passive passion with more modern thinking about the passion of love as a blaze kindled by two people's mutual seduction.

When Lucille Spira discusses child abuse in *Crocodiles, Lambs and Soul Murder* she quotes Junot Díaz discussing his experience of being abused as saying, *"That shit cracked the planet of me in half"*. This echoes Stephen Sondheim's discussion of passion. In the Stephen Sondheim play *Passion* the ugly, sickly, unpleasant woman who is passionately in love with a handsome, strong, successful man, wins his passionate love by the force of hers. Michiko Kakutani (1994) quotes Sondheim, "'Passion' is about how the force of somebody's feelings for you can crack you open and how it is the life force in a deadened world". The Sondheim view of passion is being destroyed or having one's defenses removed. This idea of passion as a cracking open invokes the trauma of being seduced.

Alizade (1999) regards passion as an overwhelming force pursued despite the consequences to self and other. For Alizade, the passion that is overcome by saints is the counterpart of the passion acted out by witches.

Spira in "Crocodiles, Lambs and Soul Murder" (Chapter 16), sees that passion leads the priest to seduce the young boy even though it is contrary to his priestly vows. When he leaves the priesthood and becomes a publisher, he pursues a young man even when he becomes aware that the young man no longer wants him. Despite knowing that it is dangerous, he pursues that man to his own death.

The director pursues his quest to find out what really happened to the man he loved when they were both boys. He learns that passion kills.

Almodóvar shows us passion that enlivens when it becomes a creative drive when the director makes his film in *Bad Education*.

Our authors emphasize Almodóvar's characters' passions. His characters deal with their passions as they move through the vicissitudes of their lives. And those vicissitudes impact the viewer; in (Chapter 10), Nancy Goodman discusses the intense feelings aroused in her by *High Heels* and *Volver*. The heroine of *High Heels* kills to keep a connection to her passionately adored mother. Here, as in *Volver*, to Goodman it is not only the narrative but the mise en scène that connotes passion. Along with Goodman, we think of those red high heels.

Psychoanalysts spend our lives connecting with and understanding our own and our patient's feelings. We look for feelings that provide unconscious motives for our own and our patients' actions. Almodóvar's highly dramatic characters express the extremes of their emotions. We watch characters who are beset by longing; they are lonely, in love, frightened, envious, joyous, and full of desire and passion. The cinematography expresses arousal with the frequent use of red. Merle Molofsky highlights the passion, and Almodóvar's use of red, in her discussion of "*What Have I Done to Deserve This?* and *Julieta* (Chapter 5). The heroine, an ignored, sexually frustrated and overworked housewife, (*What Have I Done to Deserve This?*), controls her anger until it boils over into murderous rage. She kills her husband with a ham. In *Julieta*, the passionate love of a daughter, Antia, for her father causes her to abandon her mother, whom she blames for the death of her father, even though he died by taking his boat into a storm. The mother had fought with him about his adulterous behavior.

In *Labyrinth of Passion* the hilariously named "Sexilla" is a singer in a punk band who was disappointed by Riza not showing up for a tryst when both were young. Sexilla now has sex with many men so as not to be spurned by any man. Riza tries homosexuality, but in the end finds himself in love with Sexilla and sexually desires her. The labyrinth they go through in order to re-find each other is the winding path of desire. The intensity of the desire is the definition of passion. Desire enlivens; passion can lead to death or to creation.

Passion can be transformed into compassion, as Julián Daniel Gutiérrez-Albilla considers in (Chapter 2), "Trauma and Memory in the Cinema of Pedro Almodóvar". The clinical process of psychoanalysis shares something in common with Almodóvar's movies. Both are open to the individual, the unusual, the far out. Though Almodóvar spoofs psychoanalysis in *Labyrinth of Passion* and in *What Have I Done to Deserve This?*, Gutiérrez-Albilla points out that in *Matador* the psychologist responds compassionately to her patient's traumatic circumstances.

Compulsion

Like addiction, compulsion is felt as irresistible. It drives the sufferer into a frenzy that demands enactment immediately. Characters in several of Almodóvar's movies are addicts, for example Ignacio in *Bad Education*, the Mother Superior, Sister Manure and Yolanda in *Dark Habits*, the father Esteban (Lola), the actress Nina in *All About My Mother*, and Marina in *Tie Me Up, Tie Me Down*. The matador and the lawyer in *Matador* are compulsive killers. Compulsive masturbation, compulsive sex, self-cutting, and compulsion to kill are all totally compelling.

Compulsion to act on the immediate wish can be a reaction to overly strict repression as happened in Spain under Franco.

In (Chapter 4), *Dark Habits*, Arthur Lynch, Lourdes Rigual-Lynch, and Arnold Richards discuss how extreme reactions to the trauma of extreme suppression can become compulsive self-abuse and addiction to pain. They point to the defensive aspects of such behaviors.

In "*Matador*: Death in the Eclipse" (Chapter 6), Philip Matyszak shows how the compulsion to kill becomes erotic; it becomes irresistible. The trauma of loss of the matador's power when he can no longer be a bullfighter leads to a compulsion to kill people. The lawyer's traumatic loss of her idealized matador when she sees that he can no longer be a bullfighter-killer leads her to kill until she kills him as he watches her kill herself. For this pair, ritualized killing is the pleasure—the ultimate orgasm. Sabbadini, (2014) in his discussion of *Matador*, points out that the pleasure in the fantasy of dying together lies in the false idea that death will forever unite lovers. He sees this as rooted in the fantasy of symbiotic union with the maternal object.

Albert Brok, considering *Talk to Her* (Chapter 15), discusses the fixation Benigno, a male nurse, has on Alicia, as he was fixated on his mother. He compulsively attends to her comatose body as he cared for his mother. Is it only the trauma of the loss of his mother or, as Brok suggests, the lack of a father or Other that results in his compulsion?

Passion exists in the space between desire and compulsion. In Chapter 17, Sandra Cohen, through a Kleinian lens, gives us a starkly Oedipal understanding of *Broken Embraces*. She shows how desire born of infantile need and compulsion turns back into the original life or death intensity of the triangle of mother, father and baby. In this depiction of seemingly normal, rational and creative people, the raw force of the boy baby's wish to have mother to himself and the girl baby's wish to have father and keep him alive for herself fuels adult behavior. It is the intensity of the desire that turns it into compulsion, and the mere fact of the death of the original object of that desire and the original subject of that passion does not diminish either the passion or the compulsion. When it threatens to swallow the other, passion repels; Lena becomes repelled by Ernesto Martel, Sr.

Volver tells the story of a woman raped when she was a teen by her father. Years later her teenage daughter, who was born from the rape, kills her stepfather to prevent him from raping her. Nancy Goodman, (Chapter 10), suggests that by murdering the stepfather the daughter was enacting her formerly victimized mother's desire for revenge. While the mother thought that what she most wanted was revenge, Goodman shows how she came to see her desire was to have her trauma witnessed by her own mother as she witnessed her daughter's.

Compulsion is most powerful when it is fueled by the desire for revenge, by rage and by failure to mourn. In *The Skin I Live In* (Chapter 18), Arlene Kramer Richards finds a plot for revenge fueled by all of these filtered through intellectual pride. A surgeon's trauma of losing his wife and his only daughter has left its traces on him. He who changes a man's body into a woman's body has invented a superior skin with which he covers his victim. The surgeon is meticulous but has a wild, beastly brother. The brother rapes the woman the surgeon has created. He gets revenge on her for his mother's abandonment of him. The surgeon is compelled to operate; the beastly brother is compelled to rape.

Compulsion contrasts with desire in that it is felt as an outside force like passion. But compulsion goes beyond passion in erasing the self and erasing desire. Compulsion is selfless. Even as the person feels that she is coughing, short of breath, having irregular heartbeats, and knows that these symptoms come from smoking, she must continue killing herself by smoking. The anxiety produced by quitting a compulsion or habitual self destructive behavior overcomes the rational self preservative understanding. No one can convince Esteban in *All About My Mother* that he is going to get AIDS when he has sex with many anonymous men in the roadside. No one can convince Nina that she is going to die if she keeps taking drugs. But in this movie, as described by Arlene Kramer Richards, she goes to her hometown, marries and becomes a mother. The audience feels this as a betrayal, but it is also a foreshadowing of the happy ending when Manuela goes home with a baby in her arms, to raise him as her own, protect him and cure him of his AIDS. The baby is rejected by his maternal grandparents because they could not accept a baby being illegitimate and having AIDS.

Could Almodóvar be suggesting that it is the nurturing and compassionate behavior of an other that is the cure for compulsion?

In Conclusion

Almodóvar searches for meaning in the emotional life of his characters. He moves the audience to tears of pity, shivers of fear, and outbursts of laughter. He shows and creates desire, passion and compulsion in his beautiful, always lively, sometimes lurid scenes by his cinematography, use of music, costume, furniture, and outdoor settings. By moving us to these feelings, he illuminates the passion and compassion in human interaction. We experience vicariously what his characters portray onscreen. We relate to his work because we have experienced trauma as well as joy in our lives. Even when it is outlandish, his work reflects what we experience in dreams, thoughts and associations. We agree with Sabbadini (2014) that reflecting on a film adds to the pleasure of watching the film. That is what we are trying to do in this book. Narrating one of Almodóvar's movies is like analyzing our own dream. The movie gives us a little entree to our own unconscious. We are left with a desire to see his next movie.

References

Alizade, A. M. (1999). *Feminine Sensuality.* London: Karnac.

Kakutani, M. (1994). *Passion* by Sondheim Review in *NY Times Archive.*

Luhmann, N. (1987). *Love as Passion: the Codification of Intimacy.* Boston: Harvard University Press.

Sabbadini, A. (2014). *Moving Images: Psychoanalytic Reflections on Film.* London: Routledge.

www.ingramcontent.com/pod-product-compliance
Lightning Source LLC
Chambersburg PA
CBHW051712020426
42333CB00014B/945